INSIDE THE CAMPUS

Inside The Campus

MR. CITIZEN
LOOKS AT
HIS
UNIVERSITIES

BY

CHARLES E. McALLISTER, D.D.
President of the Association of Governing Boards
of State Universities and Allied Institutions and Regent
of the State College of Washington

NEW YORK

FLEMING H. REVELL COMPANY

Printed in the United States of America

New York 10 : 158 Fifth Avenue
London, E. C. 4 : 29 Ludgate Hill
Glasgow, C. 2 : 229 Bothwell Street

CONTENTS

PART I

PART II

CONTENTS

PART III. TABLES AND CHARTS

The charts listed below will be found following page 248.

FOREWORD

PLENTY of courage was displayed by American youth on Iwo Jima and Okinawa and at Salerno and elsewhere. There was also plenty of confusion in connection with the war effort. The phrase, "too little or too late," found its way into our thoughts on too many occasions. The military phase of World War II is now a thing of the past. The battle of ideas which precipitated that war still goes on. It remains to be seen whether we will face our educational problems with a courage parallel to that of American youth in battle. It also remains to be seen whether stumbling confusion will characterize the determination of policies of higher education in the United States for the next few years. The decision will depend very largely upon the governing boards of our colleges and universities. This is particularly true of state-controlled institutions of higher learning. Which will it be—courage or confusion?

INTRODUCTION

THE Association of Governing Boards of State Universities and Allied Institutions is an organization made up of members of boards of trustees, regents, curators, and members of state boards of education. The Association held its 25th Annual Meeting at the University of Michigan, October 2, 3, and 4, 1947, when a report covering the study embraced in this volume was presented. This study was made possible through the generosity of Mr. and Mrs. George Frederick Jewett of Spokane, Washington.

This survey is unique in that it is one of the few educational studies available based on personal interview and not largely assembled by correspondence. It proceeds on the assumption that no questionnaire is foolproof and that the results of many earlier educational surveys contain certain inaccuracies, due to lack of clear understanding on the part of the surveyor and on the part of those who answer the questions which have been prepared. In the present instance, with the exception of three, the author personally interviewed presidents, board members, staff members, deans, and faculties of the eighty-nine institutions surveyed.

The procedure was to send out a prepared questionnaire well in advance of a visit by the author. This visit was also prepared for sufficiently ahead of time, so that arrangements could be made for the author to interview the various individuals most concerned in furnishing accurate information on the points to be covered.

The study is also unique in that never before in the history of American education have so many institutions been visited within a span of one year, so that comparable conditions could be examined without the lapse of unnecessary time and without delay. It was of the utmost importance to be able to consider the

9

facts at one institution and also to consider similar facts at a neighboring institution within a comparatively short period, especially in view of the change in conditions that the passage of even a year would involve.

The survey began in September, 1946. The author had a year's furlough from his normal duties in order to devote his time exclusively to this project. The institutions in New England were visited first, followed by visits to the colleges and universities of the Middle Atlantic states and along the southern Atlantic seaboard. A second series of visits included institutions on the West Coast and along the southern tier of states from California to Florida. The third section of the tour began at the University of Utah and included colleges and universities in the area generally known as the Middle West. Covering this vast territory was possible only because of the rapid traveling facilities offered by aviation. The schedule provided for approximately two days at each institution with preparation in advance so that every moment of the time allotted could be programmed and waste of motion or effort be avoided.

Again, the study is unique in that it is the first of its kind attempted from the point of view of governing boards. The few studies previously made of governing boards have concerned themselves almost exclusively with the composition of these boards, and have been conducted entirely by correspondence. The first was made by Scott Nearing in 1913.[1] It was based on 189 institutions, 143 of which replied. These replies were concerned largely with occupational and sex distributions. In 1927, George S. Counts published a study entitled "The Social Composition of Boards of Education: a Study in the Social Control of Public Education."[2] This survey was also based on correspondence. It dealt primarily with members of city, county, and state boards of education, mostly on the elementary and secondary school level. These boards were compared briefly with state college and university boards. Once more, major attention was

---

[1] See "Who's Who Among College Trustees," *School and Society*, VI (September 8, 1917, p. 297-99).
[2] Chicago: University of Chicago Press, 1927.

directed to the composition of the boards, with emphasis on the
fact that they were made up mostly of businessmen and professional persons, with no representation from labor. A third study,
by J. L. McGrath [3] devoted itself to the occupations of trustees of
fifteen private colleges and universities and five state institutions
at ten-year intervals, from 1860 to 1930. One of his interesting
discoveries was that in 1860, 39 per cent of the membership of
the governing boards of these private institutions were clergy-
men, but by 1930 the number had dropped to 7 per cent; while,
during the same period, the representation of businessmen rose
from 23 per cent to 32 per cent, and that of bankers from 5 per
cent to 20 per cent. In addition to these three studies, there were
several unpublished studies devoted to investigation of the occupations of governing board members.

The last published work on this subject is that of Dr. Hubert
Park Beck,[4] entitled, "Men Who Control Our Universities." Dr.
Beck's study was likewise conducted by correspondence. It was
concerned exclusively with the composition of the boards rather
than with their powers and the issues confronting them at the
present time. Following the lead of his predecessors, Dr. Beck
calls attention to the heavy representation of bankers, industrialists, and professional men, and the lack of representation of what
he calls the public and manual laborers. He presents an ideal
board as one made up of thirteen members, eight representing the
public and five the university. This membership would be
divided into two representatives each of business, professions,
agriculture, wage-earners, the faculty, and the alumni, plus one
student representative. There is an underlying assumption in all
four of these studies that the predominant representation of business, industry, and the professions on governing boards is of itself
an undesirable arrangement. It is intimated that professional and
business representatives are so devoted to a narrow, partisan, class
point of view as to be incapable of unselfishly forwarding the best

[3] "The Control of Higher Education in America," *The Educational Record*,
XVII (April, 1936, pp. 259-72).

[4] *Men Who Control Our Universities: The Economic and Social Composition
of Governing Boards of Thirty Leading American Universities.* King's Crown
Press, Morningside Heights, New York.

interests of the institutions. Faculty representation is capable of introducing campus politics to a degree detrimental to the interests of an institution. Any board member who has had to deal with student representation has some doubts also as to the value of such membership on a board. In the institutions visited in this study, there is constant and abundant opportunity for the faculty and student point of view to be heard, without their participation in board membership. It was suggested also that the wage earners select not necessarily one of their own number to represent them, but rather some highly capable, thoroughly prepared individual. Inasmuch as even governors are not always altogether wise in their nominations for board members, there is little reason to assume that the type of representatives selected by wage earners would reflect a higher level of ability and a complete absence of selfish partisanship. However, the chief difficulties with all of these studies is that they are based on correspondence, do not include personal interviews to any considerable extent, and also present facts on the composition of these boards based on data at least ten years before the present. The changes that have taken place in a ten-year period in the composition of boards, to say nothing of policies and precedures, completely alter the picture. It is very evident that Dr. Beck himself has never been a member of a governing board, for reasons outlined later in this report. However, Dr. Beck's work is scholarly and deserves serious study, whether one agrees with its conclusions or not.

The administrative and policy-making groups in charge of our great state colleges and universities carry a heavy responsibility. There is much misunderstanding of the functions of regents, trustees, supervisors, curators, and members of state boards concerning their relation to the institutions with which they are connected, their powers in relationship with the actual administration of the affairs of these institutions, their financial responsibility, their caliber, and the importance of the attitudes they adopt with reference to many of the great issues before American higher education at the present time.

At Stanford University an administrative officer remarked that this study was both timely and necessary because of the fact that in recent years colleges and universities have been so exclusively engrossed with meeting problems of housing, rapidly increasing enrollments, the recruiting of additional faculty, and other technical administrative details, that sight has been lost of the great issues that every American college and university must face during the coming decade. The answer to many of these problems will rest with the governing boards. However, these problems are of such a character that the facts underlying modern trends in higher education are of equal value to presidents and administrative staffs, to faculty members, to state legislators, to those interested in the preservation of the American form of government, to those concerned with the areas of morals and religion, and to those interested in industrial relations and workers' education.

While this study is primarily concerned with the governing boards and policies of the great state colleges and universities, visits were made to some privately controlled institutions for purposes of comparison and in order to evaluate correctly the relationship between publicly controlled and privately controlled higher education. These schools were selected on the basis of variation in size and objective. The privately controlled institutions visited included Harvard, Yale, Amherst, Vanderbilt, the University of the South, the University of Southern California, Leland Stanford, the College of Wooster, Tuskegee Institute, and Cornell (partly privately controlled). It will be noted that there are vast areas of privately controlled higher education, particularly schools under denominational auspices or church-related colleges, which are not included. It would scarcely be fair to compare a small weakly financed church-related institution with great state universities like the University of Michigan or the University of Wisconsin or the University of Minnesota.

The author prepares this manuscript with a feeling of deep humility. He is not a professional scholar. The very fact that these problems are being faced by a member of a governing board rather than by a professional educator has the advantage of a fresh point of view, divorced from dedication to any particular school of educational theory. This is a fact-finding study. In con-

sidering the findings opinions will be expressed and certain conclusions suggested. These opinions and conclusions are offered as
a basis for discussion rather than as authoritative statements beyond dispute. The study indicates certain definite trends, the existence of which is beyond serious question. However, the interpretation of facts is subject to variation, depending on the point
of view of the student. A professional educator's reaction to certain conditions may differ widely from that of the man on the
street or a member of a governing board. The members of the
boards themselves are deeply conscious of the need for improving
their capacity to carry on the responsibilities imposed on them.

It has been suggested by high educational authorities that this
study, prepared for the Association of Governing Boards of State
Universities and Allied Institutions, should be referred to carefully selected administrative and faculty groups for further consideration with the idea in mind that a year hence a revised presentation might be offered which would be capable of making a
"tremendous impact" on publicly controlled higher education.

The subjects to be considered are in many instances controversial. One conviction, however, is beyond dispute, and that is
that selfish interests must not be dominant in the control of
American higher education. This conviction is sound whether it
involves political considerations, church loyalties, or vocational
emphasis. The challenge before us is whether the situation in our
colleges and universities will be marked by a courageous attitude
and an attempt to meet their problems squarely, or whether the
confusion so apparent in many educational centers will continue
and eventually operate to the discredit of education itself.

The author wishes to express his deep appreciation of the
splendid courtesy and co-operation offered by the authorities in
the various colleges and universities visited. Everywhere there
was an eager desire on the part of those involved to discover any
light on some of the present confusing problems and to make
adjustments, even at the cost of personal sacrifice. A powerful dis-
content, combined with a serious dedication to the task, was apparent everywhere. Again and again after the study had been completed at a university, the question was asked, "When will this

report be available?" This does not mean that the report need necessarily be accepted in its present form. It can scarcely do more than present the issues to be resolved and trust to wiser minds to determine their ultimate solution.

At each institution visited, a record was kept of those who so kindly offered their services in helping to determine the facts on which this study is based. The author wishes to express his deep appreciation to the following individuals who were particularly helpful:

Alabama Polytechnic Institute—L. N. Duncan, President (deceased)
    John N. Baker, Public Relations
    Ralph B. Draughon, Director of Instruction
    Marion J. Funchess, Dean of Agriculture
    C. W. Edwards, Registrar
    Roger Allen, Dean of Arts and Sciences
    Marion W. Spidle, Dean of Women
    W. T. Ingram, Business Manager
    The entire faculty
University of Alabama—Ralph E. Adams, Acting President
    Clifton H. Penick, Secretary Board of Trustees
    Stewart J. Lloyd, Dean of School of Chemistry, Metallurgy and
        Ceramics
    R. W. Cowart, Education Professor
    W. E. Pickens, Comptroller
    Lee Bidgood, Dean of Commerce
    William J. Hepburn, Dean of Law
    James R. Cudworth, Dean of Engineering   ,
    A. B. Moore, Dean Graduate School
Amherst—Charles W. Cole, President
Arizona, University of—Alfred Atkinson, President
Arkansas, University of—Lewis W. Jones, President
    Robert A. Leflar, Dean of Law School
    Herbert L. Thomas, Chairman of Board
California, University of at Los Angeles—Clarence A. Dykstra, Provost
    William C. Pomeroy, Registrar
    Chandler Harris, Public Information
California, University of at Berkeley—George A. Pettit, Assistant to
    President

San Francisco State College—P. F. Valentine, Vice President
  Florence Vance, Registrar
San Jose State College—T. W. MacQuarrie, President
  J. H. West, Registrar
  E. S. Thompson, Controller
  Paul M. Pitman, Dean of Men
  J. C. DeVoss, Dean of Personnel and Guidance
  Margaret Twombly, Health Service Director
University of Southern California—Albert S. Raubenheimer, Educational Vice President
  Robert D. Fisher, Financial Vice President
  Elton Phillips, Comptroller
  R. D. Williams, Assistant Registrar
Leland Stanford University—T. A. Spragens, Assistant to President
  Fred Glover, Public Relations
The Citadel—Gen. Charles P. Summerall, President
  Col. L. A. Prouty, Registrar
  Col. John P. Thomas, Chairman of Board of Visitors
  Col. J. R. Westmoreland, Board of Visitors
  Col. James F. Risher, Board of Visitors
Clemson Agricultural College—R. F. Poole, President
  F. M. Kinard, Arts and Science
  J. C. Littlejohn, Business Manager
  G. E. Metz, Registrar
Colorado Agricultural and Mechanical College—Roy M. Green, President
  Joseph M. Whalley, Treasurer
  Gerald T. Hudson, Assistant Professor of Sociology
  Herb Heilig, Director of Vocational Education
  C. W. Ferguson, Director of Admissions
  James R. Miller, Secretary of State Board of Agriculture
Colorado, University of—Robert Stearns, President
  W. F. Dyde, Dean of University
  Clifford Houston, Dean of Students
  E. C. King, Dean of Law School
  R. W. Dunham, Dean of School of Music
  C. F. Poe, Dean of Pharmacy
  Elmore Petersen, Dean of Business
  Jacob Van Ek, Dean of Arts and Sciences

Merritt H. Perkins, Regent
Ralph L. Carr, Regent
Roy M. Chapman, Regent
Richard Fox, Head, Testing and Evaluation
John B. Schoolland, Counselling
Ralph Prator, Director of Admissions
Calvin Grieder, Department of Education (School Board Association)
Connecticut, University of—Albert N. Jorgensen, President
Arwood S. Northby, Director of Student Personnel
Walter Kulp, Professor of Bacteriology
Walter Stemmons, University Editor
Cornell University—Arthur S. Adams, Provost
Edward Graham, Secretary of University
Robert Meigs, Secretary of Trustees
H. E. Babcock, Chairman of Board
Wright Gibson, College of Agriculture
Delaware, University of—W. S. Carlson, President
Florida State University—Doak S. Campbell, President
Florida, University of—John J. Tigert, President
H. W. Chandler, Dean of University
Delton L. Scudder, Professor of Religion
R. C. Beaty, Dean of Students
Entire faculty
Georgia School of Technology—Col. Blake R. Van Leer, President
Georgia, University of—Harmon W. Caldwell, President
Georgia, Board of Regents of the University System of—L. R. Siebert, Executive Secretary, Board of Regents
Robert Strite, Comptroller
Elizabeth Koenig, President's Secretary
Harvard University—J. B. Conant, President
David W. Bailey, Secretary to the Corporation
Idaho, University of—W. F. McNaughton, President, Board of Regents
Illinois, University of—George D. Stoddard, President
Albert J. Harno, Dean of the College of Law
Harrison E. Cunningham, Secretary, Board of Trustees
George P. Tuttle, Registrar
Fred H. Turner, Dean of Students
Herbert O. Farber, Assistant to the Comptroller

Indiana, University—Herman B. Wells, President
  Judge Ora L. Wildermuth, President, Board of Trustees
  Robert T. Ittner, Assistant Dean of Faculties
  Herman T. Briscoe, Dean of Faculties
  All Departmental Deans
Iowa, State University of—Virgil Hancher, President
  Richard H. Plock, State Board of Education
  Elmer T. Peterson, Dean of College of Education and Acting
    Dean of Graduate College
  Carlyle F. Jacobsen, Dean of Division of Health Sciences and
    Services
  Earl J. McGrath, Dean of Liberal Arts
  Allin W. Dakin, Administrative Dean
  Mason Ladd, Dean of College of Law
  E. W. MacEwen, Dean of College of Medicine
  Rudolph A. Kuever, Dean of College of Pharmacy
  Alvin W. Bryan, Dean of College of Dentistry
  Chester A. Phillips, Dean of College of Commerce
  C. Woody Thompson, Dean of Students
  Bruce Mahan, Dean of Extension Division
  Fred Ambrose, Business Manager
  Entire Board of Education
Iowa State College of Agriculture and Mechanic Arts—Charles E.
    Friley, President
Kansas, University of—Deane W. Malott, Chancellor
  E. B. Stouffer, Dean of University
  P. B. Lawson, Dean of College of Liberal Arts and Sciences
  Raymond Nichols, Assistant to Chancellor
  D. M. Swarthout, Dean of School of Fine Arts
  F. J. Moreau, Dean of School of Law
  J. O. Jones, Dean of School of Engineering
  J. Allen Reese, Dean of School of Pharmacy
  F. T. Stockton, Dean of School of Business
  H. G. Ingham, Director of Extension
  Margaret Habein, Dean of Women
  Willis Tompkins, Assistant Dean of Men
  E. R. Elbel, Director of Veterans Office
  J. K. Hitt, Registrar
  Irvin Youngberg, Director of Dormitories

Kansas State College—Milton S. Eisenhower, President
C. O. Price, Assistant to President
A. R. Jones, Comptroller
A. L. Pugsley, Dean of Administration
S. A. Nock, Director of Admissions
R. I. Throckmorton, Director of Agricultural Experimental Station
R. A. Seaton, Director of Engineering Experimental Station
R. W. Babcock, Dean of School of Arts and Sciences
Kentucky, University of—H. L. Donovan, President
Leo M. Chamberlain, Dean of University and Registrar
Louisiana State University and Agricultural and Mechanical College
    —Fred C. Frey, Acting President
Frances Mims, Secretary of Board of Supervisors
Kelly McKnight, Alumni Secretary
James McLemore, Chairman of Board of Supervisors
Entire Board
Maine, University of—Arthur A. Hauck, President
Edward E. Chase, President of Board of Trustees
E. E. Weiman, Dean of Men
Charles F. Virtue, Professor of Philosophy
Maryland, University of—H. C. Byrd, President
Massachusetts State University—Hugh P. Baker, President
Philip Whitmore, Trustee
William L. Machmer, Dean of Men
Helen Curtis, Dean of Women
M. O. Lanphear, Registrar
Robert D. Hawley, Treasurer
Miami, University of—Bowman F. Ashe, President
Jay F. E. Pearson, Vice President
Michigan, University of—Alexander G. Ruthven, President
James P. Adams, Provost
Frank E. Robbins, Assistant to President
Arthur L. Brandon, Director of Information Services
Alfred B. Connable, Junior Member of Board of Regents
Robert L. Williams, Administrative Assistant Provost's Office
Michigan State College—John A. Hannah, President
James H. Denison, Assistant to President
Karl H. McDonel, Secretary
William H. Berkey, Chairman State Board of Agriculture

S. E. Crowe, Dean of Students
Ernest L. Anthony, Dean of Agriculture
Col. Dorsey R. Rodney, Dean of Business and Public Service
Ward Giltner, Dean of Veterinary Medicine
Howard C. Rather, Dean of the Basic College
W. G. Armstrong, Member of State Board
Clark Brody, Member of State Board
P. J. May, Comptroller and Treasurer
Eugene B. Elliott, State Superintendent of Public Instruction
H. B. Dirks, Dean of Engineering
Marie Dye, Dean of Home Economics
Lloyd C. Emmons, Dean of Science and Arts
W. H. Combs, Head of Department of Public Administration
Minnesota, University of—James L. Morrill, President
William T. Middlebrook, Vice President, Business Administration
Malcolm M. Willey, Vice President, Academic Administration
Robert E. Summers, Dean of Admissions and Records
William L. Nunn, Director of University Relations
Ernest B. Pierce, Field Secretary, Secretary, General Alumni Association
James F. Bell, Chairman of Board
Daniel C. Gainey, Member of Board
Richard L. Griggs, Member of Board
George W. Lawson, Member of Board
Albert J. Lobb, Member of Board
E. E. Novak, Member of Board
A. J. Olson, Member of Board
J. S. Jones, Member of Board
Ray J. Quinlivan, Member of Board
F. J. Rogstad, Member of Board
Fred B. Snyder, Member of Board
Sheldon V. Wood, Member of Board
Mississippi, University of—John D. Williams, Chancellor
Pete K. McCarter, Administrative Assistant and Dean of Men
Mississippi State Board of Higher Education
Mississippi State College for Women—Burney L. Parkinson, President
G. T. Buckley, Registrar
Mississippi State College—Fred T. Mitchell, President
Herbert Drennon, Dean of Graduate School

Missouri, University of—F. A. Middlebush, President
  Leslie Cowan, Vice President in Charge of Business Operations
  Thomas A. Brady, Vice President in Charge of Extra Divisional
    Educational Activities
  C. W. McLane, Director of Admissions
  Carl Agee, Dean of Bible College
  Thelma Mills, Director of Student Affairs for Women
  Paul A. Hanna, Business Manager
  Ray H. Bezoni, Auditor
Montana State University—James A. McCain, President
Nebraska, University of—Stanley D. Long, President of Board of
    Regents
  John K. Selleck, Comptroller
  C. H. Oldfather, Dean of College of Arts and Sciences
  T. J. Thompson, Dean of Student Affairs
  R. W. Devoe, Regent
  Frank M. Johnson, Regent
  C. Y. Thompson, Regent
  George Round, Publicity
  Bruce Nicoll, Publicity
Nevada, University of—John O. Moseley, President
  Silas Ross, Chairman of Board
  Albert L. Hilliard, Member of Board
  John Cahlan, Member of Board
  Chris H. Sheerin, Member of Board
  Mary Henningsen, Member of Board
  Leo A. McNamee, Member of Board
  Paul Sirkegian, Member of Board
New Hampshire, University of—Harold W. Hoke, President
  John Davis, Assistant to President
  Everett B. Sackett, Admissions
  Ella S. Bowles, Publications Editor
  E. W. Christensen, Member of Board
New Mexico, University of—J. P. Wernette, President
  William E. Hall, Alumni Director
  Keen L. Rafferty, Public Relations Director
New York State College for Teachers—John M. Sayles, President
  Milton G. Nelson, Dean of College

North Carolina State College of Agriculture and Engineering of University of North Carolina—John W. Harrelson, Chancellor
 Edward L. Cloyd, Dean of Students
Woman's College of the University of North Carolina—W. C. Jackson, Chancellor
 John C. Lockhart, Assistant Controller
 Mildred Newton, Secretary of Admissions
North Dakota, University of—A. F. Arnason, Commissioner, State Board of Education
 John C. West, President
 John H. Longwell, President, Agricultural College
 E. W. Olson, Auditor
 State Board of Higher Education:
 A. S. Marshall, President
 R. A. Trubey, Vice President
 Howard Henry, Member
 Roy Johnson, Member
 Lars Frederickson, Member
 Fred J. Traynor, Member
Ohio State University—Howard L. Bevis, President
 Harvey H. Davis, Vice President
 Norval N. Luxon, Assistant to President
 Harlan Hatcher, Dean of College of Arts and Sciences
 R. B. Thompson, Registrar
 F. W. Davis, Professor of Photography
 Joseph A. Park, Dean of Men
 Charles F. Miller, Assistant Comptroller
Oklahoma College for Women—Dan Procter, President
 Virginia Embree, Registrar
 J. D. Sneed, Business Manager
Oklahoma Agricultural and Mechanical College—Henry G. Bennett, President
 Earle C. Albright, Assistant to President
 John C. Monk, Administrative Assistant
Oklahoma, University of—George L. Cross, President
 Emil R. Kraettli, Secretary of Board of Regents
 Joe W. McBride, Member of Board of Regents
Oregon State College—A. L. Strand, President
 Charles A. Mockmore, Dean of College
 Ernest W. Warrington, Professor of Religion

Oregon State System of Higher Education—Paul C. Packer, Chancellor
    Charles D. Byrne, Secretary
    Earl M. Pallette, Registrar
Oregon, University of—Harry K. Newburn, President
Pennsylvania State College—Ralph D. Hetzel, President
    W. E. Kenworthy, Executive Secretary and Assistant to President
    Elton Jones, Electrical Engineer
    Elizabeth Farrow, Christian Association.
    James Seaman, Chaplain
Purdue University—Frederick L. Hovde, President
    F. C. Hockema, Vice President and Executive Dean
    R. B. Stewart, Vice President and Controller
    Allison E. Stuart, President of Board of Trustees
    A. A. Potter, Dean of the Schools of Engineering
Rhode Island State College—Carl R. Woodward, President
Rutgers University—Robert C. Clothier, President
    Albert E. Meder, Jr., Dean of Administration and Secretary
University of the South (Tennessee)—George M. Baker, Dean of the
    University
South Carolina, University of—Rear Admiral Norman M. Smith,
    President
    Capt. Fred K. Elder, Assistant to the President
    Francis W. Bradley, Dean of Faculty
South Dakota, University of—I. D. Weeks, President
    J. H. Julian, Vice President
    William H. Batsen, Director of Summer School
    Members of Summer School Faculty
Southwestern Louisiana Institute—Joel L. Fletcher, President
    J. A. Riehl, Dean of Admissions
    Frank A. Godchaux, Chairman of Board
Tennessee, University of—James D. Hoskins, President (resigned)
    Fred C. Smith, Dean of Faculty
Texas Agricultural and Mechanical College—Gibb Gilchrist, Presi-
    dent
Texas Technological College—William M. Whyburn, President
    R. C. Goodwin, Dean of Arts and Sciences
    Margaret W. Weeks, Dean of Home Economics
    O. V. Adams, Dean of Engineering
    T. C. Root, Dean of Business Administration
Texas, University of—Theophilus S. Painter, President

Texas College of Mines and Metallurgy—D. M. Wiggins, President
    J. F. Williams, Dean of Student Life
    J. T. Haney, Registrar
    Allen Sayles
Tuskegee Institute—Albon L. Holsey, Director, Public Relations
Utah State Agricultural College—Franklin S. Harris, President
    Russell E. Berntson, Executive Secretary-Treasurer
    Vera Carlson, Secretary to President
Utah, University of—Roy D. Thatcher, Chairman, Board of Regents
    George Thomas, President Emeritus
    Jacob Geerlings, Dean of Faculty
    Paul W. Hodson, Assistant to President
    Leon D. Garrett, Secretary Comptroller
Vanderbilt University—Charles M. Sarratt, Vice Chancellor
    Aileen Bishop, Secretary and Assistant to Chancellor
Vermont, University of—John Millis, President
    Lyman Allen, Trustee
    William Lockwood, Trustee
Virginia Military Institute—Gen. Richard J. Marshall, Superintendent
    Col. William Couper, Executive Officer
    Gen. Stewart W. Anderson, Dean of Faculty
Virginia Polytechnic Institute—John R. Hutcheson, President
    Walter S. Newman, Vice President
Virginia, University of—John L. Newcomb, President
West Virginia University—C. T. Neff, Jr., Vice President
Washington, State College of—Wilson Compton, President
    Robert Sandberg, Executive Assistant
Washington, University of—Raymond B. Allen, President
    Helen E. Hoagland, Executive Assistant
William and Mary, College of—John E. Pomfret, President
    Charles J. Duke, Bursar
    Lawrence Leonard, Public Relations
Wisconsin, University of—E. B. Fred, President
    LeRoy E. Luberg, Assistant to President
    Kenneth Little, Registrar
    A. W. Peterson, Director of Business and Finance
    John Callahan, Regent
    Frank J. Sensenbrenner, Regent
    John D. Jones, Regent
    Walter J. Hodgkins, Regent

W. J. Campbell, Regent

Leonard J. Kleczka, Regent

Wooster, College of—Howard Lowry, President

H. W. Taeusch, Dean of Students

Arthur Southwick, Registrar

Bruce Knox, Treasurer

John D. McKee, Director Public Relations

Wyoming, University of—O. H. Rechard, Dean of College of Liberal
    Arts

J. A. Hill, Dean of College of Agriculture

J. R. Sullivan, Member, Board of Trustees

Yale University—Carl A. Lohmann, Secretary of University

Rev. John C. Schroeder, Head of Department of Religion and
    Master of Calhoun College

Rev. Sydney Lovett, Chaplain

Daniel Merriman, Master of Davenport College

Frank McMullan, Department of Drama

Paul Vieth, Yale Divinity School

In the hope that regents, trustees, supervisors, curators, and members of state boards of education may prove more worthy of the responsibility reposed in them and be wisely guided in the momentous decisions they must make within the next few years, this report is respectfully submitted.

C. E. McAllister

Spokane, Washington.

1

THE OVER-ALL PICTURE

UNLESS one is careful, the over-all description of the tour necessary to produce this study will sound like an American Baedeker. I might even borrow John Gunther's title, *Inside the United States*. There is not a corner of the country that has not been covered. The Executive Committee of the Association of Governing Boards and Allied Institutions is made up of representatives of the universities of Michigan, Indiana, Iowa, Oklahoma, Colorado, Massachusetts, and the state colleges of Rhode Island and Washington. But there are some one hundred other colleges and universities active in the Association. This is only the beginning, for this study has nationwide significance in that many additional institutions were visited which are not members of the Association.

The book is divided into three parts. Part I is devoted to an over-all picture of the study and consideration of fundamental issues which are raised by it. These include keeping politics out of the state universities and the state universities out of politics; the relation between publicly controlled and privately controlled colleges and universities, involving as it does the question of federal aid; communism in the colleges and universities; the teaching of religion and morals in publicly controlled and privately controlled institutions; the importance of the establishment of schools of industrial relations and provision for workers' education; and the problem of entrance requirements and what that involves. The final chapter in this section is devoted to the contributions being made by state colleges and universities to our nation's welfare and to our national economy.

Part II is devoted to a number of technical and practical problems, such as the relation between boards of regents and presidents, faculty, non-faculty personnel, and alumni; the methods by which the various institutions are financed, their total assets and how these assets are held. There is also a chapter on administrative functions. President Truman's Commission on Higher Education has been particularly interested in certain questions covered in this section. Among these are: increases in tuition rates in state universities and colleges, present salary scales for faculties and administrators, increase in teachers' salaries since Pearl Harbor, the participation of faculty members in state, regional, and national professional associations; the relations of the various institutions to the national Congress, and the use of audio-visual aids. Part III is taken up with tables and charts which will be useful for reference in connection with Parts I and II.

One of the first problems to be faced in connection with visiting eighty-nine colleges and universities in a period of ten months is the mystery as to why the various institutions are located where they are. To investigate the reasons for the establishment of some of our great colleges and universities in their present locations would produce some very interesting material. In some states, difficult locations were selected because more favorable ones were preferred for the establishment of the state penitentiaries. In other states, the unwillingness of local communities to make even slight contributions towards the establishment of these institutions was a determining factor. In some others, it was thought that the location of the colleges or universities away from a great center of population had the advantage of removing the students from the temptations of larger cities. But to find many of these places required combined attention to atlases, maps, guides, air-line schedules, bus-line schedules, one-track railroads, and any other mode of transportation available. It would be interesting to note how many towns there are in the United States named "State College." When I inquired at the Pennsylvania Railroad Terminal in New York how to get to State College, Pennsylvania, the attendant asked sweetly, "What state college?"

I answered, "Pennsylvania State College."

The next question was, "Where is it?"

The answer was, "State College."

And then the comment of the attendant was, "Are you kidding me?"

Even in the case of an institution as widely known as Pennsylvania State College it was necessary for this highly trained railway consultant to refer to a guide to find the town of State College, Pennsylvania.

Transportation difficulties were faced again and again. Places within striking distance of air-line terminals were easy to reach, but when one tries to arrive at Storrs, Connecticut; or Sewanee, Tennessee; or Clemson, South Carolina; or Morgantown, West Virginia; or Columbia, Missouri; or Logan, Utah, the problem becomes somewhat complicated. In spite of these difficulties, every institution except one on the original schedule was visited.

The importance of obtaining a personal interview rather than depending on a questionnaire was evidenced by the fact that not a single questionnaire sent out in advance could be used as it had been prepared before the author's arrival. The disadvantage of correspondence studies in education becomes apparent through the experience at a university where a questionnaire had been sent to all members of the faculty. Here, when an attempt was made to digest the material thus made available, the confusion was so great that the president in despair consigned the entire lot to the waste basket. A recent book which is based on the correspondence method, further illustrates the difficulty of this procedure. I opened the book at random and discovered a major table which listed the number of board members of the institutions studied. Of the eighteen institutions thus listed, which were visited in this present survey, nine were found to have the number of board members, as they are at present constituted, incorrectly listed on the table mentioned.

Every questionnaire had to be rewritten after the arrival of the author at each institution. This was not because of any lack of clarity in the questionnaire, or because of any lack of intelligence on the part of those questioned. It was simply an indication that studies based solely on the use of the United States postal system are not accurate and that conclusions based on them are not apt to be sound.

The institutions visited can be divided into two classes: those interested in increased enrollments and in becoming great universities, numerically, overnight, and those interested in restricting enrollment and faculty recruiting in order to preserve some semblance of academic integrity. It is safe to assume that no institution today, with present faculty shortages, can expect to maintain high academic standards if it more than doubles its enrollment in a single year. Yet there are some institutions [1] which have tripled enrollment and thus incurred the danger of a consequent lowering of standards.

Another interesting phenomenon of the present "Veterans' Bulge" is evidenced in the frantic effort to provide housing. There have been frightening estimates of prospective enrollments, particularly of veterans. Originally, these estimates were based on optimistic reports from hopeful colleges and universities of the number of applications they had been unable to consider. They did not take into consideration that many of these students had applied to several institutions and that many of them were provided for elsewhere without any reference to the original college involved. While the effort to house the greatly increased enrollments within a short period constituted a grave problem, some of the estimates of further housing projects, except in certain highly congested areas, are open to serious question. Regents and trustees and the public must guard against undertaking the enormous expense of expansive building projects until we have something more than estimates based, at least to some extent, on guesswork and assumption. The housing is remarkably good, considering the difficulties under which it was constructed. It is reasonably priced. Early in the emergency, some men were compelled to live in great discomfort. I visited one university where several hundred men were quartered in the "field house," which had a dirt floor, double-decker bunks, and no work tables or other equipment. They presented a tragic picture, which could have been avoided had it not been for scarcity of building materials

[1] See Table 19 on Enrollments, in Part III.

in some instances, and scarcity of labor in others, and difficulties due to strikes and industrial disturbances. In many instances, the percentage of students living on or near the campus, whether in trailers or in private houses, fraternity houses or dormitory rooms, is as high as 90 or 95 per cent. In addition, it is interesting to note that frequently the forecasts for summer-school enrollments for 1947 showed a higher figure than actually resulted. Undoubtedly this is due to the fact that many veterans find that they cannot study for twelve-month periods without interruption and do effective work. Also some of them, particularly the married veterans, are under financial stress and are compelled to augment their incomes by leaving college temporarily. One student expressed it aptly when he said that he was afraid to leave, because if he did, he would be subject to pressures, including that of his wife, which would prevent his ever returning. While it is necessary to provide housing actually needed for present increased enrollment, gigantic plans for building expansion made on the assumption that enrollments will continue to increase, "world without end," should be subjected to the most careful scrutiny. It is difficult enough at the moment to maintain our existing institutions, and if we overbuild, with the consequent maintenance expense, we may find ourselves in a position far from solvent.

There are several methods by which members of governing boards are selected. In some states, they are party candidates and are elected by popular vote. In other states, they are appointed by governors, subject to confirmation by the state senate. In still others, they are elected by the state legislature; and there are even a few boards which are, either in part or as a whole, self-perpetuating. The number of members of boards varies from five at Washington State College, Florida, Nevada, and New Mexico to 105 at the University of North Carolina, where all living ex-governors are ex-officio members, for what reason no one has yet been able to explain. The length of terms of boards varies also, ranging from four years to sixteen years, to life. The significance of this in connection with possible political interference is discussed in a later chapter. Most boards have ex-officio members; others have not. It is interesting to note that, in spite of these apparently haphazard methods of selecting board members, with all the dangers involved, a vast majority of the present members of governing boards are themselves college graduates.[2]

The organization of the boards differs also. In some of them, the president of the college or university is not a member of the board. In others, he is the presiding officer. Some function with a considerable number of standing committees. Others appoint committees only as necessity arises. The average board today, even though by law it must have but two stated meetings a year, meets on an average of once a month.

Then there is the question of the difference of administration under what is known as the joint state board or under a separate board for each institution. The American Youth Commission makes this rather amazing statement:

"So far as higher education is concerned, it has become accepted in principle that all state institutions of higher education, including teacher training institutions of college grade but not including junior colleges which are parts of local school systems, should be administered under a unified state board of regents and a single chancellor of higher education, to whom the executive officers of the various institutions would be responsible. Within recent years a number of states have shifted part or all of the way toward this pattern of organization for higher education. The Commission recommends that other states follow this example in moving, when appropriate, toward the unification of control over state institutions of higher education."[3]

Personal investigation reveals that the Commission's opinion is scarcely based on fact. The number of states with joint boards, that is, a board having control of all the public institutions of higher learning is ten. The number of states with separate boards for its major institutions of higher learning is thirty-five. North Carolina, Louisiana, and Texas have both joint and separate boards. There are, of course, some states where a combination of the two systems is desirable, where a joint board is in charge of

[2] See Table 10, Part III.
[3] *Youth and the Future*, American Council on Education, 1942, p. 225.

teachers' colleges whose problems are rather identical. In the states where a joint board operates, great variation was found in the functions of the joint board. Some states have a chancellor with authoritative powers. In such states, the president of the university or state college has above him a sort of educational overlord, with powers almost Hitlerian in character. It is unnecessary to say that under such conditions the functions of the university or college president take on less and less significance, and that the presidents are not particularly happy under the system. Because the advocates of the joint board system are largely members of such boards and administrative officials appointed by them, they have almost the zeal of crusaders. The agitation for the creation of such joint boards is far more vocal than the internal conditions in the states where they operate would always imply. In other states, the chancellor is a kind of executive secretary, and in these states the university and college presidents have a little greater opportunity to exercise the powers normally reposed in them. In still other states, under the joint board, the use of the term "chancellor" is largely figurative, and the board employs a kind of chief clerk, who acts as messenger and liaison officer between the various institutions. Theoretically, the joint board can be presented most attractively. Actually, it proves difficult in operation. The various college and university presidents who have to operate under such a system are hesitant about incurring the disfavor of the joint board and its sometimes powerful appointive administrators. As a result, little is heard within the confines of the state of the disadvantages under which the institutions operate. These disadvantages are due to arbitrary decisions as between the various institutions regarding financing, to distribution of courses to be taught, and to restrictions placed on institutions which allow little right to self-expression. The affairs of a single institution with an enrollment of several thousand students are sufficiently complex and detailed as to require the constant attention of the members of a single board, and the attempt by a joint board to administer anywhere from five to twenty-five institutions means that many of the policies are delegated to paid employes of the joint board, who constitute a sort of educational supergovernment.

The functions of the boards of the various states differ but little. Most of them are empowered to determine educational procedures and policies, to pass on faculty and administrative appointments, to approve entrance and academic requirements, and to avoid political interference. President Conant of Harvard stated that he felt the boards should not be called on to pass on faculty appointments, on the ground that many on the board are not competent. Investigation, however, would seem to reveal that the boards' check on faculty appointments is preventive of inbreeding, a weakness of institutions where the constitution of the faculty is very largely in the hands of the administration or of faculty committees.

Presidents of colleges and universities constitute a class by themselves. After interviewing eighty-five of them, it is my opinion that there should be a special place reserved for them in heaven, although some people have been so unkind as to suggest that I must not be too sure of their ultimate destination. As a group, they reveal a high sense of dedication to their task. Few men are subjected to as great pressures, anxieties, unending concerns, rivalries, financial responsibilities, and all the many other obligations that are peculiarly theirs. Because of the necessity of tactful handling of delicate problems, they tend to lead a rather lonely life. They are constantly under scrutiny, not only by legislators and the general public, but by their own faculties and by the students. They must be exceedingly careful in their public utterances. As a result, they are characterized by deep searchings of heart and a grave concern for the thoroughness with which they perform their task. The relation between the university and college presidents and their governing boards is of the greatest importance. The business of the governing boards is primarily to determine policies and procedures. However, emergencies arise when it is necessary for a president to act on his own initiative, trusting that his actions will be confirmed by the board at a later date. It is here that the severest test comes for the average university executive. The need for sympathetic understanding between presidents and boards is paramount. Having laid down a framework of policies and procedures, the board should have enough confidence in the man they select as president to allow him some discretion in carrying out the administrative details of the program approved. Details of administration should be left primarily to the president and to his staff. Overzealous regents and trustees can frequently prove a handicap to an institution. If they are convinced that they are more capable at details of administration than the president whom they have selected, they should have the moral courage to dismiss him and to secure the services of a man in whom they have confidence. Constant interference in details of administration by trustees is something that must be avoided at all costs.

Then the matter of approach to the board by faculty members, non-faculty personnel, and students has its dangers. A hearing before the board of regents should always be the privilege of everyone connected with the institution, but the normal channel of approach should be through the president. An interesting recent trend is the appointment of the alumni secretary in many institutions as a member of the administrative staff, to be financed by the university. This provides an antidote to the merely football-minded alumni who, having forgotten most of the education they achieved during their undergraduate days, are sometimes overconfident of the value of the judgments they pass on the management of the institution. The alumni should be a loyal supporting group, with their affairs in the hands of a member of the administration who has a detailed knowledge of what is going on in the institution, so that harmonious relationships between the alumni and the university may be increased.

There are two general methods of financing the state universities and state colleges. One is known as the "lump-sum appropriation," under which the funds furnished by the state are expended by the regents or trustees at their discretion or, at least, under large heads, such as maintenance, capital improvements, operations, salaries, etc. Of the institutions visited in this survey, seventy-eight operate under the lump-sum appropriation. The other institutions suffer under what is known as "line-item." This means that every specific expenditure must be indicated on the budget as submitted, and that the money may be expended only according to these items. In Delaware, for instance, there is an antiquated law which provides that if the regents expend funds other than as proposed by the detailed line-item budget, which even goes into such matters as postage, telegraphic expense, fuel, and stationery, they shall be held criminally liable. While other states which operate under the line-item arrangement do not provide so severe a penalty, the regents, as responsible financially, suffer under a serious handicap. Emergencies constantly develop, and funds appropriated over a biennium frequently cannot be used in that biennium because of the lack of necessary equipment being available for purchase; while, on the other hand, new developments and requirements for instruction deserve expenditure, which expenditure is made impossible under the line-item system. Fortunately, a major portion of the states have become conscious of the serious disadvantage under which their regents are placed by this system, and it is to be earnestly hoped that all the state colleges and universities can operate under the lump-sum appropriation method in the very near future.

A much-discussed subject, in which the President's Commission on Higher Education is interested, is increases in tuition, particularly in the state colleges and universities. With only a few exceptions, tuition has been increased for both in-state and out-of-state students, particularly for the latter. This is due to increased costs in operations, and though appropriations have been increased also, the increase in appropriations has not been sufficient to offset the increased operating cost. Here we face the danger of defeating a purpose of publicly controlled higher education, which is to offer equality of opportunity to all students, irrespective of their economic backgrounds. In Part III will be found a table showing the rate of increase in tuition, not only in the publicly controlled colleges and universities, but also in the privately controlled schools visited. This increase ranges from nothing to 139 per cent. There is a growing tendency also to make fees all-inclusive so that they cover not only tuition, but athletic fees, library fees, matriculation fees, health fees, and other special expenses. It is interesting to note in passing that some of the states provide free tuition for in-state students, at state-controlled institutions. However, it is also interesting to note that those very states are guilty of at least a gentle hypocrisy, in that while they do not charge tuition, they manage to evade the law by charging a matriculation fee which sometimes is higher than the tuition fee required in other states.

The President's Commission on Higher Education also has been interested in the salary scales in the various institutions. Tables on these salary schedules are available in Part III. Unfortunately, college presidents, in spite of all their virtues, also can be described as among the "worst sheep stealers in the world." Some of them apparently are without conscience when it comes to making raids on the faculties of neighboring institutions when they are in a position to offer greater financial inducements. In order to protect the less fortunate colleges and universities, these salary schedules are grouped in the table according to size of enrollment and described by numeral rather than by name.

There has been a very considerable increase in faculty salaries since Pearl Harbor. This increase varies from 15 per cent in some ranks to over 50 per cent in others. For this reason, for the first time, the great state universities can compete successfully in attracting highly skilled educators, many of whom until recently have found it to their advantage to teach at privately controlled institutions.

An apparent grave difficulty, particularly in the larger schools, has to do with exceedingly large classes, on the theory that it is better for a student to be one of a multitude listening to the voice of a "name" professor than it is for him to sit under younger and less well-known instructors. This has gone so far that some institutions have resorted to mechanical devices to reproduce the voices of the better known teachers. It is true that while these large classes are divided into sections, there is a grave question whether they can provide thorough instruction by this mass production method. In some institutions, the size of certain classes is limited only by the size of auditoriums available. One institution reports as many as 1500 in a single lecture class. It is unnecessary to discuss at length the disadvantage under which students labor where this condition exists. The answer, of course, is to recruit additional competent teachers, which is difficult because of the present shortage of trained men. However, active steps must be taken promptly to correct this situation.

The President's Commission on Higher Education has been seriously concerned with whether there has been any appreciable increase in the teaching-hour load, that is, the number of hours an instructor actually holds classes or conducts laboratory periods. In the country at large, there has been but little appreciable increase in the teaching-hour load of the individual faculty member. However, there has been a very considerable increase in student-hour load, that is, the number of students for whose instruction the individual faculty member is responsible. While the teacher does not spend more hours on the lecture platform or in the laboratory, he must pass on the qualifications of a far greater number of students than normally, and there is at least a possibility that his work in this connection will not be so thorough as it would be if classes were smaller. President Truman's Commission is also concerned with whether faculty members are active in state, regional, and national professional associations in their various fields. The institution where this is not the case is exceptional, and there is a tendency on the part of a majority of the colleges and universities to make more generous expenditures to cover such memberships and to pay the expenses of faculty members who represent the institution, or who read papers, or who are officers of the association involved.

One of the most critical problems confronting American higher education is the question of federal aid. Under the head of land-grant appropriations, federal aid for state colleges engaged in teaching agriculture and the mechanic arts has been provided for a number of years. However, this aid is comparatively small as compared with the heavy financial responsibilities accepted by the various states and counties in these fields. The pattern of land-grant appropriations has been so clearly set over a long period that there is practically no indication of the slightest effort at federal control in connection with such grants. However, if federal aid is extended to all the states, to include not only the college level but the elementary and secondary schools as well, the possibility of federal control and federal interference is very real. It is undoubtedly true that in certain areas the need for adequate financial support cannot be met from the present resources of the state. Consider, for example, a state like Mississippi, with a population of 2,000,000, approximately 1,000,000 of whom are Negroes and "poor whites" who pay no tax. This state has to maintain not only a state university, a state college, a state college for women, and Negro institutions, but must also furnish instruction on elementary and secondary school levels. One cannot help but feel pride in the splendid achievement of such a state in view of the heavy responsibility placed on it. If any provision for federal aid is adopted, it should be based, first of all, on need. The proposal that federal aid be extended to all states, whether there be special need or not, is an open invitation to federal control, and federal control is definitely contrary to the American democratic concept of education. It also involves the danger of political interference in state education to a high degree. If any plan of federal aid is adopted, it should be limited to the states which are incapable of adequately supporting educational institutions on all levels, and there should be a time limitation requiring these states to move as rapidly as possible toward self-support. The importance of this provision is evident in the case of a state like Louisiana, which at one time was possessed of rather meager resources, but now, with the development of oil production and new industries, is reaching a point where it can compete effectively with many states formerly more prosperous than Louisiana.

Involved here also is the question of financial provision for privately controlled as well as publicly controlled institutions of higher learning. There are 1694 colleges and universities in the continental United States; of these 1137 are privately controlled or church-connected institutions, and 557 are publicly controlled colleges and universities. Because of financing by the national government for war education in various colleges and universities, very considerable appropriations have gone to all institutions, both public and private, in recent years. This was true under the V-12 program for the Navy, the ASTP program for the Army, and now is true under the educational benefits provided by the G.I. Bill of Rights. In some instances colleges which had weak financial support, are now "living in a style to which they were not accustomed," and naturally are very anxious not to surrender this style of living unless it becomes absolutely necessary. For them to continue to maintain their present standards after the G.I. Bill of Rights' provisions are exhausted will require a subsidy, either from the state or from the Federal Government. A few years ago, a survey of the presidents of independent colleges and universities showed about 98 per cent definitely opposed to federal subsidy. A recent survey of the presidents of the same institutions indicates practically 100 per cent favoring a federal subsidy of some sort. This brings us directly to the point where we must face two important questions. First, can we endanger the enormous investments we have in our great state universities and colleges by spreading our tax educational income too thinly? It is undoubtedly true that there are limits to which this tax educational burden can be stretched. In the second place, we need to remember that many of these privately controlled colleges are church-connected and rather small and have for years revealed an intense rivalry in their effort to attract students. Great educational foundations like Princeton and Harvard and Yale do not enter into this picture to any considerable extent, but there are many small colleges whose very existence will be threatened by the present cost of operation if there is not a subsidy of some sort. We then have to determine whether these institutions can be subsidized with state funds without surrendering a proportionate part of their control. Indications are that most of the church-connected colleges, as well as other privately controlled institutions, are quite willing to accept subsidies but equally unwilling to surrender even partial control to the state. It must be insisted here that the preservation of independently controlled higher education is essential to life in a democracy. Entirely publicly controlled education presents certain dangers, particularly if that control be federal rather than local.

The other grave question that has to be faced is whether the principle of separation of Church and State will be violated if subsidies to privately controlled institutions, whether direct or indirect, come to play a prominent part in our national educational life. If one institution is helped, all must be helped, or once again we shall violate a basic tenet of democracy. If all are helped, irrespective of equipment, capacity, or ability to turn out capable graduates, it is almost impossible to estimate the funds which would be necessary to carry on such a program. It is no reflection on anyone to point out that the treatment of certain subjects varies greatly as between different types of schools. While religion is a necessary part of education, *when religion colors the pursuit of truth in the interest of sectarian ends,* one can be pardoned for raising a conscientious objection to federal or state subsidy to denominational institutions.

There has been a rather widespread impression that communism is rampant in our colleges and universities. On every possible occasion the public press has magnified alleged cases of disloyalty on the part of both faculty members and students. One would almost be led to believe that the colleges and universities are breeding-grounds for communistic thought. At every institution visited in this survey the direct question was asked, "Have there been any instances of subversive activity in your institution in the past five years which have attracted public attention?" The result is bound to be reassuring to those whose fears have been aroused. Out of eighty-nine institutions surveyed, there were only five cases in which the answer was yes. A study of these cases reveals that in some instances there was practically no ground for the assertion that there had been subversive activity on the part of either faculty members or students. In others, investigation revealed that the number of persons involved was so few in comparison with total enrollments as not to cause occasion for alarm. This matter is covered rather fully in the chapter on "Communism on the College Campus." We can be assured, however, that there is no occasion for serious concern in regard to radical teaching of a communistic character on the part of faculties or in regard to any considerable communistic activity on the part of student groups. It can safely be said that there are few groups more loyal to the American form of government than the men who make up the faculties and the student bodies of our American colleges and universities.

A study of statistics of in-state and out-of-state enrollments in the various colleges and universities shows a surprisingly large number of out-of-state students. This is true in spite of the claims made that, owing to the increased veterans' enrollment, the average institution would be severely limited in the number of out-of-state students who could be admitted. A table in Part III reveals the figures.[4]

Another interesting discovery has to do with the breakdown of student populations according to religious affiliations. Of the students enrolled in the institutions considered in this study, 12.6 per cent are Roman Catholic; 75.2 per cent Protestants; 5.3 per cent Jewish; and 6.6 per cent of no religious preference. Twenty-four universities of those visited did not furnish information on the religious breakdown of their student populations. It is important to note that the vast majority of students in state colleges and universities have some sort of religious affiliation. It is important also to remark that in certain areas minority religious groups are much more strongly represented than in others. For instance, there is a very high percentage of Latter Day Saints in the colleges and universities of Utah, and a high percentage of Roman Catholic students in certain institutions in Massachusetts and Rhode Island. Perhaps the highest percentage of Jewish students, outside of New York City, is at one institution in Florida.

There have been persistent rumors of laxity in morals in our colleges and universities, a condition which might be expected as a reaction to the war affecting many levels of life. Those concerned with the future citizenry of the country are eager and anxious to determine the truth as to moral conditions on the college level. When they were interrogated on this point, presidents and administrators felt a natural hesitancy to appear critical of the student bodies of their own institutions. Two facts stand out

---

[4] See Table 5, Part III.

rather clearly. Instances of excessive alcoholism and sex offenses are noticeably less than one would have reason to expect, and this survey refutes irresponsible utterances by occasional visitors, widely quoted in the public press. The administration of every institution visited was confident that while excessive alcoholism and sex offenders always have been, and probably always will be, a problem, conditions are better than one would have expected after the kind of war through which we have passed. This is undoubtedly due, in part, to the fact that many married veteran students have their wives with them on the campus, and so are less apt to give way to sexual temptation, and, being older, they naturally set an example to the younger students. This is also true of excessive alcoholism. The married veterans are anxious to complete their formal education as rapidly as possible, and concentrate on their studies, to avoid any possibility of failure. Most of them have had enough experience with alcohol to realize that excessive use of it reduces their effectiveness. Here again the older students serve as an example to the younger.

There is another area, however, in which there has been a very definite moral breakdown. It is so general that it is unnecessary to identify any one institution as being more guilty than another. Some schools are a bit more honest than others in acknowledging the facts, but in every institution visited, when realities were faced and fears removed, there was frank admission of an increase in cheating, lying, and stealing, but particularly in cheating. There are various causes for this increase, and they are not directly related to the vast increase in veteran enrollment. In fact, so far as the offenders are concerned, high-school graduates and women students contributed their full share of these offenses. This problem is treated in some detail in the chapter on "Religion and Morality in Publicly and Privately Controlled Institutions," with suggestions as to the best method by which it is to be solved. One dean of students said that he was concerned not only because of the increase in cheating, but because of an apparent ignorance among the students of the difference between right and wrong.

In another institution, during an all-day conference with the president on this trend, he asserted that so far as his knowledge went, there had been no increase in these types of offenses in his university. It happened that I addressed the faculty of that university that afternoon and in the course of my remarks referred to the evidence of moral breakdown which I had discovered in other institutions. At the end of my talk, the president suggested that I go back to his office and continue work on my questionnaire, as there were some routine committee reports coming up in which I would not be interested, and because I was pressed for time. The following morning, five members of the faculty made appointments with me by phone, no one knowing that the others were doing so, and in our conferences expressed appreciation of the frank facing of the moral breakdown, and told me that the unfinished business of the night before was the report of a committee on the breakdown of morals, particularly the cheating, in that university. The next day the president also acknowledged that they faced a serious problem, but expressed the fear that his institution might be considered worse than some others.

To meet this difficulty a number of suggestions deserve serious consideration. We must guard against the development of the idea that dishonesty is to be expected as one of the fruits of higher education. To achieve this, there must be concerted action by boards of regents and faculties to inculcate the students with an integrated philosophy of life which will help them to make proper use of their education after graduation and also stimulate them to preserve and maintain moral standards. How these ends can be accomplished are discussed in the chapter on "Religion and Morality in Publicly and Privately Controlled Institutions." There are several methods of approach, but it is not within the purview of this report to recommend any one as infallible. However, certain facts seem to unfold rather clearly. First, basic religious concepts must be taught as a normal part of education, whether they are called religion as such or not; second, these basic religious concepts must win back the academic respectability that conventional religion, in many instances, has lost; and, third, many of the colleges and universities, with their emphasis on "science major; everything else minor," must be made to realize that they have lost sight of the need for giving their students a design for living. Instead, they appear to be concerned with delivering education in streamlined packages of information, with little attention to the motives which will determine the use the individual student will make of his education in later life.

Another great task confronting both the publicly controlled and the privately controlled colleges and universities is the problem of how to teach industrial relations. One of the most serious difficulties confronting America at present is economic unrest and constantly recurring industrial disturbances. Labor is unacquainted with the problems of management, and management is frequently unsympathetic with the problems of labor. Leadership on both sides often has shown evidence of greater interest in selfish gain than in the common welfare. The citizen who does not have a selfish interest on the side of either labor or management (in other words the consumer) finds himself the victim of economic pressures which threaten to destroy the democratic way of life. The problem involved can never be solved until there is a common mind, equally open to the facts on both sides of these ever-recurring controversies. It would seem to be the business of colleges and universities, particularly of the state colleges and universities, to provide instruction in the problems of management and labor. This would enable them to graduate students capable of representing either side impartially, and intelligent enough to place the common good before selfish ends and thus avoid catastrophe. The chapter on "Industrial Relations and Workers' Education" goes into this matter in some detail. It is important that steps be taken to meet this great need promptly. Many colleges and universities are already offering numerous courses in the field of labor relations, but, with the exception of Cornell, Wisconsin, Illinois, Minnesota, and a few others, such instruction has not been so organized as to make much of an impression on the problem itself.

The relation between high schools and colleges deserves serious study. Just as there is inequality between the various colleges and the effectiveness of their work, so there are even greater inequalities on the secondary school level. The high schools in suburban areas can offer advantages denied high schools in rural areas, and sometimes in the congested sections of great cities. The mere acceptance of a high school diploma, with sixteen accredited units, is not proving an altogether satisfactory requirement for college entrance. This is especially true of the work in English and in the Social Sciences on the secondary level. The colleges find many of their students improperly prepared, and the mortality rate is high, often proving such a discouragement to the student as to handicap him seriously throughout the rest of his life. One university is making a study of the college records, first of veterans admitted as a result of aptitude tests and without high-school diploma, and, second, of former high-school students admitted on the same basis who have not graduated from high school. The findings thus far would seem to indicate that those thus admitted were making better average records than high-school graduates. This study is still in the experimental stage, but should be watched with interest. Another state college has accredited the high schools of the state on the basis of the records of their graduates over a period of ten years. These high schools are rated A, B, C, and D. Thus A and B are admitted without examination; a few in class C pass the entrance examination, and a very few in class D. In other institutions increasing emphasis is being placed on the General Educational Development test and similar measurements in an effort to determine just what should constitute the standard by which students are to be admitted to college. With a vast increase in enrollments, some limitation is already necessary, and there is a possibility of an even greater selection in the days ahead.

Finally, the last chapter in Part I is devoted to the contribution being made to our national welfare and to the improvement in the standard of living of the individual citizen because of the work in the various state colleges and universities throughout the country. "Basic Research" was long a prerogative and privilege enjoyed only by the privately endowed institutions. With the growth of state colleges and universities, there has been a greater emphasis on what is known as "Applied Research," and the advance of "Basic Research" has been somewhat neglected in state colleges and universities. However, the tremendous strides in "Applied Research" have contributed to the common welfare and to the advantage of the individual in a surprising way. It may safely be said that the state colleges and universities, along with their emphasis on "Applied Research," are also developing high instructional levels in certain fields, and have made a greater contribution than any other single group of interests to the welfare of the individual and to the development of resources of the particular areas in which they are located.

In this overall picture we have passed rapidly over the main issues, on the determination of which the future of American higher education may depend to a considerable extent. There is a noticeable trend toward the development of a broader general educational base. It is evident that, with the strong emphasis on the scientific method, colleges and universities have neglected teaching those intrinsic values which determine the direction of a man's life, and which rescue society from a chaotic existence where class rivalries and selfish interests conspire to destroy society itself. We must keep politics out of the universities and the universities out of politics. We must promote the most cordial relations possible between publicly controlled and privately controlled institutions, facing squarely the implications that state and federal subsidy of privately controlled institutions imply. We must determine whether our universities are breeding places of communism, as suggested by a sensational press, or whether the roots of communism are to be sought elsewhere. We must study the question of the teaching of religion in all institutions of higher learning as a means of offering a student an integrating philosophy which will determine the use he will make in later life of the various skills he achieves at the university. We must face squarely the serious threat to the economic independence of the individual implied in the unresolved conflict between management and labor, and the part the college or university must play in bringing these disputes to a just and peaceful settlement. We must determine what preparation is necessary for college or university entrance, the need for vocational guidance centers and whether they should be part of the local school system, and the type of education the university or college has as its objective to supply. And, last of all, we much consider the contribution being made by various state colleges and universities to a better living standard for the individual as a result of "Applied Research" and to the maintenance of high instructional levels in certain fields.

KEEPING POLITICS OUT OF THE
STATE UNIVERSITIES

THERE has been a rather general impression throughout the
country that state colleges and universities are governed
largely by political considerations. Instances can be cited
of political interference handicapping the educational program
of state-controlled institutions of higher learning. These instances, given wide publicity, have led to a mistaken conception
among many people that a majority of the state colleges and universities are influenced largely by political considerations in their
policies, educational procedures, and other matters involving
control. Personal investigation at the state colleges and universities visited indicates clearly that the facts do not justify this easy
assumption, which has been encouraged from time to time by the
public press, especially when that press finds an opportunity to
exploit its own political views. The number of publicly controlled institutions of higher learning now being influenced unfavorably by political considerations is so few that they are conspicuous, and public opinion in a majority of states is so strongly
set against such interference that the time may come in the near
future when it will be visited with heavy penalties. When public
opinion becomes sufficiently stirred—and it is rapidly nearing
that moment—institutions primarily governed by political considerations may find their national accreditation seriously threatened. Therefore it will be to the advantage of every state institution to keep itself so clear of political involvements that no
finger of suspicion may be pointed at it.

In order to examine fairly the opportunities for, and instances
of, political interference, we may well consider the methods by

which the various boards of trustees, regents, supervisors, curators, and members of state boards of education are chosen. These
methods vary widely in the different states. There are four principal means by which these boards are constituted: (1) appointment by the governor of the state, subject to confirmation by the
state senate or the general assembly, (2) election by popular vote
from candidates nominated by the political parties, (3) self-
perpetuation, and (4) election by the state legislature. The opportunities for political intrusion into the affairs of a state university or college are apt to be affected by the method used in the
selection of regents or trustees. In order to offset this danger,
there is a definite movement toward establishing boards of regents
or trustees as constitutional boards. Where this method is in
operation the boards are so protected by constitutional provisions
that the opportunity for political interference is definitely les-
sened. No state government or state legislature can by statute
change the nature of such a board, or the method by which its
members are chosen, or the powers conferred upon it. It is interesting to note that where there has been excessive political
interference in the affairs of state boards the reaction of the public
has been so strongly condemnatory as to bring into being constitutional provision for protecting the boards from this abuse of
power. Perhaps the best-known instance of this is in Louisiana,
where, under the administration of the late Huey Long, there was
evidence of strong political domination of Louisiana State University.[1] The immediate result of this, after Governor Long's
death, was the creation of a constitutional board consisting of
fourteen members to serve terms of fourteen years each. These
terms are staggered, so that two new members are added each
biennium. Inasmuch as a governor of Louisiana may serve only
two terms, he normally names only four members of the board
during his incumbency. It has been found that this restriction
of the power of the governor led to much greater care in the
selection of supervisors, with a consequent improvement in the
government of the university. Other instances could be cited

[1] *Louisiana State University:* A Survey Report, American Council on Education,
1940.

showing that public opinion, when given an opportunity to express itself, is strongly opposed to political control or political interference in the affairs of the state colleges and universities. It may be stated that one of the definite aims of the publicly controlled institutions of higher education is "to keep the state universities and colleges out of politics and politics out of the state universities and colleges," which cannot be repeated too often.

That the governors of the states possess great responsibilities in the selection of the men who make up boards of regents and trustees is beyond question. Because the college training of the citizens of the future is largely under the control of the governors in the states where they have appointive powers they should be held to strict accountability for the type of men selected for the boards. Wide publicity should be given such appointments and the qualifications of the men selected be carefully examined to determine whether they are capable of undertaking the responsibility conferred on them. When one considers the vast powers given these boards by law, one realizes the importance of other than political considerations entering into their selection. The widest publicity should be given the governors' selection of men about whom there is the slightest question. Appointments have been made for political reasons and to repay political debts. There is a kind of traditional honor associated with these appointments, and the type of governor who is so unworthy of his opportunity to serve education as to appoint men from ulterior motives should be exposed to public criticism and denunciation. There is also a grave question whether men should be appointed on boards of regents or trustees to represent special interests.[2] In many states where there is a land-grant agricultural college it has long been the tradition to appoint representatives of agriculture. There is a good argument for this, that because of the vast expenditures for agricultural education some of the men in control of such expenditures should have agricultural knowledge and experience. However, the same theory carried out in other fields frequently leads to an unfortunate situation. In one state university three members of a rather large board are appointed to

[2] *Men Who Control Our Universities*, Hubert Beck; King's Crown Press, 1947.

represent agriculture; three, management, and three, labor. Curiously enough, while the agricultural and management representatives are named for three years, the labor representatives are named for only one, because the turnover in the internal politics of the unions is so great that any man appointed for a three-year term would be apt not to represent his organization during a second or third year. The primary consideration, however, is that regents or trustees be representative of the higher educational interests of the entire citizenry of the state, inasmuch as all citizens through their taxes contribute to the maintenance of state institutions. In addition, the matters brought up for consideration on the agenda of boards of regents or trustees are of such varied and comprehensive character that each regent or trustee should be capable not merely of representing a special partisan point of view, but a point of view which embraces matters as far removed from each other as educational procedure and policy, the work of a graduate school, agriculture, the humanities, industrial research, finance, and the problem of morals on college campuses.

The most popular method of selecting state boards of regents or trustees is appointment by the governor, subject to confirmation by the state senate or the general assembly. This is the method for fifty-nine of the eighty-nine colleges and universities included in this study. There are a few instances where only some members of the board are appointed by the governor subject to confirmation by the state senate. In one case the governor appoints five members only of a board of fifty-eight; in a second case, one to eight members of a board of thirty-two; in a third, one to six out of thirty-two; and in a fourth, one to five out of forty-five. The boards in these eighty-nine institutions vary tremendously in size. They range from boards of five members to a board of 105. The states in which this method of appointment by governor and confirmation by the state senate prevails are (for one institution) Alabama, Arizona, Arkansas, California, Colorado, Connecticut, Delaware, Florida, Georgia, Indiana, Iowa, Kansas, Kentucky, Louisiana, Maine, Maryland, Massachusetts, Mississippi, Missouri, Montana, New Hampshire, New

Jersey, New Mexico, New York, North Dakota, Ohio, Oklahoma, Oregon, Pennsylvania, Rhode Island, South Dakota, Tennessee, Texas, Utah, Virginia, Washington, West Virginia, Wisconsin, and Wyoming. A table in Part III [3] indicates the number of members on each board and the number appointed by the governor, subject to confirmation in each instance. In a majority of cases, all the regents in these states are appointed by the governor and confirmed by the state senate or general assembly; however, in the instances where all the members are not so named, there is a provision whereby the balance of the board is chosen by some other method. For instance, at the University of Connecticut nine are appointed by the governor and two are elected by the alumni. At Cornell five of a board of forty-five are appointed by the governor, eighteen are chosen by the board itself, ten are elected by the alumni, and there is one life member. At the University of Delaware, with a membership of thirty-two, eight are appointed by the governor and twenty, or a majority, are elected by the board itself.

A few states where the governor appoints, provide by law for a bipartisan board. Yet men who are eligible for appointment as regents or trustees should be of such caliber that a mere change in political administration from one term to another should not mean the removal of an especially capable man. It would be desirable if political considerations could be entirely eliminated from the composition of boards of regents and trustees. Nine boards among the institutions visited which the law provides shall be bipartisan are located in Iowa, Kansas, Missouri, Montana, New Hampshire, Utah, West Virginia, and Wyoming. While terms of office frequently overlap, the bipartisan provision does not normally strengthen the membership of a capable board of regents. Therefore, it would be a decided advantage if the bipartisan provision were eliminated entirely. Another method of choosing regents and trustees is by popular vote, the candidates being nominated by the various political parties and running for election on partisan platforms. Surprisingly enough, the men chosen by this method have been of a reasonably high quality.

[3] Part III.

This method is followed by seven of the eighty-nine institutions included in this survey—the University of Colorado, the University of Michigan, Michigan State College, the University of Nebraska, the University of Nevada, Southwestern Louisiana Institute, and the University of Illinois. There is a grave danger, however, in this method of selection. Members so chosen testify to the fact that names to be presented to the electorate are usually selected at a party caucus. In view of the many other nominations to be made at such a caucus, the nomination of regents is an item far down on the agenda, which usually comes toward the end of the second day, when a great many of the delegates have already left for home. This means that a small, well-organized group can control the naming of the candidates, with some special and not altogether unselfish objectives in view. This method was employed in the election of a school board in one of the larger cities recently, and it nearly precipitated disaster for the elementary and secondary schools of that city's system. It has the additional unfortunate feature of frequently changing the composition of the board of regents because of the fluctuation in the political fortunes of the candidates. This method has the same disadvantage as the legal requirement for a bipartisan board, which sometimes makes a man's political label more important than his qualifications for the position of regent or trustee. It should be said that the system has worked reasonably well so far, but considering the almost insane hunger for control occasionally displayed by partisan political leaders, this is no indication that the dangers inherent in the system should be ignored. In addition, interviews with citizens of the states where this system is followed, brought out that very little attention is paid to the qualifications, or even to the names, of the men nominated, and that a majority of those who vote in such an election vote blindly along strictly party lines. It would seem well therefore to question whether the selection of regents or trustees by popular election is a satisfactory method for constituting these boards.

A third method, which also has certain disadvantages, is that of the entirely self-perpetuating board. This method is used in some six institutions of those visited, along with five partially self-perpetuating. Such a board governs the University of Alabama, although Alabama Polytechnic Institute, in the same state, has a board appointed by the governor and approved by the state senate. The board of the University of Southern California, a private institution, is self-perpetuating, and it is interesting to note that out of a membership of thirty on this board, only ten have had previous college experience. The board of Stanford, another private institution, is also self-perpetuating, and all of its members are college graduates. Out of a board of thirty-two at the University of Delaware, eight are appointed by the governor and twenty are elected by the board itself, without any confirmation, thus making a working majority of this board self-perpetuating. The Fellows and Corporation at Harvard University have five out of seven members self-perpetuating. The University of Miami, which is a privately controlled institution but which receives a small appropriation from the county in which it is located, also has a self-perpetuating board. The Rutgers Board, with a membership of fifty-eight, one of the larger boards of the land-grant institutions (for Rutgers is the State University of New Jersey) elects all of its members except sixteen, which means that an overwhelming majority of that board is self-perpetuating. Vanderbilt, a private institution, has an entirely self-perpetuating board of thirty-three. Yale's board has ten self-perpetuating members out of a total membership of nineteen. Thus it will be seen that the boards of private institutions are largely self-perpetuating, with a part of the membership elected in some places by the alumni. In the state universities and colleges the practice is not so common, and the only instances visited were at Rutgers, Alabama, Clemson, Vermont, and the University of Delaware. At one institution where the self-perpetuating system of election to board membership prevails, the administration frankly confessed that they felt this method could be improved upon. They testify that it has the danger of son succeeding father in too many instances, or a lawyer or a doctor being appointed to replace some other lawyer or doctor who had resigned or died. Another disadvantage of this system is that with the self-perpetuating feature membership is apt to be for life. This means that such boards sometimes are rather heavily overloaded with older men and have a tendency to carry on conventional practices rather than to seek out new avenues of service and usefulness in the pursuit of truth.

Still another method of determining the membership of boards of regents or trustees is to have them named by the state legislature. This system is followed in six institutions of those visited. These institutions include the Citadel, the Military College of South Carolina, where seven out of thirteen members are elected by the General Assembly. Ninety-eight members of the joint state board of North Carolina are elected by the legislature. It is interesting to note in this case that there are two ex-officio members out of the first hundred and that all living ex-governors of the state are also ex-officio life members, the reason for this never having been clearly stated. Inasmuch as there are five living ex-governors of North Carolina at the moment, the present membership is only 105. At the University of South Carolina, fourteen out of eighteen are elected by the legislature, and at the University of Vermont nine out of twenty are chosen by the General Assembly. At Minnesota there are no ex-officio members, and the board of twelve is elected by the legislature. Clemson in South Carolina has six out of thirteen members elected by the General Assembly.

There are certain variations of the four major patterns of selecting board members. It has been indicated that in the majority of states and institutions the members are appointed by the governor and confirmed by the state senate or general assembly. The next largest number of boards is self-perpetuating. There are seven elected by popular vote, and six elected by the legislature independently of the governor. In one institution, Pennsylvania State College, twelve out of thirty-two members are elected by delegates from county agricultural and industrial societies. At New York State College for Teachers a college board is named by the New York State Board of Regents, while at Southwestern Louisiana Institute three are appointed from public service commission districts and confirmed by the Senate. In Indiana five out of eight are chosen by the State Board of Education with the approval of the governor.

In contrast with this, among the private institutions visited, three had a considerable number of the board elected by the alumni, and a major number of each board was self-perpetuating. On the other hand, there is alumni participation in only six state colleges or universities. In three of these cases the alumni elect two members to the board; in one case, three members; in one case, nine members; and in one case, ten members.

In regard to qualifications, the private institutions select trustees from a country-wide area. State residence is required for practically all publicly controlled state colleges and universities. There are thirteen institutions which select members from the various congressional districts.

There are certain restrictions in some states. One requires that board members hold no other public office. Another requires a member from each judicial district, and still another, that no university employe shall be a board member. Five require alumni members, and two have representatives of labor, agriculture, and industry. Only one institution requires that the board members themselves be college graduates. It is interesting to note, however, that out of a total membership of 1025 board members in seventy-two institutions, 815 are college graduates, while 210 are not. At nineteen colleges all board members are graduates, and at sixteen, all are graduates but one. It is worthy of comment in this connection that the vast majority of those not having previous college experience are distinguished citizens and outstanding leaders in their states. It would be possible to place within a small compass the number of men who have been appointed for purely political reasons or whose capability is open to serious question. Wide publicity of the backgrounds of such appointees would be highly desirable.

An interesting question is raised as to the advisability of having ex-officio members. A careful examination of the make-up of the boards indicates that forty-two states provide for these ex-officio trustees, regents, supervisors, or curators. On a number of these boards there are only two ex-officio members, the governor and the State Superintendent of Public Instruction. This arrangement operates in Alabama, Arizona, California, Connec-

ticut, the Citadel, Illinois, Maine, North Carolina, Pennsylvania
State, Rutgers, South Carolina, Tennessee, Utah, Virginia, Wyoming, Florida, Kentucky, Massachusetts and Montana. In some
other states, however, there are a considerable number of ex-
officio members, ranging all the way from the Adjutant General
to the State Director of Agriculture. U.C.L.A. has eight ex-officio
members and the University of California has eight. Cornell has
eleven out of a possible total membership of forty-five. The University of New Mexico has two out of a membership of seven.
Rutgers has eleven out of fifty-eight. North Carolina is the outstanding instance of ex-officio and inactive members. The joint
board in that state has 105 members, which include seven who are
ex-officio—the governor and living ex-governors and the Superintendent of Public Instruction. This means that the majority of
the board does not regularly attend meetings and that the work is
done by an executive committee of twelve, which has full interim
authority. There is serious question of the desirability of ex-
officio membership. They can be divided into two classes, those
who almost never attend, and those who are active in contributing to the work of the board. In most states the governor, because
of other responsibilities, is not usually present at board meetings.
Only one ex-officio member can be counted upon generally to be
a useful and helpful member of a board, the State Superintendent
of Public Instruction. It is interesting to note that in almost every
instance the ex-officio members are either appointees of the governor or members of the governor's political party. In some states
ex-officio members are denied the right to vote. Ex-officio members, if they are not active, should not hold office. If they are
active, there is a possibility, with the exception of the Superintendent of Public Instruction, that they may constitute a solid
block of votes which can be counted on in any controversy between the regents and the governor, or between the governor
and the administration of the institution. Instances could be cited
where inactive ex-officio members, without previous experience
or background, have hurriedly taken over in time of crisis
and, moved mainly by political considerations, have been a
factor not always for the best interests of the institution. There

is no particular reason for even a governor to be an ex-officio member of a board of trustees or regents. Except as an honorary title and because of the prestige of his actual office, this seems rather unnecessary. He should be able to trust the men who make up the board or take steps in his official capacity to remove them for cause. The same applies to his relation to the president of the college or university. It might be well to consider seriously a move to abolish all ex-officio members of boards of regents except the State Superintendent of Public Instruction, thus eliminating a possible channel for political interference.

The length of term for the regents in the various states is also important as a factor in the opportunity it presents for the exercise of political influence by outside sources. The length of terms vary from three years to sixteen years to life. The terms are staggered in forty-three of the eighty-nine institutions visited. This means that in the case of a board of five members appointed for a six-year term, two will have their terms expire at the end of two years, two more at the end of the following two years, and one at the end of the sixth year. There are two advantages to this arrangement. One is that there is always a majority of experienced regents or trustees on the board. A second is that it prevents a governor from arbitrarily replacing an entire board with largely inexperienced men. In practically all states board members are eligible for reappointment or re-election. A few provide for the expiration of a short period before such members may be reappointed or re-elected, but in most states competent regents are reappointed or re-elected term after term. In most states vacancies due to death or resignation are filled by appointment by the governor, subject to confirmation at the following meeting of the legislature. Even with the staggered term arrangement there is the possibility of a governor, with the help of ex-officio members, controlling by appointment a majority of a board. With governors non-politically minded in regard to education this arrangement can be made to work; but not all governors are non-politically minded when it comes to as powerful an institution as a great state college or a great state university. Once again steps should be taken to protect the boards from political interference:

(1) by insisting on staggered terms, with eligibility for reappointment for all men who have demonstrated their ability; (2) by the abolition of the bipartisan feature; (3) by a restriction on governors so that no governor shall be able during his term in office to name a majority of members of a board. The governor always has the right to remove board members for cause. This protects sufficiently against the retention of incompetent men over a long period. Unfortunately, there have been instances when, for political reasons, governors have replaced competent regents with less competent men because of a change in the political complexion of the state. In order to protect publicly controlled higher education, such action should be made impossible.

A governor can be guilty of treason to the youth of his state by appointing regents or trustees for partisanship reasons rather than for their ability and capacity. The sums invested in publicly controlled education add up to an enormous total. It is a grave temptation to men who are for party first and for public welfare second to be swayed by political preference when an opportunity for control presents itself. The slogan, "To the victor belong the spoils," should never be applied to appointments to boards of regents or trustees. Any governor to whom this is a major consideration is disloyal to education and to the public welfare.

In several states visited, concern was expressed by educational administrators and by members of governing boards over the possibility of the use of what is known as the joint-board system as a method by which a governor can secure political control. There was a time when the joint-board system, which is a single board for all the higher educational institutions of a state, gave promise of rather widespread use. In theory, the joint-board plan appears to offer many advantages. In practice, however, it proves exceedingly difficult to operate. This is evidenced by the fact that there are few orthodox joint-board systems in operation. Even in the minority of states which have the joint board instead of a separate board for each institution there have been such modifications of the joint-board system that it is scarcely accurate to say that ten states employ this system in the full sense of the term.

The advocates of the joint-board system are most persuasive in their arguments that it reduces the cost of higher education by eliminating duplication of courses in the higher educational institutions, promoting good will and avoiding rivalry among the institutions, and so arranging enrollments of students as to produce the maximum benefit to the state. It is also claimed that administrative costs are reduced by vesting authority in a single board for all publicly controlled institutions of higher learning. This is carried even so far as to advertise very small reductions in the comparative costs of catalogues, in the cost of extension courses in the various institutions, and in other details.

The unmodified joint-board system provides for the creation of a chancellor or commissioner who has absolute and complete authority. It also provides for a joint-board administrative staff of paid employees, usually including a secretary, whose authority is second only to that of the chancellor himself. This rather totalitarian setup is effective only in a few states, such as Oregon and Georgia. It has certain marked disadvantages. In the first place, it sets up a kind of super-president in the person of an authoritarian chancellor, and the presidents of the state universities and state colleges are placed in a subordinate position and deprived of a considerable amount of initiative and authority. In the second place, it gives occasion for considerable dissatisfaction in awarding to one state institution the right to teach and to offer certain subjects, and denying that same right to another state institution in the same system. This has the merit of apparently avoiding duplication. Actually, it forces students to go to a certain institution rather than to one of their choice, and it places a severe limitation on the present trend toward a broader general educational basis, especially in land-grant colleges under the joint-board system. It also presents serious financial problems in that the joint board, under the leadership of a powerful chancellor, arbitrarily decides on the division of funds among the state university, the state college, and the state teachers' colleges. For instance, in a state where there is an unusual number of state teachers' colleges, with rather small enrollments and high per capita overhead, funds which are needed for properly carrying on the work of the university and the state college can be diverted to maintaining these smaller institutions. This may apply even to fees and receipts, which should be the property of the university earning them, but which, under this system, can be diverted to other purposes. The chancellor of such a system must be a person of unusual patience, tact, charm, and sympathetic understanding. Someone once asked an old Episcopal priest whether the Presiding Bishop of the church was an autocrat. His answer was, "Yes, but a rather benevolent one." Well, the same thing might be said of chancellors. Under the highly efficient joint-board system we have, in essence, a totalitarian form of government for higher educational institutions. While it is possible for such a system to operate with every appearance of efficiency and economy, we need to be reminded that there is a considerable overhead in connection with the maintenance of joint-board offices, and salaries for the chancellor and secretary and for the additional office help that may be required. It is putting it rather mildly to say that the lot of college and university presidents under such a system (while it may mean relief from certain responsibilities) is apt to be marked by considerable unhappiness and disappointment because of their inability to exercise the authority normally vested in them. However, the assumption that the entire college and university world is moving toward the establishment of a state joint-board system of control is scarcely justified by the facts, when we consider that there are three times as many states operating with separate boards as there are states operating under the joint-board arrangement. It is true that in certain states there has been a considerable accumulation of separate institutions and separate boards. For instance, at one time in Georgia there was a separate governing board for each of twenty-one institutions. In such a case a reduction in the number of boards would seem logical. The present tendency would appear to be toward the establishment of a separate board for the state university, a separate board for the state college, and a joint board for the teachers' colleges, whose programs are rather identical and whose problems are much alike. It has also been proved that it is possible for separate boards to work in harmony and co-operation and thus to avoid one of the difficulties the joint-board system was supposed to resolve.

Anyone who has ever served as a regent or trustee on a separate board for an institution of 5000 or more students is fully conscious of the demands on his time and thought if he would do his work effectively. To place on a single board the responsibility for outlining policies, educational procedures, confirming faculty and administrative appointments, passing on academic standards, and assuming financial responsibility for anywhere from half a dozen to twenty-five such institutions means that these duties have to be left largely to the salaried chancellor and such staff as he may require. In the average institution having a separate board monthly meetings are the rule. If such a schedule becomes necessary for a separate board, a joint board would face an almost impossible task if the work had to be done by the board members themselves with the same thoroughness as under the separate board system.

The autocratic type of joint-board system just outlined is in effect in very few states. Charles B. Byrne says, "A single governing board controls the entire state educational systems in Florida, Idaho, Montana, New York, and North Dakota; a single board controls all state higher institutions in Georgia, Iowa, Kansas, Mississippi, Oregon, and South Dakota." [4] However, the type of board which operates in Oregon and Georgia is entirely different from the type of joint board in a state like Florida, or in North Dakota. Oklahoma is also listed as a state operating under a joint-board system. However, the system in Oklahoma differs radically from that in Oregon. Oklahoma has a state board of regents for higher education. This board employs a chancellor, who acts as a kind of executive secretary and as a liaison officer between it and the various institutions in the state. Each constituent institution has its own board of control to supervise administration of its program, employ the faculty, and operate the institution. The state board of regents of higher education (or joint board) simply functions as a co-ordinating agency for all. The Oklahoma

[4] *Co-Ordinated Control of Higher Education in Oregon*, Charles David Byrne—Stanford University Press, 1940.

system also provides that privately controlled institutions may become affiliated with the system. In other words, although there is a joint board which considers the allocation of funds and assignment of functions, there are separate boards for the University of Oklahoma, Oklahoma A. & M., Oklahoma College for Women, the teachers' colleges, Northern Oklahoma Junior College, and the Oklahoma Military Academy. There are eighteen state-owned senior and junior colleges in the state, as well as two state-controlled graduate schools. The Oklahoma system is, in principle, a separate board rather than a joint-board system, with the joint board acting as a kind of co-ordinating committee to consider problems which affect all institutions, but leaving the supervision and normal powers of regents to separate boards in each institution involved. When we speak of a joint-board system as operating in Oklahoma, we have such modification of the original joint-board arrangement as, in principle, to make its operation almost a separate board system.

In Florida we have still another modification. The state board of education is an ex-officio body composed of the governor, secretary of state, attorney general, state treasurer, and the superintendent of public instruction. This make-up of membership has definite weaknesses in that (1) for all members of the board except the state superintendent education is not their particular concern; (2) the board has a great many other responsibilities and can devote little attention to education; (3) the state superintendent, the executive officer of the board, is elected by the people, and because of his political status is subject to pressures as between various educational interests. But supervision of education does not end with this board, for there is another agency, known as the state board of control, which is made up of five members and to which is delegated administrative supervision of the institutions. The members of this board of control are appointed by the governor; they have charge of the University of Florida, Florida State University, Florida A. & M. College, and the School for the Deaf and Blind. In view of the complications resulting from this cumbersome arrangement—and it will be noted that there is no authoritative chancellor in the Florida system—it was recommended that a new state board of education, composed of nine non-salaried lay citizens, be established, and that it be empowered to appoint a state commissioner of education, a state superintendent of public instruction, and a chancellor of higher education. Such an arrangement would scarcely be in the nature of an economy, and the proposition was defeated by the people at a recent election.[5]

In North Dakota we have a still different version of the joint-board arrangement. Here there is a board of seven members, appointed by the governor and confirmed by the state senate. No more than one member can be a graduate of any one North Dakota institution. The method of choosing these members is rather involved. One is selected each year. The president of the North Dakota educational system, the chief justice, and the superintendent of public instruction must unanimously recommend three persons for each position. The governor then nominates one of the three, who is subject to confirmation by the state senate. There is no chancellor in the North Dakota system, but an official called the commissioner acts as liaison officer between the board and the presidents of the various institutions. In addition to the University of North Dakota, this single board has jurisdiction over North Dakota Agricultural College, four state teachers' colleges, a normal and industrial college, a school of science, and a school of forestry. It is to be noted here that final authority does not rest with the commissioner. He acts as a kind of executive secretary during the interims between meetings of the board. Under this system, the presidents of the various institutions have much larger freedom of action than under an authoritative chancellor. The North Dakota law provides that the board elect a competent person as secretary, who shall reside during the term of his office in the city of Bismarck. The board is also empowered to "appoint for a term not to exceed three years a state commissioner of higher education, whose principal office shall be in the state capitol in the city of Bismarck. Such commissioner of higher education shall be the chief executive

---

[5] *Florida's Future in Education,* Florida's Citizens Committee on Education, Tallahassee, 1947.

officer of the state board of education and shall perform such duties as shall be prescribed by the board." It is to be noted in the case of North Dakota that the total enrollment in the nine state colleges and the university was at the time of writing only 8347, or about the size of that in one state college or university in a populous state. Five of these institutions had enrollments of less than 400 and four of these less than 250. This modified joint-board system, with a competent executive officer in the person of the commissioner, operates rather effectively; however, there are marked differences between it and the joint system in Oregon or Florida.

In Mississippi the state board consists of fifteen members, who have jurisdiction over the University of Mississippi, Mississippi State College, Mississippi State College for Women, Mississippi Southern College, Delta State Teachers College, Alcorn A. & M., and the Mississippi Negro Training School. There is no provision in the state law for the election of an authoritative chancellor or commissioner. The board does have a paid secretary who maintains an office for handling the correspondence and relationships between institutions. The state by-laws provide for an executive secretary to inquire into the problems of higher education, to survey and study carefully the organization, management, and all other affairs of each institution; and to make reports of all findings and recommend such changes as will increase efficiency and economy in operation. However, this secretary has no administrative authority whatever. A peculiar outgrowth of the Mississippi joint-board arrangement is that the presidents of the various institutions are forbidden by law to appear before appropriation committees, except with the approval of the board or on invitation of the legislature itself. In practice, no president ever appears even before the board when another president is present. It is not quite clear why this atmosphere of secrecy has to be maintained. One result of this policy was the setting up of a separate scale of salaries for persons teaching the same subjects in the various major institutions in the state. The title of chancellor appears in the Mississippi system, but it is an honorary title only, conferred on the man who occupies the office of president of the University of Mississippi. He is not a member of the board, nor is he treated on any level other than that accorded the other college and university presidents. South Dakota also has a joint board, which has nine institutions under its direction, including the school for the blind and a school for the deaf. There is no provision in the South Dakota system for a chancellor or a secretary, or the rather elaborate machinery necessary under the arrangement in Oregon. Kansas also has a joint board, with no provision for a chancellor other than the honorary title conferred on the president of the university, but the state does have a full-time paid secretary.

Thus it will be seen that there are considerable variations in the joint-board system. Iowa has a joint board of nine members, who control six state institutions, including a school for the deaf and a school for the blind and a tuberculosis sanitarium. This system also has no authoritative chancellor, but has a salaried finance committee. The institutions' presidents are not members of the board. While in some states the joint-board arrangement appears to work satisfactorily, investigation beneath the surface reveals that there are many instances of administrators and faculty members feeling strongly that the interests of their institutions are militated against under this arrangement. Even if it provided a more efficient system of operation, discontented presidents and faculties do not contribute to the most effective work in education. The tendency to include institutions other than those of higher learning under the joint-board system should also be noted. Schools for the deaf and schools for the blind are frequently included, and in Iowa expansion has reached the point where a tuberculosis sanitarium is placed under joint-board jurisdiction. It would seem wise, therefore, first, to examine very carefully what is meant by a joint-board system, in view of the claims that the joint board plan of operation is expanding; second, to examine critically those states where very wide powers are conferred on the chancellors; and, third, to determine whether it is possible for a joint board to do as effective work in the interest of higher education as can be accomplished by a separate board for the state college or university and perhaps a joint board for the group of teachers' colleges, whose problems are almost identical.

The survey of the methods of selection of the governing boards and their functions in the various states disclosed certain weaknesses due to the danger of political interference. It would appear, first, that the presence of ex-officio members on governing boards offers a possible avenue for the exertion of political pressure; second, that the joint-board system is viewed with some suspicion in states operating under the separate board arrangement as a possible channel for political domination; third, that governors should be held to strict accountability for the caliber of the men they appoint as regents or trustees; fourth, that the bipartisan system frequently invites appointments with a political flavor, when the primary consideration should be to secure men competent from an educational or administrative point of view rather than men distinguished for political activity; fifth, that the reaction to political pressure on boards has become so strong that there is reason to hope that, with the interests of education paramount, states tolerating political interference may be made so conspicuous as to invite penalties for their offenses.

There are various opportunities for the misuse of political power. In one Southern state, one hundred faculty members were dismissed through the influence of a governor who had control. This wholesale wrecking of the faculties of the university and the state colleges constituted a disastrous attack on the public welfare. The reaction of the people resulted in the establishment by law of a constitutional board of regents, with full powers and complete protection from governmental interference. The board in this state now consists of fifteen members, appointed by the governor with the consent of the senate. There are no ex-officio members. The board itself fills its vacancies. The members are appointed for a term of twelve years, the appointments being staggered so that no governor can appoint a majority. These members come, one from each congressional district of the state; one from each supreme court district, and two from the state at large. One-third of the members complete their terms every four years. This method has brought about the almost complete eradication of political interference with the board in this state.

A similar serious situation was produced by political pressure in Louisiana. A survey of Louisiana State University,[6] prepared by a commission of the American Council on Education, says in part of the situation it found:

"To understand the first of these causes one must look at certain political, economic and social changes in Louisiana during the years since the World War. . . . The most striking of these was the people's awakening consciousness of their political power. . . . The second cause of the present difficulties arises from internal disorders. . . . But here the members of the staff had been so long unaccustomed to the consideration of educational problems and for so many years deprived of the rights and duties of self-government that they were impotent in the face of new conditions. . . . It was during this period that the management of the institution got out of hand. Administrative posts and educational units were capriciously created, shifted about, or abolished. New courses of study were inaugurated. New schools were established. All this was done, with cavalier disregard of existing facilities at the University, or at other institutions in the state. Thousands of new students surged into the University. Only ineffective attempts were made to place them in courses suited to their varied talents, interests, and needs. Few were dismissed; many were permitted to remain for several years without making substantial progress. Under the pressure of time, faculty members were added to the staff with only scant attention to their qualifications. Inefficiency in the academic branches of the University was matched by irregularities in the business office. This combination of circumstances led inevitably to the debacle of June 1939."

Again the result was the establishment of a constitutional board, this composed of fourteen members serving terms of fourteen years each, the terms of two expiring every two years, thus making it possible for a governor to appoint only four of fourteen members during his term of office, provided the governor was re-elected.

A letter received from a prominent citizen of a state in which

[6] "Louisiana State University: A Survey Report," American Council on Education, 1940.

one of the universities studied in this survey is located contains the following:

"A few months ago a small group of students of the university burned a small building on the campus, after applying oil to assure its destruction. When this group was expelled from the university by duly constituted authority, a meeting was held by the regents of the university and at least one student, the son of a state official, was reinstated by the regents. Another instance in which politics was injected into university affairs occurred more recently. A member of the faculty who is married to a politician was suggested by the board of regents for the deanship of the law school. Investigation of the individual revealed that he had resigned from the state bar of a neighboring state after being brought up for disbarment procedure and had been allowed to resign 'with prejudice.' This fact was brought to the attention of the board of regents and formed the basis for an attempt by the regents with the co-operation of the governor and other politicians for the ouster of the president of the university."

This statement, made by a reputable citizen who is deeply interested in keeping politics out of state universities as a matter of principle, is offered on his authority and not as a result of personal investigation; but there is every reason to believe it is accurate. Here we have an instance of appalling political interference.

That the facts as outlined by this interested citizen are correct, is evidenced by events which have now taken place. The university president was notified that he was dismissed and a successor was elected at the same meeting, the act of dismissal taking place at a meeting at which the dismissed president was not allowed to be present. The chief charge against this educator is "he declined invitations to speak at Rotary clubs, could not bring himself to gladhand state politicos." As an actual fact, the president in question made eighty-one addresses before service clubs and similar organizations all over the state in a period of about two years. The institution had increased enrollment under his direction, administrative processes had been modernized, a new Law School and a new School of Pharmacy had been opened. Thirteen Harvard Ph.D.'s had been added to the faculty. An earlier effort had been made to dismiss the president, but there was sufficient protest from disinterested sources to prevent action at that time. Later the action was taken. The student paper of the University said, "The dismissed president is an educator and a scholar and evidently could not play politics."

Another great state college has recently been subjected to a legislative investigation. This was apparently due to an effort to enforce discipline and to stop hazing. Encouraged by political interests, the hazing continued, and the duly empowered authorities of the institution were publicly defied. The result was a chaotic situation on the campus, followed by an investigation by an especially appointed committee of the legislature.

After a thorough investigation covering seven general charges and six questions raised by the Veterans Student Association, the findings of the Committee are as follows:

1. The A. & M. College of Texas is a constitutional, tax-supported institution of the State. (Art. VII Sec. 13, Const. 1876.)

2. The sole governing authority of the College is vested in a Board of Directors composed of nine members appointed by the Governor, by and with the advice and consent of the Senate. (Art. IV Sec. 12; Art. 2610 R.C.S. Texas 1925.)

3. The duties of the Board of Directors are fixed by statute. (Art. 2613 R.C.S. Texas, 1925.)

4. Seven of the current Board of Directors are ex-students of A. & M. College and three thereof have served as President of the Ex-Students Association of A. & M. College.

5. There was no evidence of any official corruption of or by the administration or the President.

6. There was no evidence of any misapplication or misappropriation of any funds of the College by anyone.

7. There was no evidence of any "ineptness" in the school administration.

8. There was no evidence of any coercion, intimidation or duress of either students or faculty or staff members.

9. The rental charged for rooms was reasonable and necessary and in compliance with law for the retirement of outstanding revenue bonds. (Art. 2613a-1, 2613a-4, R.C.S. Texas, 1925.)

Texas has won for itself a reputation for political activity in connection with publicly controlled higher education. The people of this state burn with the "fierce spirit of Texan independence." However, the unfavorable publicity given Texas in connection with the resignation of President Homer Rainey of the University of Texas was not altogether deserved. The facts appear to be as follows:

A distinguished committee of the Association of University Professors made a thorough investigation and reported on academic freedom and tenure. In the opinion of this committee the board responsible for the dismissal of Dr. Rainey was guilty of repressing freedom of teaching and research, and of threatening dismissal of members of the faculty without due trial and opportunity for defense. The report said, "It is the considered judgment of Committee A that Dr. Rainey was dismissed because he refused to yield to pressures by the board concerning teaching and research and, also, because of his philosophy of freedom in education." The report took up not only the difficulties at the University at Austin, but vindicated Dr. Rainey of charges of maladministration as former president of Bucknell University. It pointed out, however, that a reconstituted board later reinstated several of the teachers who had been dismissed, some being given promotions in rank and salary. The Committee felt that these reinstatements were motivated by expediency and "by a desire to becloud the issues with reference to Dr. Rainey." Also Dr. Rainey's reported difficulty with the medical school, located at Galveston, had little to do with his removal. It was pointed out that the university faculty was strongly desirous of having him retained at the time of his dismissal. The Committee also referred to criticism of Dr. Rainey, that "he made public his difficulty with the board of regents," and defended him on the ground that he enjoyed this privilege because of academic freedom. The conclusion of the report recommended that the University of Texas be placed on the Association's list of Censored Administrations." [7]

There are two sides to every controversy. Apparently the feel-

[7] *American Association of University Professors Bulletin,* Vol. 32, Summer 1946, Nov. 2, p. 374.

ing in Texas at the time of this disagreement was so intense that facts sometimes were overlooked, even by as painstaking a body as the Committee of the American Association of University Professors. A statement by a responsible officer now connected with another university, but at that time playing an active part in the Texas difficulty, contradicts the committee's assertion that the trouble in the Medical School had nothing to do with Dr. Rainey's dismissal. He says:

"A careful study of the long controversy between President Rainey and the University's Board of Regents will show that the trouble really started over differences among them on the management of the medical school. In 1941 a member of the Board requested the President not to renominate the Dean of the School of Medicine. It developed that this majority had 'met' without the knowledge of the full Board or of the President and had come to this decision. President Rainey pointed out that this was in violation of the Board's own regulations. While I presume there had been some earlier differences between Dr. Rainey and some of his Board, it was this action that started the trouble that grew into such a great one, with results that are familiar to you."

On my visit to the University of Texas, the present board of regents discussed the difficulty with Dr. Rainey freely. They were unanimous in agreeing on two facts: first, that the controversy between that board and Dr. Rainey had reached a point where it was impossible "for Dr. Rainey to trust the board or the board to trust Dr. Rainey." The present president of the university was chairman of a committee which brought in a compromise proposal, by means of which Dr. Rainey could have retained his position as president and the board could have "saved its face." This proposal was rejected by the board of regents. The second unanimous conclusion of the present board had to do with facts not contained in the Association of University Professors' report. These were that, in an effort to increase faculty salaries, the board proposed a reduction in the appropriation for publicity. This proposal was fought by Dr. Rainey and the public relations officer of the university. There was a frank admission that the faculty was still divided to some extent in its loyalty to Dr. Rainey. However, the present president is a man of recognized scholarship, has the confidence of the board and of a majority of the faculty, and the work of the university is progressing satisfactorily. It was felt that the attempt to capitalize on the university's difficulties in connection with Dr. Rainey's campaign for nomination to the governorship when he was overwhelmingly defeated contributed to a renewal of peaceful relations at the university and the restoration of public confidence in the institution.

The same authority quoted as contradicting the findings of the American Association of University Professors Committee on the Texas Medical School also feels that the present Board was misinformed as to the actual part played by the Public Relations Director in the controversy. His statement is:

"What actually happened, as the records show, is that the Board in 1943 'transferred' the then Director of Public Relations to a professorship in journalism without discussing this with the Director and against the wishes of the Vice-President and the President, the usual channels of nomination. This action proved to be very unpopular and it was a few days after the action had been announced that one of the members of the Board claimed it had been taken in order to make more money available for teachers' salaries, 'especially low-paid teaching instructors,' and had the resolution on the action rewritten. Actually the action of the Board would have increased the combined budgets for public relations and journalism and not effected an economy, inasmuch as another journalism teacher was not then needed; nor was the University's financial situation such that it could not have maintained the publicity budget and also increased teachers' salaries if the Board desired to do so."

As to the charge that the Public Relations Director had influenced press releases in favor of Dr. Rainey, this responsible official says:

"Such action by the director would have been a definite violation of professional standards, as you know. It simply did not happen, as more than one investigation has shown. The Board might more truthfully have said 'The public relations officer held the confidence of the press and he had earned that confidence because of his ethical handling of University news and publicity.' . . . The controversy that concerned the Board was not handled directly by the public relations officer at all. The record will show that with the director's help press interviews were set up so that reporters had access to the Board and to others at times when there were matters involving the Board in controversy. They explained their own actions and made their own statements."

It should be added that Texas is unique in many ways. After visiting several institutions in the state and finding evidence of a rather belligerent attitude on the part of individual Texans, both laymen and some professionally interested in education, one might lightly assume that if Texans cannot find someone outside the state to fight with about the superiority of everything Texan, they resort to the device of fighting with each other. This is not intended to be a harsh judgment, but an acknowledgment that the rugged pioneer fighting spirit of the Texan still lives. The controversy in Texas was most unfortunate, but it is my conviction that there was definite partisanship on both sides of this controversy. Without the services of the American Association of University Professors, grave injustice would have been done to education. On the other hand, the present board of regents is making an honest effort to correct such injustices as may have existed, and there is reason to believe that, whatever repression of expression and violation of tenure may have taken place, there is a strong determination on the part of the present regents to see that the governing board of the University of Texas measures up to reasonable standards of fairness in its dealings.

Public education is a sacred responsibility for a democracy. The conduct of that education must be beyond reproach. With the enormous resources of the states behind publicly controlled higher education, there is every reason that the quality of the work done in state colleges and universities should be the highest. To achieve this objective requires unselfish dedication to the unfettered pursuit of truth by regents, trustees, faculties, and all right-minded citizens. Every college president interviewed in this study, with the exception of one, expressed himself as unalterably opposed to the use of political pressure and political interference in the conduct of his institution. On the great majority of campuses, the report shows, there is now no political interference, nor has there been for periods of from five to twenty years. The general atmosphere is healthy. Steps should be taken to see that this wholesome atmosphere prevails in the few questionable areas. The one president who stated that he thought political influence was a good thing in his institution spoke from a thoroughly selfish point of view, the implication being that by the use of such influence he might possess an advantage over a sister university in the same state. His testimony should not be taken too seriously, since this same president, when questioned about a requirement in American government for all graduates of state colleges and universities, replied, with particular emphasis on engineering, "Engineers are so much smarter than other people that they could get all the general education they need on the outside." Fortunately, this individual is not representative either in his opinion of politics in state universities or in his opinion of the general mental "brilliancy of the average undergraduate engineering student." Politics must be kept out of the state colleges and universities, and the state colleges and universities out of politics.

3

THE RELATION BETWEEN PUBLICLY CONTROLLED AND PRIVATELY CONTROLLED INSTITUTIONS

INDEPENDENTLY controlled higher education is essential to life in a democracy.[1] Exclusively state-controlled education would be contrary to basic democratic principles. The earliest educational ventures in the United States were privately controlled institutions. They had as their objective training for the so-called learned professions. They were limited in scope and enrollment, yet on the foundation they laid has been built the great system of publicly controlled state colleges and universities, a system which is making a tremendous contribution to higher education in the United States today. For many years the privately controlled schools jealously guarded their independence. They felt that they were possessed of a certain freedom and could lay down requirements and disciplines in a sense not permitted the publicly controlled institutions. This led to the assumption that they possessed greater power of selectivity in accepting or rejecting students.[2] The privately controlled colleges did well in basic research and won high respect for their academic achievements. As time went on, the earlier foundations of Harvard, William and Mary, Yale, and Princeton were joined by a host of small and frequently poorly financed institutions. Many of these smaller colleges were church-related or church-controlled.

[1] *The Educational Record, Supplement Number 16,* January, 1947, pp. 148, 149, 150.
[2] *The Educational Record, Supplement Number 16,* January, 1947, p. 99.

In many instances they were limited in their program to a four-year course in liberal arts. They had few facilities for research [3] in the exact sciences, and many of them have been poorly equipped in this respect up to the present moment. The rapid increase in the number of these small independent colleges led to a rather intense rivalry in obtaining students. Many and various were the devices used to make one smaller institution more attractive to prospective students than another.[4] Fantastic claims to academic standing, equipment, ability of the faculty, and other educational features were made.[5] Meanwhile, the old, well-established, and rather heavily endowed private educational foundations went on improving their work, producing scholars, and making contributions to American education which compared favorably with those of the best universities in the world. That this race among competing smaller colleges continues to the present day is evidenced by a report of one such institution which recently announced a highly inflated enrollment, examination of which revealed that a majority of those claimed as students were taking special classes in nursing and would not have been counted as full-time students in the average institution. The offering of work of high quality in these independent schools was not limited, however, to the great "name" universities and colleges. Some of the smaller institutions, under the guidance of inspired leaders, gradually won more and more support, and today stand in the forefront of colleges and universities in the United States. Meanwhile, the less favored colleges, being inadequately financed, struggling for survival in a race for existence with other weakly manned institutions, continued to multiply and increase.[6] The question has been raised more than once, "Are there too many small colleges in the United States?" The small college that is doing reputable work possesses an advantage, in that, with small classes and with a competent faculty, it can do a better job than great universities which, with thousands and thousands of students,

[3] The Educational Record, April, 1947, p. 161.
[4] The Educational Record, Supplement Number 16, January, 1947, p. 148.
[5] Studies of Higher Education in the South, Southern Association of Colleges and Secondary Schools, 1946, p. 4.
[6] General Education in Free Society, Harvard, 1945, p. 178.

are faced with recruiting satisfactory faculty material in these days of shortage of properly equipped teachers.

Because of their independence, the smaller privately controlled colleges, some of them church-related or church-directed, are not subject to the same restrictions and requirements as are the larger state universities and state colleges. In many instances they are only locally accredited and neither have the facilities nor show immediate promise of reaching the point where they will become entitled to national accreditation. The rapid increase of schools of this type has been most unfortunate, in that it serves to discredit reputable independently controlled colleges and universities, particularly those with smaller enrollments, which are doing thoroughly good work.

There are some 699 Class A accredited colleges and universities in the United States. Those nationally accredited total 311, and in this national accreditation list are eighty-one state colleges and universities. Of the smaller private colleges, 225 are nationally accredited and 264 are regionally accredited, that is, within the limited area where they are located. The following are facts based on Carter Good's report.[7] In 1940-41, in the state of Massachusetts we find an exception. There were seven publicly controlled colleges and universities, and thirty-eight private colleges, not including junior colleges. This was before the enrollments were swollen by the influx of veterans, a factor which has distorted enrollment figures in both publicly and privately controlled institutions. Because of their size, the increase in enrollments in the publicly controlled institutions of higher education has been greater than that in the privately controlled institutions. In 1940-41, the enrollment in the thirty-eight privately controlled schools in Massachusetts was 36,190 and the enrollment in state colleges and universities was 2,911. In another state, the picture is reflected among eleven publicly controlled colleges and universities and twenty-six independently controlled institutions. In this state the enrollment in the state schools was 47,648, while the enrollment in the twenty-six private schools was 21,780. Present figures

[7] *Guide to Colleges, Universities and Professional Schools in the United States,* American Council on Education, 1945.

show that the publicly controlled institutions are carrying a very heavy share of the burden of higher education in the various states. In Tennessee we have Vanderbilt University, an outstanding institution with a splendid record, with an endowment of $40,000,000, while the University of Tennessee, a publicly controlled institution, with an enrollment of twice that of Vanderbilt, has an endowment of $400,000. Of course, the University of Tennessee, in turn, has state funds on which to rely. In addition, this state has nineteen privately controlled colleges and one other publicly controlled institution.

The College of Wooster in Ohio is a good instance of a fine privately controlled smaller college, with an enrollment of 1300. It has an endowment of $3,500,000. Ohio State University, at Columbus, with a present enrollment of 65,000, has an endowment of $2,160,000. Ohio State's prewar enrollment was 13,000. Stanford University, at Palo Alto, California, another privately controlled institution with a splendid reputation, has an enrollment of 7200 and an endowment of $38,000,000. Near by is the University of California, with a full-time enrollment of 40,800 and endowments amounting to $36,000,000. Southern California, another privately controlled school, with an enrollment of slightly under 24,000, has endowments of something over $3,000,000. Yale University, in Connecticut, with an enrollment of 8500, has an endowment of $123,000,000, while the University of Connecticut near by, with an enrollment of 9200 has a very much smaller reserve in endowment funds. These instances are suggested to show that there is every reason to believe that independently controlled education in well established institutions is in sound condition in the United States. Such assurance, however, is not indicated in the case of many smaller colleges and universities, particularly in those of recent origin, some of which are church-related and church-controlled.

It is of the utmost importance that the most cordial possible relationships be developed between the state universities and colleges and the privately controlled institutions. Wherever possible, interchange of faculties should be encouraged. Every effort should be made to strengthen these less prosperous schools, provided the work they are doing measures up to reasonably high academic standards. However, with our present expenditures for education, there is no good reason for encouraging the useless multiplication of small and struggling schools which cannot measure up to standard requirements.

Immediately after the war, of course, there was a vast influx of veterans enrolling in every type of institution, private and public. One fact which has been largely overlooked is that, for the past five years both private and public institutions have benefited largely from federal subsidies. This aid came first in connection with the V-12 training program for the Navy and the ASTP program for the Army. This was followed by the appropriations made available to all colleges, public and private, under the provisions of the G.I. Bill of Rights. As a result of this subsidy, many colleges found themselves possessed of greater resources than had ever before been available to them. They expanded building programs and hurriedly recruited faculties, and once more the race was on and many of the earlier rivalries revived. There was a great temptation for hitherto small and weak colleges to attempt to attain university stature overnight. The benefits of the G.I. Bill of Rights for education will not last forever. Having shared in public funds for a period, however, the privately controlled colleges, which formerly were extremely proud of their independence, are now almost unanimous in their requests for federal subsidy. That there are dangers in connection with federal aid cannot be disputed.[8] If that aid becomes large enough there will be an inevitable trend toward federal control. This would affect not only the independently controlled colleges thus subsidized, but also would gradually affect the state universities and colleges as well.

Two very serious questions have to be faced. The available income from taxation, whether from federal or state sources, has certain limits. Do we dare to spread this income so thinly among a multitude of small competing institutions as to endanger the great investment the states have in their publicly controlled col-

[8] *Educational Record*, April, 1947, p. 213; *General Education in Free Society*, p. 178.

leges and universities? Even assuming the critical increase in enrollments and the expiration of the period during which G.I. educational benefits will be granted, there is bound to come a time when these enrollments will level out, when we may find ourselves assuming financial obligations heavier than it is possible for the average state to bear. A second grave question has to do with the relationship of the state to sectarian-controlled colleges. The principle of separation of Church and State still prevails in the United States. If subsidies, federal or state, are granted to privately controlled institutions they cannot be granted to one and not to another. That would be contrary to democratic practice. If one private institution is helped, all should be helped. Undoubtedly, if federal aid were extended there would be private heavily endowed educational foundations which would insist on preserving their independence, and rightly so. However, with increased costs of operation, there are many of these privately endowed schools which might possibly face liquidation unless aid of some sort is forthcoming.[9] The only other answer would be to increase fees beyond any reasonable figure. Meanwhile, the public has become accustomed to low tuition rates in the state-controlled colleges and universities, which offer equality of opportunity to students seeking entrance irrespective of financial background. Then, too, in the church-related and church-controlled colleges instruction is frequently affected by the doctrinal position of the dominant church. The type of philosophy or of history taught in a state university can differ widely from the teaching of the same subject from a special point of view in a church-related or church-controlled institution. Here we are faced with the problem of whether or not the state has any right to subsidize the *ex parte* presentation of subjects which are taught from an impartial point of view in the state college and the state university.

The whole question of federal aid places on regents and trustees the necessity for very clear and unprejudiced thinking if such aid is found necessary in order to maintain reasonably high edu-

[9] *Educational Record,* April, 1947, p. 215; *Educational Record, Supplement No. 16,* January, 1947, p. 151.

cational standards, not only on the college level but also in elementary and secondary schools in certain states. The offer of such aid should be based on need and need alone. Coupled with this extension of federal or state grants, there should be a provision looking toward the assumption by the state or private institution of self-support by degrees over a period of years. Of course, there are some areas, including particularly elementary and secondary school education, where that period would of necessity be rather prolonged. On the other hand, experience shows that it is exceedingly easy to pauperize agencies as well as individuals by extending benefits on which people become dependent unless there is a constant incentive toward self-support. For the more prosperous states to expect federal aid because the less fortunate areas cannot exist without it opens a way for the intrusion of political influence to a degree that may mean a general lowering of educational standards. It makes little difference whether the aid be direct or indirect, whether it be in the form of special appropriations or in the form of scholarships to individuals who, in turn, subsidize the institutions they attend. If there is to be federal aid it should, first of all, be directed to deserving areas and institutions at present incapable of maintaining themselves; and, second, it should be accomplished by some plan whereby the aided areas and institutions could, over a period of years, achieve self-support.

Once more it must be stressed that efforts be made to encourage the most cordial relationships between publicly controlled and privately controlled colleges and universities. When the question has to be faced of whether or not there is to be a federal subsidy of privately controlled institutions, the decision must be made entirely free of prejudice, religious, political, or any other. The preservation of high standards of education is fundamental. It is necessary that sufficient funds be available to preserve these standards, but it will be fatal to education if funds are made available and there is no investigation of each request and no strict supervision of performance.

Unfortunately, while a considerable number of privately controlled colleges are desirous of obtaining public funds,[10] there is

[10] *After Black Coffee*, Robert I. Gannon, McMullen Press, 1946, p. 36.

little disposition on their part to surrender any degree of private control. When public funds are made available to private institutions every citizen becomes a contributor to them, just as every citizen shares in maintaining our state colleges and universities. It is only natural then that the citizens should be represented on the governing boards of these institutions and have a share in the control proportionate to the amount of public funds involved. The reaction of the privately controlled institution to this suggestion is apt to be unfavorable. A very good instance of it may be found in a pamphlet [11] prepared by the president of Tuskegee Institute, Dr. F. D. Patterson. He wrote:

"There are not now or have plans ever been considered whereby the State of Alabama would exercise administrative control over Tuskegee Institute. The Governor responded to a proposed quarter of a million dollar program of graduated and professional education by stating that he was willing to recommend to the Alabama legislature that it take the first step by appropriating $100,000 toward the amount needed and that six trustees (three more than the Tuskegee charter now provides) should be set up as an instrument through which the state funds could be transferred. The governor stated specifically that he did not wish to interfere with the control of Tuskegee Institute."

Dr. Patterson wrote further:

"Tuskegee Institute has felt it desirable to examine its claim for support in terms of public funds—public funds which might be sought both at the state and national level. The $100,000 voted by the state legislature of Alabama is in terms of current operating costs only. The additional trustees should function in such a way as not to constitute a board within a board. To prevent this from happening, the governor agreed that there should be no chairman of the state trustees. They are to have all the rights and powers of other trustees, no more and no less, with one exception: this exception related to the appointment of the rest of the board, which is self-perpetuating. In this instance the state trustees specifically are entitled to no voice."

The statement goes on to say that while Tuskegee looks forward to appropriations from the state of Alabama well in excess

[11] "Co-operation between Tuskegee Institute and the State of Alabama," 1943.

of $100,000, the expectation is that state representatives on the board shall be limited to six out of twenty-five, no matter how great the appropriation. From this, it is apparent that we have here a privately controlled institution which does not hesitate to speak of its claim for public funds, but resents very directly any suggestion of public control. Institutions which have been privately controlled for years will naturally hesitate to surrender that control in exchange for public funds. However, there is also a grave question whether the state has a right to appropriate public funds without protecting them by active representation on a board. To add six state-appointed trustees to a self-perpetuating board of nineteen, and to refuse those six representatives the right to share in the self-perpetuating feature in the election of the nineteen presents an area of possible conflict which might be difficult to resolve.

In view of the fact therefore that if one privately controlled institution is subsidized they must all be, it seems evident that public subsidization of privately controlled institutions may easily endanger the great investments the people have in their publicly controlled colleges and universities. Even considering the factor of need, there are so many of these privately controlled institutions that the drain on the public purse would be enormous. In the second place, public funds must never be used for promoting sectarian versions of education, no matter how highly we respect the institution in which such teaching is offered.

It should be borne in mind that the generous provision philanthropy has made for the endowment of privately controlled colleges and universities has not been extended to the publicly controlled institutions. A comparison of the endowments of the great privately controlled schools with the endowments of state colleges and universities shows a great disparity. With the state colleges and universities bearing the major burden in "Applied Research," the expense of conducting these institutions is mounting constantly. At the present moment most of the state colleges and universities have before them research projects they are unable to carry on because of lack of public funds. They are also lacking in income from large endowments. A few state universi-

ties, such as Michigan and Delaware, have been the recipients of
large gifts from the public. However, there is no good reason why
philanthropy should not provide for education under public
auspices just as liberally as it provides endowments for privately
controlled institutions. If the state universities and colleges are
to measure up to their full opportunity the trend of philanthropy
toward providing more adequate gifts for their endowment must
be encouraged. Such an extension of philanthropy toward publicly controlled higher education need not interfere with the con-
tinuation of the generosity already shown the privately controlled
schools. There is plenty of wealth available, and the publicly
controlled and the privately controlled institutions must join
forces and endeavor to interest persons of great wealth in providing endowments for specific purposes for both publicly and
privately controlled colleges and universities.

As far back as 1905, President Charles R. Van Hise of the
University of Wisconsin, speaking before the Association of
American Universities,[12] said:

"But suppose I am wrong in reference to the support by the state
of advanced instruction and research. Still, the question as to the place
which these higher lines of work are to take in the state universities is
open. Why should not a state university receive help from private
funds for such purposes as well as other universities? No good reason
can be assigned for the belief that state universities in the future will
not receive liberal support from private funds. It is true that in the
past this has not been the case, but the same was also true of private
institutions until very recently. As already intimated, the great sums
in the United States for advanced work in private institutions have
been given within the past thirty years.

"When the alumni of the state universities become numerous and
some of them wealthy, why should they not give to these institutions
as do the alumni of private universities? Indeed, if there be any difference between the two it should be in favor of the state institutions,
for the men who have obtained their education at such universities
have returned a considerably smaller proportion of its cost than have

[12] "The Opportunities for Higher Instruction and Research in State Universities," by Charles R. Van Hise. Address before meeting of the Association of American Universities at Baltimore, January 18, 1905, pp. 10, 11, 12.

those educated in private institutions. I hold the conviction firmly that in the future the alumni of state universities will give liberally to their support.

"Nor do I believe that the gifts to state institutions will be derived from alumni alone. What valid reason can be assigned for the belief that the men who have gained their wealth by taking advantage of the natural resources of the states will not turn back some portion of this wealth for higher education? Indeed, this has already begun. It is only within the past score of years in the Middle and Far West that we have seen large accumulations of capital, and have had the feeling of assured prosperity. Now that this situation has come about, gifts from private sources have begun to flow to the state universities. The largest recipient has been the University of California. At Wisconsin and in other states there have been the small beginnings of the flow of private funds to the state universities.

"In the past many of the men who have given money to educational institutions have been inspired by a religious motive. But in the United States at present there are a large number of men of wealth who are moved by the educational and ethical impulse and who are not impelled by the religious motive. In the future such men, I doubt not, will give largely to state universities. To such persons it can be made to appear that a state is at least as safe a trustee as any individual or corporation. The wealth of the people of an entire state is surety for such funds."

__ 4 __

COMMUNISM ON THE COLLEGE CAMPUS

UNINFORMED conservative business men are easily alarmed by recurring reports that there is considerable communism in American colleges and universities.[1] These reports involve both faculty and students. From time to time there are rather lurid newspaper accounts which would seem to indicate the existence of communistic activity and communistic teaching. It is of the utmost importance that the facts behind these reports be known. For that reason the following query was included in the questionnaire used in this study: "Have there been any instances of communistic teaching or activity in your institution which have attracted public attention during the past five years?" This question was answerable in only one of two ways, yes or no. When the answer was yes, a statement of details was requested, and in every instance there was compliance. While eighty-nine colleges and universities represent only a carefully selected cross section of American higher education, they offer a sampling which carries with it considerable authority. If there is a definite trend either toward or away from communism, it would certainly have been disclosed by investigation at so many institutions as these. It was evident that the problem of com-

[1] *Educational Record, Supplement Number 16,* January, 1947, Henry M. Wriston, p. 101.

munistic teaching and activity was faced frankly and that there was an earnest desire to allow full opportunity for liberal political thought, as well as a unanimous determination that liberal teaching should not take the form of disloyalty to the American form of government.

One president of a very well known American university stated that America was never better prepared for a "witch hunt" than it is at the present moment. He expressed the hope that, while a definite stand would be taken against communism as a menace to the American way of life, steps would also be taken to guard against carelessly attaching the communist label to a person who shows the slightest liberal tendency. There have been various definitions of communism, ranging from describing as a communist one with whom one disagrees, all the way to so labeling anyone holding a political philosophy which one does not understand. The situation has reached the point where honest scholars engaged in studying the political problems of the day are called communists because they dare to include the study of communism as one of the great questions to be faced in our generation.

It should be stated, in the first place, that no respectable school of political science can avoid reference to communism as an existing form of government, which, no matter how thoroughly we disagree with it, has forced itself on the attention of the world and become a power with which to be reckoned. In the study of political science the colleges are faced with the question whether they will leave their students to pick up inaccurate ideas about communism from partisan propaganda, or from the casual conversation of the street corner, or at a cocktail party. We must face the fact that, if the claims of communism are to be considered, the instruction should be in the hands of educators whose loyalty to our own government is unquestioned, and who are sufficiently scholarly to place before their students accurate facts and a picture that is sternly realistic. The same thing can be said about fascism, which, while not so immediate a danger as the communistic trend, also has to be considered as a factor in world politics today. If, therefore, an institution offers courses which include references to communism given by reputable teachers, there is no occasion to assume that these teachers are necessarily communistic or disloyal to our form of government. They would be unworthy of their mission if they did not give their students the background of communism, not only as a political theory but as a world force. It is to be hoped sincerely that the fear that even the use of the word communism implies disloyalty, a fear conjured up in so many minds, will not be allowed to interfere with the honest teaching of all political theories.

The situation in the colleges visited reveals the following facts: of eighty-nine institutions studied, the number responding with a flat "no" or "none" to the question, "Has there been any communistic teaching or activity in your institution in the past five years which has attracted public attention?" was fifty-six. It is interesting to note that in almost every case where there had been "public attention" there was more discussion of communism as headline material in the public press than actually existed on the campuses of the institutions involved. It is quite safe to state that if one looks for the breeding places of communism in the United States he will find that the campuses of our American colleges and universities do not furnish a very fertile field for it. America is accustomed to a sensational press. There is little that makes for more sensational news today than rumors of communistic teaching and activity in colleges and universities. We need a careful and thoroughgoing investigation of every reported instance of communism on the campus, and authoritative statements should be issued by the universities themselves, especially when the facts stand out in contradiction to some of the reports in the public press.

It should be observed that in some of the institutions investigated there were instances of faculty members being charged with communistic utterances. Curiously enough, an examination of these cases shows that most of them fall into a single category. Many of the colleges and universities today are operating on the basis of "up or out." This unusual expression means that a faculty member should reveal his ability for promotion within a stated number of years. If he fails to do so he is considered no longer desirable as a member of the faculty and is notified by the administration that it might be well for him to seek employment elsewhere. Strangely enough, although there are not many in any case, there are a certain number of instances of instructors or faculty members whose standing in the institution was rather doubtful taking the opportunity to make speeches sufficiently inflammatory to attract comment, usually in some town or city adjacent to the institution with which they are connected. The distinction must be made that when a faculty member speaks on the lecture platform on a campus he speaks in the name of the university. On the other hand, in order that he may enjoy full opportunity for freedom of speech, he has the right to express his views as a private citizen, and not as a representative of the institution, away from the campus. This distinction is lost sight of in many instances when teachers, speaking as private individuals, express views which are merely personal, and do not in any sense represent the attitude of the institution. When this occurs there is usually a rather violent reaction by the press. This is followed by an attempt on the part of the university authorities to ascertain what the facts actually are. Inasmuch as many such addresses are extemporaneous the attempt sometimes involves difficulty. If the administration finds cause for action there is apt to be a protest to the American Association of University Professors. This organization, which is naturally interested in academic freedom, frequently investigates such cases. A study of its records would reveal some interesting facts concerning the flimsy grounds on which many of these charges of communistic activity are based. In a good many cases the result has been that the instructor in question is acquitted of communistic teaching but loses his position as a member of the faculty at the end of the current term, or perhaps in the following year, for reasons allegedly having to do with his teaching ability. Frequently, after thorough investigation, such a disposition of the case has the full approval of the American Association of University Professors. College teachers, like many other weak human beings, sometimes feel the necessity for attracting attention to themselves, especially if they believe that their status or tenure is in danger. This

frailty is responsible for many of the so-called reports of communistic activity.

However, it is beyond question that communism has appeared
in the teaching staff and among the students in some colleges
and universities. But there has been no attempt at "white-wash-
ing" in any instance where an investigation was made. There are
probably few groups more loyal to American standards of government than the members of the faculties of our colleges and
universities. There are men of liberal thought, of course, on
every faculty. There would be no progress in education if this
were not the case, but there is a wide gap between an inquisitive
mind conscientiously searching for truth and one secretly disloyal
to the national government. Academic freedom must be preserved if education is to be worthy of its name. Academic freedom
must also be guarded as a precious possession and not abused.
The distinction between utterances in the name of the university
and the utterances of an individual must be strictly insisted upon.
To assume that a university of 10,000 students is a center of communistic activity because one faculty member may be careless in
his utterances as a private citizen is scarcely just.

It needs to be remembered that charges of communism are
easily made in the heat of political campaigns. They furnish
opportunity for politicians seeking office to point out the horrible
example supposedly set by others in contrast to the highly advertised Simon pure Americanism of the interested candidates seeking public office. General accusations against institutions are
easily made, but substantiated with difficulty. However, the dam-
age is done so far as the public is concerned. We must guard
against "witch hunts" on the one hand and see that loyalty to our
own form of government is emphasized on the other. We must
make provision for honest liberal thought and yet see that those
calling themselves liberals are not communists in disguise.

The colleges and universities have been at fault in that they
have given too little attention to courses in American government and American history. Too often, a high-school requirement in the history of the United States is accepted as evidence
that a student has been so inculcated with American principles

that further attention to this aspect of his education is unnecessary. The general trend today is toward a broader general educational basis. Such a basis should include courses in American
government, American history, and the American way of life.[2]
There is good ground for advocating a course in American government and American history for every student of every college
and university, private or public, in the United States. The purpose of such a course should be not to encourage jingoistic nationalism but to make sure that the student has an intelligent
concept of the system of government under which he lives and
thus be able to compare it intelligently with other ideologies,
such as communism and fascism. In the present state of the world
it is absurd to take the position that the student can ignore the
existence of any form of government other than his own. If he
does become familiar with the principles of communistic teaching, whether favorably or unfavorably presented, he must have
some knowledge of his own system with which to compare communism. Of all the presidents, deans, trustees, and faculty members interviewed, only two questioned the advantage of having
such a requirement. One university in the East has gone even
farther by requiring teaching in American history, American
literature, American philosophy, and American economic backgrounds. This curriculum is still in an experimental stage, and
it is too early to determine whether quite so strong an emphasis
is needed. In the two instances where educational authorities
were unsympathetic with such a requirement, the reasons given
were, in one case, that such teaching implied indoctrination. This
objection is hardly valid, since it could be raised against all other
branches of education and thus end in confusion. The other
objection was that general education was not important for
technical students, since those studying subjects such as engineering have so many scientific details to master that it would be
easier for them to pick up their knowledge of the American

[2] *Public Education and the Structures of American Society,* by James B. Conant,
1946, p. 31; *Studies of Higher Education in the South,* 1946, p. 33; *General Education in Free Society,* pp. 143-145; *Youth and the Future,* American Council on Education, 1942, p. 211.

system of government along the way. The illogic of this objection becomes apparent when one considers what its effect would be not only on teaching loyalty to government, but also on teaching morals and religion. Therefore, it would seem wise for every faculty to consider seriously the possibility of adopting a requirement for the study of American government and American history. This is especially necessary in the case of the state colleges and universities, and would have equal value if the courses were offered in the privately controlled institutions of higher learning.

Alabama Polytechnic Institute requires two years of American history, and American government is required in a number of professional curricula. American history is also required at the University of Arkansas, at U.C.L.A., San Francisco State College, San Jose State College, the University of Southern California, Stanford, The Citadel, of nearly all students at Clemson, at the University of Connecticut, Florida State University, the University of Florida, the University of Georgia, Iowa State College, the University of Kansas, Kansas State College, University of Maryland, Massachusetts State University, Mississippi State College for Women, North Carolina State, Ohio State, Oklahoma College for Women, Oklahoma A. & M., University of Oklahoma, Rutgers, University of South Carolina, Southwestern Louisiana Institute, University of Texas, Texas Tech, Texas Mines, University of Vermont, Virginia Military Institute, University of West Virginia, and the University of Wyoming. Texas is unique in that it requires a course on the constitution of the state. Georgia also requires a course on the state constitution. In view of the political difficulties sometimes associated with these two states, it is probable that a little more emphasis on American government and a little less emphasis on the state constitution would be desirable. Among the institutions with no requirements in American history or government are the University of Alabama, Colorado A. & M., University of Colorado, Cornell, University of Delaware, Harvard, University of Illinois, Indiana University, Iowa State University, University of Kentucky, Louisiana State, University of Michigan, University of Minnesota, University of Mississippi, University of Missouri,

University of Nebraska, University of Nevada, University of New Hampshire, North Carolina Woman's College, North Dakota, University of Oregon, Oregon State, Pennsylvania State, Purdue, South Dakota, University of Tennessee, Utah Agricultural College, University of Utah, Vanderbilt, Virginia Polytechnic Institute, University of Wisconsin, the College of Wooster, and the State College of Washington. In practically every one of these institutions there are generous electives or provisions for courses in American history, American literature, American philosophy, American economic backgrounds, etc. It will be noted of the institutions cited that forty-six have requirements in American history or government for graduation in certain departments; and thirty-eight do not have such requirements.

Of the institutions where there has been subversive teaching or activity which has attracted even slight public attention, three out of eight are privately controlled institutions visited and thirteen out of seventy-seven are publicly controlled colleges and universities studied. Yale University is outstanding in offering a series of courses called "American Studies," the object of which is to teach the American way of life. This can be offered as a major for the Bachelor of Arts degree. Outstanding courses on early American literature are offered by Dr. Ralph Gabriel, author of *American Thought and Culture,* and Dr. Stanley Williams. These courses are not just glorified civics, and the university has unusual library resources to back them up.

As for subversive teaching by faculty members, the ratio is so small and the areas of influence so limited as to cause little concern. Much of the newspaper publicity has concerned itself with communistic activity among students. The organization known as the "American Youth for Democracy" has been identified by the Congressional Committee on un-American Activities as a communistic group.[3] It has been stated that the organization has active chapters in some sixty-six American colleges and universities. Among the institutions visited in this survey the ratio is not so high as this would suggest. In fact, there were more dead than

[3] *Report on American Youth for Democracy,* U. S. Government Printing Office, 1947.

live chapters of AYD in the schools included in the survey. In only one institution, the University of Minnesota, did the AYD group receive a clean bill of health. It was described there as an "honest liberal group." In all other cases where the organization exists or has existed there have been difficulties of one kind or another. The extent of the influence of this organization has been vastly overestimated. For instance, in one institution which received very wide newspaper publicity as being a center of communistic activity careful investigation revealed a membership of thirty students out of a student body of 12,893, only six of whom were communists.

Curiously enough, the turbulence caused by the AYD group has varied according to the policy of the administration in the institution involved. Student groups normally have to be recognized and granted a charter by the college administration. In many cases where the AYD has applied and the institution's policy was to refuse to grant a charter until the organization had demonstrated that it was an honest liberal group, not interested in the overthrow of the American government by force, the chapter died a natural death before the probationary period expired. The general pattern seems to have been to have a young communist student enroll in an institution and endeavor to be the organizing center of the AYD. In most instances, if the group were not officially recognized by the university the organizer, after a period of six to eight months, moved on to try other fields. On the other hand, institutions which granted charters to the AYD generally had trouble. After a period, communistic activity on the part of a minority of these students became apparent. It then became necessary for the institution to rescind or withdraw the charter. The cry of interference with freedom of speech was immediately raised. In some instances, there was criticism of the college administration. However, once the charter had been withdrawn, there were no instances of a revived interest in the movement.

Amherst College, a private institution, reported "complaints by alumni and others on public speeches and radio broadcasts by faculty members on controversial economic problems." However, the report adds that there were "no real difficulties."

California, which is believed to be normally a center for various vagaries of political and religious thought has had some difficulty because of subversive activity. At the University of California, at Berkeley, a small group of communistic students have taken part in local strikes and other activities. The same has been true of the U.C.L.A. branch. However, in each of these instances the number of students involved was almost unbelievably small when we consider the total enrollment. Some members of the University of California faculty joined an organization known as the Hollywood Writers Mobilization. It is believed that these faculty members joined in good faith, for on discovering that the Hollywood group had the reputation of being communist dominated, they withdrew. However, this action led to a legislative investigation and the adoption of a rule by the regents that "no one advocating the overthrow of our government by force will be enrolled or employed by the University of California." At the University of Southern California it was discovered that one student was a Russian spy who had attempted to organize subversive activities. The report from the University of Washington says, "Some concern currently over studies of Legislative Committee on un-American Activities. No charges have yet been made against faculty members."

The University of Colorado had some difficulty in connection with the withdrawal of the charter of the AYD. There have been no charges of subversive teaching at Colorado, but a group of the students, masquerading as a liberal group, revealed evidence of communistic tendencies. After investigation, President Stearns withdrew the charter and was subjected to considerable criticism for doing so. A letter addressed to President Stearns by the deans of the faculty is worth quoting as a reflection of the attitude of responsible educational authorities when this issue is raised. It reads as follows:

April 14, 1947

President Robert L. Stearns
University of Colorado

Dear President Stearns:

We have read with deep concern certain statements which we need not identify, regarding the motives and purposes which, it is alleged, prompted you to withdraw the charter of the organization known as American Youth for Democracy. While several members of the faculty have publicly expressed approval of your action, and there has been some favorable editorial comment, you must have felt at times that here on the campus you were standing alone, or at best must have entertained doubt as to the attitude of the faculty and students of the University.

There were some of us who did at one time entertain some doubt as to the wisdom of withdrawing the charter of the AYD. The subsequent actions of the members of the AYD and their supporters have thoroughly dispelled those doubts. We are now convinced that your action was wise as well as proper, and we feel sure that this same opinion is entertained by the vast majority of both faculty and students.

We are, accordingly, taking this means of commending your decision, and assuring you of our wholehearted support. We feel that your decision reflects accurate recognition and careful evaluation of issues, and, above all, an appreciation of what is right and good and what is wrong and dangerous. We feel that approval of the AYD would have meant a compromise with truth and honesty that you could not properly have made. We concur in your belief that liberal thought should be welcomed on the campus, provided, of course, that there is no intentional concealment or distortion of the sponsorship or purposes of such organizations.

Your attitude on freedom of speech and academic freedom is too well known to us to require comment or defense, but we do wish to express our opinion that withdrawal of the charter of the AYD did not constitute any infringement of academic freedom or any deprivation of civil liberties.

Sincerely yours,

/s/   W. F. Dyde
Dean of the Faculties

Ward Darley, M.D.
Dean of the School of Medicine

P. G. Worcester
Dean of the Graduate School

Mary Ethel Ball
Dean of Women

Rowland W. Sunham
Dean, College of Music

C. L. Eckel
Dean, College of Engineering

Harry Carlson
Dean of Men

Cliff Houston
Dean of Students

Edward C. King
Dean, School of Law

Charles F. Poe
Dean, College of Pharmacy

G. G. Fullerton
for the School of Business

At Colorado also there was an instance of the refusal of the regents to approve the nomination of a candidate for a deanship allegedly on the ground of his liberal views. The regents maintained their position, but subsequently appointed the same man as director of research in the institution. Apparently the alleged reason for his being denied promotion in the first place was not sound.

Cornell University has been criticized because of the use of Russian teachers. This scarcely suggests communistic activity, as it is usual to have native teachers as instructors in the Russian language and civilization. If the presence of Russian teachers on our university faculties is an indication of communistic activity, there are few great universities in the country which are not open to such accusation. Just as there are a few Americans who are not democratic, so there are a few Russians who are not communistic. The fact that a man is a Russian by birth does not necessarily indicate that he is communist.

An interesting situation developed at Indiana University. During a political campaign the governor demanded the investigation of three professors on grounds of alleged communistic teaching. There was a very thorough investigation by the board of regents. Faculty members were interviewed, and even the leaders of student political groups were called in and questioned. Only flimsy evidence resulted, including a statement by one student that he had overheard another student say that Professor Blank was a communist. The investigation revealed no evidence whatever of subversive teaching. One professor under inquiry resigned of his own volition, but was specifically cleared by the board of any charges. The other two professors in question are still members of the faculty and have been completely exonerated of any charges of subversive teaching. The following report to the governor is self-explanatory:

Bloomington, Indiana
December 15, 1946

The Honorable Ralph F. Gates,

Governor of Indiana:

Agreeable to the request in your letter following a resolution by the American Legion, Department of Indiana, the Board of Trustees of Indiana University has made a good faith investigation of the possibility of communistic or any other subversive or un-American activity at Indiana University, and begs to submit this, its report thereon.

Records are available which indicate that, during its proud history of 127 years, including its active participation in most of the great wars and the social and political resurgences preceding and following them, Indiana University has attempted to prevent on its campuses (1) subversive, un-American or unpatriotic activity or the dissemination of such philosophies, and (2) any undue cramping of the type of academic freedom of thought and speech which is so essential to the success of any educational institution. The university, recognizing consistently the importance of freedom and liberty of thought has constantly drawn a sharp distinction between liberty and license. Several years ago this Board adopted a resolution bearing on the subject, which is still in effect in this and many other universities. It is as follows:

"No restraint shall be placed upon the teacher's freedom in investigation, unless restriction upon the amount of time devoted to it becomes necessary in order to prevent undue interference with other duties. No limitation shall be placed upon the teacher's freedom in the exposition of his own subject in the classroom or in addresses and publications outside the classroom so long as the statements are not definitely anti-social. No teacher shall claim as his right the privilege of discussing in his classroom controversial topics obviously and clearly outside of his own field of study. The teacher is morally bound not to take advantage of his position by introduction into the classroom of provocative discussions of completely irrelevant subjects admittedly not within his field of study, is entitled to precisely the same freedom, but is subject to the same responsibility, as attaches to all other citizens."

The investigation included: (1) many interviews of students and faculty members by individual members of the Board, (2) a two-day hearing by the full Board at Bloomington. This hearing was an executive session in the absence of press and public so that witnesses would be more inclined to speak freely. Witnesses were put at ease, informed that the hearing was informal, that the technical rules would be ignored, with hearsay or rumor evidence being welcomed. Witnesses were all informed that the Board would guarantee protection against any reprisal which might be attempted from any source. (3) After adjournment of the hearing a statement was given to the press that the matter would be held open until the next meeting of the Board on December 15, 1946. This was to give opportunity to any additional witnesses to present anything bearing on the subject.

Invited to the hearing for the presentment of any relevant matter were representatives of the Department of Indiana, American Legion, the Logansport post of the Legion, and many other organizations of large and representative membership throughout the state or in Indianapolis and Bloomington. Many representative students, including presidents of principal campus organizations, were also invited. Most of these invitations resulted in acceptances, including the Legion, whose department commander, adjutant, magazine editor, Americanization chairman, a post commander and others honored us by their attendance, and their cordial and friendly attitude of co-operation. Two of these are graduates of Indiana University and two are former residents of Bloomington. Four of the eight members of this Board are members of the Legion. Under these circumstances, there could not have been and was not any clash of interests, but rather a sincere co-operative effort to get to the bottom of a troublesome subject.

At the hearing it was announced by the Legion representatives that they had no evidence of communism or subversive activities generally but would limit their discussion to the single matter of three members of the law school faculty signing a petition for the inclusion of the Communist Party on the state ballot at the November election. The Board did not, however, confine itself to this one issue, giving it due and extended consideration but also going far afield into the general subject matter of your letter.

The Board gave its principal consideration to the following questions:

(1) Whether teachers at Indiana University have used their positions of advantage to promote any communistic, un-American, unpatriotic or subversive philosophy.

(2) Whether any such philosophies which are communistic, un-American, unpatriotic or subversive, have existed or exist among faculty or students.

(3) The specific charge relating to the signing by three law professors of the petition to include the Communist Party on the state ballot at the last election.

The Board, after hearing and seeing all of the evidence, a transcript of which from the stenotype recording would be approximately four hundred typewritten pages, makes the following finding of facts:

(1) No evidence, direct, circumstantial or hearsay, was presented showing or tending to show that communism or any subversive philosophy was being or had been taught or propagandized by any member of the faculty in any school or department on any of the campuses of the university. The evidence was unanimous that no such thing had existed.

(2) The Communist Party has apparently had no party organization in Bloomington or Monroe County. It polled 21 votes at the last general election in Monroe County as against an average of around 2,000 votes polled by the Prohibition Party, the only other minor party appearing on the County ballot.

(3) No communistic, subversive or un-American activity outside the

classroom could be discovered, by individuals, in groups, or organizations among students or faculty.

(4) Prior to the last election, Dean Bernard C. Gavit, Professor Fowler V. Harper and Associate Professor Howard Mann signed an informal petition which reads as follows:

Governor Ralph Gates and the Indiana State and Marion County Boards of Election Commissioners

Gentlemen:

Perhaps the most precious right of citizens in a democracy is the right to vote for candidates and principles. We are proud of the fact that in the United States we are able to effect the most profound political changes by simple use of the ballot.

We the undersigned, citizens and voters of Indiana, are convinced that any limitation on the right of citizens to use the ballot to vote for candidates or principles they support is a direct danger to our democracy.

For that reason we support wholeheartedly the right of every minority party which can fulfill the statutory requirements to have its place on the ballot.

On July 29th, the nominees of the Communist Party filed a petition signed by 11,000 electors requesting that the said nominees be placed upon the ballot. The Communist Party in Indiana is a tiny minority and none of the undersigned are either members or political sympathizers with the Communist Party. However, its members and those other citizens who wish to support that party cannot in justice be deprived of that opportunity.

Accordingly, we call upon the State and Marion County Boards of Election Commissioners to cause the names of those candidates to be printed on the ballot, as provided in Section 106 of the Official Election Code of Indiana, and the Governor to certify the names of said candidates to the various clerks of courts, as provided in Section III of the Election Code.

This is a matter affecting deeply the civil liberties of all citizens which constitute the very cornerstone of our democratic system:

Signed:

Bernard C. Gavit
Dean of School of Law
Indiana University

Starling W. James
President, Federation of Associated Clubs, Indianapolis

Joseph K. Shepard
President, Indianapolis Industrial Council, C. I. O.

James McEwen
President, Indiana State Board, Congress of Industrial Organization

H. L. McNamara
Field Representative
C. I. O.

Walter Frisbie
Secretary-Treasurer, Indiana State Board, Congress of Industrial Organization

Rev. Frank S. C. Wicks
Minister Emeritus, All Souls Unitarian Church

Charles F. Fleming
Indiana State Senator

John R. Shannon
Professor of Education, Indiana State Teachers College, Terre Haute

James H. McGill
President, McGill Manufacturing Co.

Fowler Harper
Professor of Law
Indiana University

Powers Hapgood
Regional Director
C. I. O.

James S. Hunter
Indiana State Representative

W. Howard Mann
Professor of Law
Indiana University

The above persons have signed this letter as individuals, and their organizational connections are given only for identification.

End of Petition

At the time of such signing there were no titles appended beneath the signatures. Such titles were subsequently added without knowledge of the signators.

Professor Harper, who has since tendered his resignation and is no longer teaching at the university, tendered the document to Professors Gavit and Mann with the request that they join him in signing, advising that to do so was simply an expression of political freedom on behalf of a minority party of which none of them was a member. The three signed. These three, each a veteran of one of our world wars, appeared at his own request, testified that they were not members of the Communist Party and detested its philosophy. Two of them testified that they were regular members of one of the two major political parties. The other said that he had voted independently for candidates of one or the other of such parties. Each earnestly asserted his profound admiration for the Constitution and the American way of life. During World War II each of them was in the service of the government of the United States and, as a condition of their employment, underwent the customary investigation by the Federal Bureau of Investigation. Professor Harper offered in evidence certificates of merit signed by the secretaries of War and Navy, of opposite political faith, which commended him for his service as chairman of the Joint Committee on Recreation of the Army and Navy. This evidence was undisputed by anyone, and, with no evidence tending to dispute it, the Board accepts it as true.

In the meantime, the Communist Party had filed a formal petition fashioned as required by the election laws of Indiana with the state election officials, containing some 11,000 names. This petition was not signed by these three professors. The state election board held that the petition was legal and ordered the Communist ticket included on the ballot. It is interesting to note that the party polled only something over 800 votes at the election.

Because of the importance and sincerity of purpose of the American Legion and your own continuously friendly activity in favor of education generally, including Indiana University, this Board has taken extra time to conclude this investigation as it completes what is probably the most ambitious program for the housing and education of returning veterans in the nation, as well as concurrent care for their wives and children. The Board expresses its deep appreciation to you and the Legion for extending to it this opportunity to serve the state by clarifying the matter under consideration.

Respectfully submitted:

Ora L. Wildermuth	Paul L. Feltus
William A. Kunkel	John S. Hastings
Frank E. Allen	Mrs. Mary Rieman Maurer
C. Walter McCarty	George W. Henley

Members of the Board of Trustees of Indiana University

In the neighboring state of Iowa, the president of the State University of Iowa made a significant statement in connection with the general assumption that subversive teaching occurs in colleges and universities. It is as follows:

"I sometimes feel that the reason why there have been no active controversies in this institution with regard to academic freedom and no public charges of subversive teaching or activity is that the faculty is so aware of the witch hunts which often are directed toward the most innocent and enlightened proposals to alter the social structure in some particular that they are unwilling either personally or for the sake of the institution to embark on investigations which might result in controversy. There are many weaknesses in our federal Constitution—the institution of the Vice-Presidency is a glaring example —but I have no doubt that any proposal to eliminate such obvious defects would meet with the charge of communism from some quarter. Having gone to school in England for two years and having observed English discussion and controversy at close hand, I am often amazed at the lack of faith which Americans seem to have in the solidity and vitality of democratic institutions or of the values of free discussion and controversy. In many an American's mind there is an unacknowledged mental reservation that only that speech should be free which agrees with our point of view. We need to create a climate of opinion in which we believe so firmly in the strength of democracy and in the validity of our own institutions that men may be able to criticize them honestly with the hope of improving them without being charged with subversive teaching or action."

At Maryland, while there was no subversive teaching, there was a reaction on the part of several faculty members to the introduction of requirements in American civilization. The reason given by these faculty members was that they were opposed to the proposal for fear that it might mean "indoctrination of extreme nationalism."

Michigan has had its share of publicity in regard to supposedly subversive activity. In one state-controlled university an American Youth for Democracy organizer announced the formation of his group. The students of the School of Business Administration of the university interested themselves in the matter and attended the organization meeting in some numbers. When the election of officers of the group was held the organizer ran for every office, and was defeated every time his name was presented. He left the institution the following day and the AYD chapter died a natural death. However, even though the above facts would certainly suggest loyalty to American principles, there was an investigation of the university by the F.B.I.

There was considerable publicity also in connection with the

AYD group at Michigan State College. In February, 1947, in answer to the questionnaire, President John A. Hannah summarized the situation there in the following words:

"This matter has been given publicity out of all proportion to its importance, considering that only six of our more than 13,400 students are known to be members of the AYD. It is even more unfortunate that extraneous matters have been injected into the normal operation of democratic student government on this campus. For example, the claim has been made that members of the AYD are being penalized for their political beliefs. This is wholly untrue; they are being penalized for violations of long-standing policies governing the activities of student organizations. Specifically, they are being penalized for refusing to abide by the decision of a majority of students on this campus, as expressed through their representatives on the Student Council.

"In view of the widespread misunderstanding of the facts in the case, and of attempts to confuse the issue, it might be useful to review the circumstances.

"Student government has long been encouraged and supported by the faculty, administration and governing body of Michigan State College. The students themselves elect their representatives to the Student Council, which conducts its affairs under a written constitution and by-laws, which have faculty approval.

"One section of that constitution states that every newly-organized group of students must submit a statement of its purpose and a draft of its proposed constitution and by-laws to the Student Council for approval before it engages in any activities.

"Last fall, the American Youth for Democracy organization applied to the Student Council for authorization to carry on its program on the Michican State College campus. After deliberation and debate, the Student Council refused by a majority vote to approve the AYD as a Michigan State College organization. Approval is withheld from a number of proposed new organizations every year, and ordinarily the rejected organization disbands and its members cease their activities.

"Last week, it was called to the attention of the Student Council that the AYD had continued to carry on organized activities in defiance of the Student Council's decision. It was cited that the members had continued to meet as an organization, and that they had circulated handbills on the campus without authority in violation of another long-established College regulation.

"Confronted by this defiance of the authority of student government, the Student Council voted to recommend that the offending members of the AYD be disciplined. Probation was suggested as a minimum penalty.

"On February 4, the recommendation of the Student Council came before the Faculty Committee on Student Organizations, as do all such recommendations. The students accused of violating the rules of student government were given a hearing. Questioning was restricted to establishing their membership in the AYD, and the fact that AYD had been operating in violation of the rules of student government. Six of the seven students admitted membership and such unauthorized activity. Following the meeting, the faculty committee concurred in the recommendation of the Student Council that the members of the organization be placed on disciplinary probation.

"I have recited all this history to emphasize the point that this breach of discipline has been handled as a matter of routine college administration. As a believer in student government, I am gratified that this matter has been handled efficiently and impersonally by the Student Council. The Student Council made the original decision to refuse permission for the AYD to operate on this campus, and the Student Council originated the action to discipline offenders against that decision.

"I want to make very plain that this action is not directed against the AYD and its members because of their political beliefs or affiliations, as has been charged. That has never entered into the matter. Similar action would have been taken no matter what the background or program of the organization."

Seven or eight years ago, one man accused of subversive teaching was dismissed from the faculty of the University of New Hampshire, but there has been no further difficulty there since that time.

At the University of North Dakota the only instance was criticism by an out-of-state speaker of reference textbooks used by six institutions in the state, including one privately controlled college. While there was some newspaper publicity, the incident was ignored by the legislature and by the public at large, and it should scarcely deserve serious attention.

At Ohio State University there has been no recent instance of subversive teaching or activity. President Bevis says: "There has been no instance of subversive teaching or subversive activity during the past five years. A few vague incidents have occurred but they are not worthy of serious consideration. A former chapter of the American Youth for Democracy (known as Ohio State Youth for Democracy) was discontinued about a year ago, due to misrepresentation of objectives."

At V.M.I. the report says, "No isms at V.M.I. except Patriotism."

At William and Mary there has been no difficulty with subversive teaching, but there was one case of a conscientious objector.

Wisconsin is another state which has had considerable publicity in regard to radical tendencies. The report here says, "There have been rumors of subversive teaching from time to time but no organized attempt to investigate the university, nor have such rumors been taken too seriously by either the university or the public."

While it was not strictly a matter of subversive teaching or activity, the University of Texas has been cited because of the charge that former President Rainey was dismissed because of his liberal views. A careful study of the situation, including interviews with regents and faculty involved, would seem to indicate that Dr. Rainey's liberal attitude had very little to do with his actual dismissal. This case is mentioned, not because of subversive teaching, but because of the implication that the board of regents dismissed a president for honest liberal views. The evidence in the case, including the report of the Association of University Professors, would seem to indicate that both President Rainey and the regents had many valid reasons for the severance of this relationship.[4]

The conclusions to be drawn from the charges of communism in our colleges and universities, both public and private, are as follows: (1) If one is seeking the breeding places of communism in this country they are not to be found on the campuses

[4] See page 72.

of our colleges and universities. (2) The amount of subversive teaching and activity is insignificant when we compare the few persons involved with total enrollments. (3) The AYD has more dead than live chapters in our colleges and universities, and where it has not been admitted should not be recognized in view of its past record. (4) There are few more loyal groups of citizens in the United States than the faculties and student bodies of our colleges and universities. (5) In order that the student may have an intelligent concept of the system of government under which he lives and be able to compare that system intelligently with other ideologies which are a normal part of his education, it is recommended that there be a required course in American history and American government for all students of American colleges and universities, particularly those which are state-controlled. This recommendation is made with full recognition of the resentment of faculty members and students against compulsory courses. However, there is no reason to assume that a really good teacher cannot make a compulsory course as interesting as an elective if he is worthy of being a faculty member at all.

It should be noted, however, that the absence of communistic teaching and activity in our colleges and universities in no way disposes of the possibility of communism becoming a national menace.

It must be kept in mind that national socialism in Germany proved as great a menace as communism. In a republic the ability to pay high wages depends on wise handling of resources and competent management, and also on competent labor. This determines the wages of the individual worker, and under such a system the individual worker retains the right to exercise the privilege of his franchise unhampered and unrestricted. Socialism always has appealed to idealists. Theoretically, it can be made most attractive. Russia today suggests a national socialistic program rather than a truly communistic one. In the preservation of academic freedom and in the encouragement of honest liberal thought care must be taken constantly to determine whether any teaching can be construed as inimical to our form of government even if it does not take the form of outright communism. The preservation of democracy and the preservation of the four freedoms depend upon maintaining a republican form of government. Any teaching directly or indirectly disloyal to such a form of government in our educational institutions is a danger. We must uphold freedom of speech, but we must also sustain the democratic way of life. A republican form of government is possible only where there is individual ownership of resources and where the rights of the individual to hold these resources are protected.

5

RELIGION AND MORALITY IN PUBLICLY AND PRIVATELY CONTROLLED INSTITUTIONS

MORALITY on college campuses has been under attack on more than one occasion. Certain institutions are singled out and given the reputation of lower moral standards than prevail at others. There is a general impression that unless one goes to a church-related college the serious study of morals and religion is largely ignored during one's undergraduate career. There has even been a question as to the type of religion and the effectiveness of its relation to morality in some of the church-related colleges, where morality and religion are accepted subjects in the curriculum. In the secular colleges, with all the extra-curricular activities of the average undergraduate, it has been easy in many instances to assume that religion and morals have been somewhat neglected. In many of the professional schools the amount of technical teaching and experiment that must be crowded into a limited time has also diverted attention from emphasis on ethics and morals and religion. In a majority of colleges the development of a rather vast extra-curricular program has made it difficult for religious organizations to compete successfully with the social programs of fraternities, sororities, and other secular student groups. The idea of worship has been largely connected with the observance of Sunday, and the almost universal use of week-ends at many colleges and universities for social purposes leaves little time for religious thought and activity.

There is a growing feeling that this lack of emphasis on morals and religion leaves a serious gap in our educational program. Many of the states have laws restricting the teaching of religion; but this lack of religious emphasis is not limited to the state colleges and universities. Many of the privately controlled institutions, originally founded to educate for the ministry, are equally guilty of a similar lapse. Religion has largely lost academic respectability in many quarters, yet the motives in men's minds and hearts [1] are more important than the machines men's hands produce, for those motives determine the use to which these machines will be put, for good or for evil, for life or for death. It would be illuminating to submit all American college students to an examination on the meaning of life and the meaning of death. To be an expert in forestry or technological research or in classical studies means little unless life has meaning and death has meaning.[2] Religion offers a student the means by which he can successfully unite the warring elements of human personality into a compact unit which will enable him to face the demands of life unafraid, and to be master of his own destiny. Education which does not include such a motivating power falls short of its greatest objective. But religion should do more than bring peace of mind to the individual student. It should furnish a driving urge that impels a man to sacrifice himself in behalf of human decency and public righteousness, in behalf of honest competition, in behalf of giving every other individual a reasonably fair chance. This requires a religious motive,[3] particularly in a democracy where freedom of action gives the narrow, selfish bigot as much of a chance to exploit others as it gives the man with a faith opportunity to serve.

[1] *Youth and the Future,* American Council on Education, 1942, p. 204.
[2] *Co-operation in General Education, American Council on Education,* p. 83 ff. 1947.
[3] *After Black Coffee,* Robert I. Gannon; McMullen, 1944, p. 13.

We forget that the beginnings of American education, beginnings which have led to the establishment of our great state and privately controlled universities, had behind them a religious impulse [4] and the aim of establishing in the new world an intelligent educated ministry. Earlier, the education of clergy, doctors, lawyers, and learned clerks characterized the Middle Ages. With the Renaissance came the education of gentlemen. With the flowering of democracy came insistence that every man should be able to read and write, and be sufficiently skilled to contribute his share to the common good; and that he should be able to take an intelligent attitude toward religion, the mother of motives, education, the process of preparing to live, and democracy, the form of government under which he has a right to speak his mind, to think his own thoughts, and live his life as a son of God, a son of man, and the master of his own destiny.

With the growth of secularism in education and of sectarianism [5] in religion, the gulf between purely technical studies and basic religious concepts grew wider and wider. Church colleges of one type retired into a kind of monastic seclusion, and sometimes emphasized their particular religious beliefs at the expense of other aspects of education.[6] Other church-related colleges, in their effort to appear liberal, have practically robbed religion of its vitality. The great technical schools, some of the earlier wealthy privately controlled higher educational institutions, and many of the state colleges and universities were so characterized by secularism that religion, as a fundamental part of education, was largely lost sight of. College presidents were very careful about appearing sympathetic with religion, even in its most liberal sense. Many faculty members adopted an attitude of superiority and slyly discredited any reference to religious values in their lecture rooms and in their laboratories. This state of affairs became so general that there were occasional utterances about

[4] *Religious Counseling of College Students,* American Council on Education, Vol. 7, April, 1943, p. 53.

[5] *Religious Counseling of College Students,* American Council on Education, Vol. 7, April, 1943, p. 54.

[6] *Religious Counseling of College Students,* American Council on Education, Vol. 7, April, 1943, p. 57.

the Godlessness of our universities and colleges and of our state colleges and universities particularly. There was more and more emphasis on utilitarian education, on producing more and better jobs, making more money, inventing new machines, preventing plant diseases, in short, on exclusive dedication to the so-called practical aspects of life. Little attention was given to the motives which would determine the use of the machines and the discoveries when the student left the precincts of the campus to take an active part in a highly industrialized world.

Then a change began to be apparent.[7] The very faculty members who had referred lightly and humorously to religion began to make fewer and fewer derogatory references. More thoughtful teachers became seriously concerned over the lack in the average curriculum which provided nothing as a pattern for life or a design for living. The fear of sectarianism still persisted, and the only religion that many of them knew was the conventional orthodoxy of some particular sect or church. However long it may take truth to assert itself, a ferment was under way which was bringing more and more into focus the importance of some integrating philosophy, some motivating agency which would give meaning to life and to death other than in terms of money and of purely material values. There has been, and there still is, much confusion over how this problem is to be handled.[8] The vast majority of presidents, faculty members, and regents interviewed in this study revealed their consciousness of the importance of making a place in education for the teaching of morals and of a religion divorced from sectarian overemphasis. There is a widespread consciousness of this need, but there is an equally wide uncertainty as to how the need should be met. There is an awareness that certain types of emotional religion sometimes verge very closely on intellectual dishonesty. There is also a consciousness of the temptation to try to readjust facts so as to meet a particular theory of religious history or of religious practice. On the other hand, men also have awakened to the need for an intelligent presentation of basic reli-

[7] *Religious Counseling of College Students*, American Council on Education, Vol. 7, April, 1943, pp. 60, 61.

[8] *General Education in the Humanities*, American Council on Education, 1947, p. 79 ff.

gious concepts which have to do with belief in a divine power called God, belief in one's fellow man, belief in social responsibility, and belief in the preservation and maintenance of a moral code.[9]

Along with this revival of interest among faculties and administrators in the necessity for a serious consideration of the claims of religion as a part of education, there has been a growing intellectual curiosity among a considerable number of students.[10] This curiosity does not take the form of a particular interest in the conventional practices of orthodoxy. The students are showing comparatively little interest in conventional religion, with its emphasis on sometimes dull preaching, its misunderstandings, and, particularly, its ecclesiastical quarrels, and its routine formulas; but they are interested in trying to discover, behind all these religious expressions, the basic reasons for adopting a philosophy of life which enables one to do one's job better, to be at peace with one's self, to get along with one's fellow man, and to live the kind of life that deserves the respect of others.[11]

Along with this increase in the student's intellectual curiosity in regard to the basic concepts of religion, there is a curious contradiction, in that there has been a rather serious breakdown of morals in practically all of the colleges and universities. This breakdown takes a new and peculiar form. After any war, we normally expect, as one of the post-war by-products, a temporary laxity in the use of alcohol and a rather general looseness in sexual relations. After great masses of young men under discipline have been denied normal social expression, the temptation is to overdo and to forget moral inhibitions for a time when the moment of release comes. In addition, during war many young men who, because of the influence of family and home environment, would not normally do so, seek release in the use of alcohol and in sexual offenses. This moral looseness is apt to continue

[9] *General Education in the Humanities,* American Council on Education, 1947, Akk. A. B. & C.

[10] *Relation of Religion to Public Education,* American Council on Education, Vol. 11, April, 1947, p. 1.

[11] *Co-operation in General Education,* American Council on Education, 1947, pp. 60-65.

when students return to a campus and take up its reasonably normal social life.

Investigation reveals, however, that there is reason for congratulation that, in spite of war's effect, conditions on our campuses, so far as excessive alcoholism and an expected increase in sexual irregularities are concerned, are far better than many people assume. Alcoholism and sexual misbehavior are problems that the colleges always have had to face and probably always will have to face. Common sense dictates that everything possible be done to limit these excesses and hold moral irregularities down to the lowest possible minimum. Practically every institution visited, reported that excessive drinking and sexual misbehavior are less, if anything, than they were; and in the few instances where this does not hold they are at least no worse than they were before. In view of earlier post-war experience, this is a rather encouraging development. It is probably due, in part, to the fact that so many married veterans have their wives with them on campuses, and therefore are less exposed to sexual temptation than otherwise they would be. Not only this, but the married students, being somewhat older, set an example in this regard to the younger students who have entered directly from high school. The same influences bear on the excessive use of alcohol. Older veterans, and particularly married veterans, are exceedingly eager to complete their formal education in as short a time as possible. This means concentration and the avoidance of social interruptions which would delay, even momentarily, the time of graduation. Once more, the older and married students set an example to the younger. Therefore, there is reason to feel great satisfaction, over the absence of any marked increase in excessive alcoholism or in the number of sex offenders in this post-war period.

There is a moral breakdown, however, and it has taken another form. There has been a marked increase in cheating,[12] lying, and stealing, but particularly in cheating. This increase is so general as to prevent the singling out of any particular insti-

[12] *Educational Record,* American Council on Education, Supplement 16, January, 1947, pp. 96, 97.

tution. In practically every university or college visited, there was a frank facing of the problem and willingness to discuss it and the methods whereby it might be solved. The heads of some institutions were franker and more honest than others in acknowledging the situation, but even where there was hesitancy in discussing the facts, there was a disposition to be frank once it was assured that the institution in question was not to be held up as a horrible example, and that its experience was being shared by many others.

The question has been raised whether this increase in cheating is due, in part, to the large increase in veterans' enrollment. The answer is no. Women students and recent high-school graduates appear to be equally guilty. The instances take many and varied forms. In one institution it was discovered that a certain fraternity, which had not been conspicuous for its scholastic attainments, suddenly achieved an unusually high rating in a certain subject. This rating included some students who, as a rule, were very definitely below average, not only in the subject in question, but in all subjects. Investigation revealed that the lecture class in this particular course was unusually large. For the examination the class of hundreds was divided into small sections. One student from this group was assigned to the first section to be examined. This group had a pet dog, which accompanied the student to the examination. After creating a few moments' disturbance, the dog was indignantly sent home by the student. It was discovered that the dog went home with a copy of the examination carefully tucked beneath his collar. That house must have been a busy place, for the result was exceptionally good papers, indicating a mastery of the course that the students actually did not possess.

In another institution with unusually large classes which had to be divided into sections for examinations, one rather bright student repeated the examination in a number of different sections under the names of other students. This deception was discovered when a long-distance call came for the young man in whose name the student was taking the examination at the moment. When the cheater went to the telephone, he was, of course, not able to identify himself to the family of the boy in whose name he was writing the paper, with the result that the whole scheme was discovered. In several institutions professors' desks have been broken into and the examination papers stolen and sold. Some institutions have had special faculty committees to study the problem and to make recommendations with reference to it.

While this practice of cheating is rather general, it should be noted that it is indulged in by only a minority of students in each institution where it was discovered. The great majority of the student body resents cheating, and in many places the students themselves have taken action against it. There are instances of the abolishing of the honor system because of this increase in dishonesty in examinations. In certain institutions where the honor system is strictly enforced, there has not been the same increase in cheating as in those where the honor system does not prevail. It should be noted that in every institution visited, where cases of dishonesty were proved, strict disciplinary action was taken.

In regard to stealing, the increase has not been as general as in cheating. Instances are reported of the theft of equipment, a practice hitherto practically unknown, and the theft of books and personal belongings. In one institution there was formerly a tradition that a book could be left anywhere on the campus and it would still be there even two years later. Now that tradition has been so badly broken that students are exceedingly careful about leaving books or other personal belongings where they might be stolen. During a fire at another institution helpful students removed the belongings of those whose quarters were in danger. This happens to be an institution where stealing was almost unknown. Within a period of a few moments before the occupants of the dormitory arrived at the scene of the fire over $700 worth of goods had been taken.

As for the increase in lying, which also is less than the increase in cheating, there is reason to believe that this tendency toward telling untruths did not originate on college campuses. It goes back to the life of the family, to the high-school level, and to social life in general. There was a time when white lies were discussed

as possible moral violations. Today the white lie in social interchange is so common that the distinction between white and gray
and, frequently, black is lost sight of. There is a general disregard for truth in many quarters, of which the increase in lying on
campuses is probably only a reflection. In any case, it is an evidence of the need for moral teaching as a necessary part of education.

An examination of the causes of the moral lapse in cheating,
lying, and stealing suggests that many of them existed before
college and are not necessarily connected with campus experience
as such. First, the mishandling of so-called progressive education,
especially on the high-school level, by teachers who had never
been trained to teach progressively, has developed psychological
attitudes in the students under their care, resulting in a lack of
social responsibility and self-reliance. The policy of doing largely
what one pleases, and a feeling that the method is unimportant
and the result only is to be considered, has been responsible to a
considerable degree for this moral lapse. Second, the breakdown
in family life and the increase in broken homes also have contributed to a delinquent attitude toward lying, cheating, and
stealing. Third, the strict limitations placed on entrance to graduate schools has made competition for entrance exceedingly keen.
When a student realizes that 1/10 of 1 per cent in average may
prevent his entrance to engineering school or medical school or
to graduate school there is a strong temptation to take advantage
of illegal methods. Fourth, some of the veterans are exceedingly
anxious to master the technical details of their chosen field as soon
as possible and resent required courses of a general educational
character. These students are very careful to master honestly the
details of technical courses, but are not nearly so conscientious
when it comes to taking required courses such as history or English, the results of which they cannot measure in terms of income
in later life. Fifth, the competition among sororities to obtain
high standing for their groups was blamed in one institution for
the increase in cheating among women students. Sixth, during
the war it was a common practice when one soldier "borrowed"
another's blanket, the borrowing was from the man next to him.

This was not considered stealing. The blankets all belonged to the government, and each soldier was a part of the government, so that, although some inconvenience was caused, it was not generally considered that the question of dishonesty was involved. There was a communal attitude toward property, and as this attitude grew, the right of the individual to own property was taken less and less seriously. It must be insisted that the armed forces officially did everything in their power to promote honesty. However, in the exigencies due to unforeseen emergencies some men developed a habit of taking very lightly the appropriation of another man's property. It should be stated here that the veteran groups in our colleges can be divided into two classes. One class represents many of the finest students we have, men who have raised the general standing by their conscientiousness and highly satisfactory work. In the other class can be found a group of so-called students who were below par in the military service and who continue to be below par on the campus. The mere fact that a man has worn a uniform for a few months does not turn him into a paragon of virtue. Many of the best and some of the worst students on our campuses are veterans, and this fact must be faced frankly. Seventh, there have been indications of a growing disregard of the rights of private property in the United States during the past twelve years, and this disregard is reflected in an increase in dishonesty, not only on college campuses but in other circles.

It should be observed that no institution has been singled out as being especially marked by this lapse into cheating, lying, and stealing. With very few exceptions, the tendency has been apparent in the great majority of institutions visited, and it is a matter of grave concern to faculties and administrators as to how this difficulty should be met. The ability to live with one's neighbors, to carry on normal business transactions, to enter into holy matrimony, to assume responsibility for the upbringing of a family, all involve adherence to a sound moral code.[13] Even though this

[13] *Faith and Fire Within Us,* Elizabeth Jackson, University of Minnesota, 1944, p. 79.

lapse is found in only a minority in each institution involved, it has reached sufficient proportions to require remedial steps.

This weakness is evidence of a lack in our national higher educational program. There has been a tendency to stress the idea of "science major, everything else minor." Throughout the country there is a growing conviction as to the importance of a broader general educational base. Many of the colleges and universities frankly acknowledge that they have been failing their students, in that they have offered them no carefully thought out design for living. To limit education to the accumulation of a few technical facts, without any emphasis on the way those facts should be used in life, whether to benefit society or merely to exploit others, is a dangerous philosophy of education.

Reference has been made to the fact that along with this increase in lying, cheating, and stealing, there also has been an increase in the intellectual curiosity of students concerning the basic concepts of religion. Even in the older, highly endowed Eastern educational foundations there has grown up, over the years, a neglect of religion as a subject for serious study. Attendance at university and college chapels, formerly compulsory, gradually became voluntary, and eventually attracted only a handful out of large student enrollments. There was a time when this neglect seemed to suggest that religion was a sort of by-product of civilization and was gradually giving place to more important and practical educational disciplines. The extent of this neglect was quickly reflected in the increase of corruption in politics, of dishonesty in business, of selfish exploitation by both labor and industry, and of neglect of family responsibility, and has brought us up sharply to the realization that something more than technical information is necessary if we are to preserve the great moral values on which civilization is based.[14] This leads to a consideration of the teaching of religion in order to offer students an integrating philosophy which will determine how they will use in later life the skills achieved at college or university, and which also will serve as a motivating agency for the preservation and maintenance of a moral code.

14 *Youth and the Future*, American Council on Education, 1942, p. 289.

While this need is felt rather universally, the state universities and colleges are particularly conscious of it. There has been fairly generous provision for religious teaching in many of the privately controlled institutions. Even these schools have not escaped the moral breakdown, and serious questions are being raised as to the effectiveness of the religious teaching which they offer, teaching which, in many instances, has degenerated into the presentation of a series of conventionalized formulas. This teaching does not stimulate the students either to serious thought or to a proper understanding of the relation of religion and moral standards.

The Harvard Report [15] was conspicuous for its failure to make any adequate suggestion for the improvement of morals and of the teaching of religion. It seemed to be evasive whenever the subjects of religion and morals were touched on, a point which stood out in contrast with the carefully thought out findings in other fields of education. Yale University, never hesitant about taking advantage of any mistake that Harvard might make, determined to make a frontal attack on this problem. A committee of ten men was selected from the faculty, six of whom were scientists, which insured the use of the critical method in examining the problem of religion and morals at Yale. This committee engaged in serious study for over a year and then produced a report which deserves far wider circulation than it received.

This report was [16] directed to "the place and function of religion in the post-war life of Yale University." The first section was devoted to religion as worship. Emphasis on this aspect of the problem by a committee of whom a majority were scientists is rather suggestive of the changing attitude of many faculty members toward the place of religion in education. The report traced the history of religion at Yale. It pointed out that there was a steady increase in attendance at Sunday morning services, but a marked decrease in daily attendance at chapel services. The report said, "The mood of aggressive secularism which was evident throughout the life of the nation, notably during the 1920's, was no less characteristic of Yale. For a substantial number, probably

15 *General Education in Free Society*, Harvard University Press, 1945, p. 174.
16 *Report of Special Committee on Morals and Religion*, Yale University, 1946.

a majority of students and many members of the faculty, religious convictions appeared to be intellectually discredited. . . . The very nature of moral obligation became obscure." [17] The counseling service was criticized, and the report pointed out the lack of co-operation between religious counselors and the psychiatric service of the Department of University Health. Referring to the reaction from the war, the report went on to say, "It is a common 'code' in the armed services that one obeys the announced rules but 'anything else goes.' As a result, the attitude that it is right to break minor rules, provided one can get away with it, is widely accepted today. Striking evidence of this war-time condition has appeared in a sharp increase in the amount of classroom dishonesty." Attention is called to the fact that the Sheffield School had been forced to give up the honor system. It should be noted here that Yale University is probably no worse than any other institution visited, and even may be better. It is to Yale's credit to state that the committee is a bit more honest, perhaps.

Attention was called to the fact that while the work of the various denominational student chaplains was highly effective in some instances, the small proportion of the student body they reached placed a severe limitation on the possibility of their influencing moral standards in the university as a whole. Leaving the Yale Report for a moment, it is interesting to note that even where the denominational student chaplains are most active and effective, at best they reach only about fifteen per cent of the student body; and, in some instances, the relationship even with this fifteen per cent is nominal rather than compelling.

The Yale Committee recommended steps be taken toward avoidance of plagiarism in the study of English. It also recommended "a voluntary program of objective education on the biological, psychological, and sociological aspects of sex."

Perhaps the most significant part of the Yale Report was the recommendation for the establishment of a Department of Religion on both the undergraduate and the graduate levels. This department would be largely divorced from the Yale Divinity School, thus freeing it from some of the possible handicaps of

[17] *After Black Coffee*, Robert I. Gannon, McMullen, 1947, p. 35.

time-worn and occasionally antiquated theological trends. Its first objective would be the restoration of religion to academic respectability.[18] That religion has lost its intellectual respectability in many quarters is beyond question. The report provided, in the second place, that the department would have as an objective the offering of a motivating agency for guidance in the life of the individual student for the preservation, maintenance and practicing of a decent moral code. Its purpose would be to give the student an intelligent understanding of the basic concepts of religion, his relation to his fellow man, his relation to God, his relation to society, and of his share in the task of maintaining moral standards. The report emphasized the need for research in the field of religion and the importance of "men feeling the need for something more than hypothesis and for concrete religious experience." It stated frankly, "Traditional religious teaching has steadily been losing its hold upon the educated classes." It stressed the importance of a critical attitude toward the study and understanding of religious beliefs.

The faculty of this new department would include a teacher of the psychology of religion. This would stress the study of man, the fact of prayer, the meaning of repentance and conversion, the significance of sacraments, the place of a religious code of ethics in man's stabilization, and the varieties of religious life. There would also be a chair of anthropology and religion to study the data derived from the religions of less complicated civilizations. Also the provision would be made for specialists in religious history. This would include the religions of Asia and of the Near East, together with the "old Hebrew religion." Christianity would be taught by two men, a medievalist and a modern scholar. There would also be a study of the Jewish tradition, with emphasis on the Talmud, and a specialist in Islam, and, finally, a professor of the philosophy of religion. In the conclusion of this part of the report were these words: "If Yale is looking for a venture which will be acclaimed for its leadership and vision in the country and in the world, we believe that this is the venture."

[18] *Religious Counseling of College Students*, American Council on Education, Vol. 7, April, 1943, pp. 65, 67, 71, 73.

In 1947 the Department of Religion at Yale offered only four courses for undergraduates. The new department would be far more generous. It would stress the idea of religion being "an interdepartmental major." The report implied that a frank approach to the subject of the teaching of religion in the university is the next essential step in American education, in these words: "Your committee believes that if Yale cares to help in the present religious crisis nationally, as well as within her own doors, this proposal of all we know, is the most promising."

The President and Fellows of Yale University approved the report and authorized the establishment of the proposed new department. Yale authorities, with their usual conservatism, feel that it is too early to express an opinion as to the effectiveness of the plan. It is interesting to note that in 1946-1947, 422 undergraduates were taking courses in religion for credit. The attendance at the voluntary religious discussion groups has increased noticeably. The discussions themselves are on a higher intellectual level than before. The men selected for the faculty of this new department were chosen with the greatest care and represent a very high degree of scholarship. In contrast with the rather light and trifling courses in conventional religion which, at some institutions, are a convenient method of accumulating credit hours, these courses in religion at Yale challenge the best of which the student is capable.

It should be stressed that these courses are strictly nonsectarian.[19] Of course, it will be objected that there is no such thing as nonsectarian religion. This objection need not present any serious difficulty, as the type of man whose concept of religion is so limited to sectarian considerations that he is incapable of hearing religious truth presented under other names and by other faiths is probably beyond any help from honest education in any case. The "shut mind" has been too characteristic of certain religious teachers for all too long. There are certain basic concepts— belief in man, God, social responsibility, and a moral code— which are common to every respectable religious faith. One of the

[19] *Educational Record,* American Council on Education, Supplement 16, 1947, p. 147.

greatest obstacles to religion at the present time is that set up by various sects and denominations, frequently founded on the trivia of religion rather than on fundamentals. The hope of religion as a force in the world depends on unity of purpose rather than upon conformity in externals. The ability of men to live happily one with another is more dependent on a knowledge of areas of agreement than overemphasis on details of disagreement. Probably the restoration of religion to academic respectability, and emphasis on these basic concepts will do more to bring about unity of purpose and common agreement on the necessity for sound morality than one can imagine until the experiment has been tried.

In addition, the level of preaching in America has reached a low ebb in many places. A challenging attitude on the part of students, armed with an intelligent idea of the basic concepts of religion, will contribute toward raising this level. Any church which has an honest and sound basis for its position has nothing to fear from the teaching of nonsectarian religion of this type. In the various communions are certain backgrounds having to do with history, the sacraments, mental attitudes, the art of worship, which can be given the student who has received training in these basic concepts, and he will be a far better religionist than he appears to be under the present system. Religion is not the exclusive possession of the warring denominational churches across the street from each other, but a possession of all humanity. It deserves research and study as a necessary factor in raising life to a far higher level and as an essential part of education. The Yale plan is an experiment in a privately controlled institution, unhampered by restrictions of state law which apply to publicly controlled colleges and universities. It is a thoroughly worthwhile experiment and should be watched with the greatest interest by all who are concerned with an education which furnishes the student an integrated moral design for living. Yale's innovation is marked by courage, and is a step away from the confusion in the teaching of religion in many American institutions, both public and private.

An entirely different method of teaching religion can be

found in the experiment at Iowa State University. The School of Religion is a part of the State University of Iowa, being a unit in the College of Liberal Arts. Its courses are fully accredited toward university degrees, and its staff is made up of members of the university faculty. It has its own Board of Trustees, which is composed of members of the university faculty, representatives of the religious groups of the state, and other citizens of Iowa. This Board recommends all staff appointments and is responsible for the financial support of the Protestant, Roman Catholic, and Jewish professorships, and interfaith projects. This support comes entirely from private and denominational sources. The University provides only for the general administrative expense. Men and women throughout the state, aware of the value of religion in the lives of students, frequently remember the university by contributing to the support of this school. Founded in 1927, it presents an example of co-operation between a university administration on one hand and Roman Catholics, Jews, and Protestants, on the other, in an effort to give religion a formal and worthy status on a college campus. Here, as at Yale, there is a determined effort to restore religion to academic respectability. All the teachers, Roman Catholic, Jewish, and Protestant, hold the Doctor of Philosophy degree. They teach with full freedom of individual conviction, and there is a marvelous opportunity for real understanding and good will. It is stated that the school has two objectives. The first is to provide opportunities to study religion in a thoroughgoing and sympathetic way so as to increase understanding of its meaning, its history, its literature, and its claims on life. At first, the courses were only for members of the upper classes, but recently courses for freshmen have been introduced as well. There are about five hundred students now enrolled as freshmen in this School of Religion, and this number has been increasing from year to year. The second objective is to encourage the activities and expressions of religion. There is close co-ordination between campus activities in the religious field and the actual teaching of the courses in the classroom. Iowa is unusual in that from an early day it has made a consistent effort to teach religion. In a statement by the university there appear these words: "Culture of intellect without religion in the heart is only civilized barbarism and disguised animalism," and, again, "Character development is the great, if not the sole, aim of education." Former President Eugene A. Gilmore, at a vesper service designed especially for freshmen, said this: "Therefore make no mistake, and I say this especially to the freshmen: a vital religion is essential not only to give you happiness, but, more important, to give you the morale without which no great achievement was ever realized.[20] The University and those of us charged with its administration and with the education of the oncoming generations recognize religion as essential to a full and effective life and will constantly endeavor to facilitate it as a part of the educational program.[21] If I may be permitted to paraphrase from the language of Solomon, I can express the attitude of the university toward religion: 'With all thy getting, get religion; forsake her not and she shall preserve thee.' "

There isn't space to go into the history of the development of this School of Religion at a state university. There are several phases to the story; there was the problem of finance to be met; there was the problem of agreement among the various faiths to be represented; there was the necessity of interesting the students in religion as a subject for serious study; and there were various other problems which presented themselves from time to time. The major question in most of the state universities has to do with the relation between Church and State. In the period between 1936 and 1939 there was careful consideration of the extent to which public funds could be used to support the teaching of religion in this state university. The following statement expresses the conclusion reached:

"The school was founded on the fundamental principle that 'the responsibility for the development of religious education in a tax-supported institution should be shared by Church and State.'

"In this joint responsibility, the university's proper share is to provide the elements which are nonsectarian and of common advan-

[20] *Faith and Fire Within Us*, Elizabeth Jackson, University of Minnesota, 1944, p. 44.

[21] *General Education in the Humanities*, American Council on Education, 1947, Ch. 2.

tage to all the religious groups; the responsibility of the churches is to provide for their distinctive religious teaching.

"Hence state funds are used only for the administration and general work of the school and not for the support of the Roman Catholic, Jewish, or Protestant professorships.

"This is thought to be in strict accord with the doctrine of the separation of Church and State as defined in the First Amendment to the Constitution of the United States, which prohibits the state from favoring any particular church or form of religion, but not from supporting religion in a way that is fair to all the religious groups." [22]

Protection against any undesirable interference by the university with the free teaching of religion is provided in the school's Board of Trustees, that is, the Board of the School of Religion itself; this is separate from the State Board of Education, which has control of the University administration. On the School of Religion's Board of Trustees the churches must have at least 50 per cent of the membership and may have 60 per cent. "This Board is the school's policy-forming and budget-making body, and while its actions are subject to the approval of the university, the university deals with the school on all fundamental matters through the Board."

The faculty consists of one Roman Catholic professor, one Jewish professor, and three Protestant professors, all under an administrative director. Typical subjects taught include the Fundamentals of Religion and Ethics, the Old Testament, the New Testament, Jewish History, the Roman Catholic Church, Protestant Christianity, the Religions of Mankind, Personal Problems and Adjustment in Present Day Life, and there is research work for graduate students. The School of Religion has its own articles of incorporation, which state its objectives very clearly, the way its board is to be constituted, its relation to the trustees of the university, officers, committees, the functions of the director, the degrees to be conferred, and the power to hold property. This is a very interesting instance of how religion can be taught

[22] *The Story of an Idea*, Revised, University of Iowa Extension Bulletin No. 534, State University of Iowa, 1942, p. 9.

in a state university and public funds be used in connection with the administration of a school of religion which is an official part of the university itself. In certain features, it stands in marked contrast with the plan at Yale.

There is one objection to the School of Religion at the State University of Iowa. That objection is that the sectarian divisions, in the larger sense, between Roman Catholic, Jewish, and Protestant, are definitely maintained. There is naturally a tendency for Roman Catholic students to attend Roman Catholic classes, Protestant students to attend Protestant classes, and Jewish students to attend the classes of the Jewish professor. However, this distinction is being broken down, and more and more students are crossing denominational or sectarian lines and taking subjects which do not deal directly with the particular church or communion to which they belong. It is impossible to state dogmatically whether the Yale system or the system at the University of Iowa is the superior one for introduction into a state institution. The primary fact at Iowa is that there is frank recognition of the importance of the teaching of religion as a part of education in a state university. An Iowa statement says this:

"The study and practice of vital religion is an integral part of a sound educational program. No education is worthy of the name which does not provide ample facilities for the religious life of the students. Religious education off the campus, no matter how fine the preaching, the teaching, or the pastoral and personal guidance may be, cannot be an educational or spiritual equivalent for religious education incorporated into the university itself, and of a quality as good as any other part of the university's life."

Enrollment in the School of Religion at Iowa for 1946-1947 was 1798.

Another interesting instance of a school of religion connected with a state university is that of the University of Missouri.[23] While at Iowa the school of religion is an integral part of the university, at the University of Missouri the Bible College of Missouri is a separate institution, located across the street from

[23] *Bulletin,* Bible College of Missouri, 1946.

the university itself. This institution is nonsectarian, is fully accredited, is independent of state support or control, and has existed for fifty years. Members of the Board of Trustees and of the staff are affiliated with the Disciples of Christ, Methodist, Jewish, Presbyterian U.S., Presbyterian U.S.A., the Congregational, and the Episcopal Churches. It is to be noted that there is no Roman Catholic representation on either the Board of Trustees or the faculty. However, the college enrolls Roman Catholic students. It maintains its autonomy, has the power to grant degrees, appoint instructors, and control property. It conforms to the standards of scholarship and quality of teaching approved by the university, and most of its students are matriculated at the University of Missouri. The Bible College courses accredited by the university are listed in the University of Missouri catalogue. No courses are offered for students not qualified for entrance in the College of Arts and Sciences in the University of Missouri. The institution will admit special students over twenty-one years of age who lack the preparation necessary for college credit. At Iowa the faculty of the School of Religion are recognized members of the faculty of the university. This is not the case at the Bible College of Missouri. The professors, however, must have academic standing acceptable to the university faculty, and must have had at least three years of graduate work. The various churches which appoint a teacher on the faculty of this affiliated Bible College must be responsible for his salary. Effort is made to pay salaries comparable to those of the men on the Missouri faculty. All teachers have an equal voice in determining educational policies and plans, and any religious body supporting a full professor for one year is entitled to one membership on the Board of Trustees. This institution has passed beyond the experimental stage, and the relationship between the Bible College and the University of Missouri appears to be a permanent one. There are certain marked differences between the plans at Yale, Iowa, and Missouri. At Yale the department of religion is strictly nonsectarian, is taught by regular members of the University faculty, and constitutes a department of the University. At Iowa the School of Religion is a recognized department of the University, the state paying the administrative expenses of the school and the various churches supporting the Roman Catholic, Protestant, and Jewish professors who represent their points of view. Therefore the teaching is to a considerable degree sectarian. At Missouri we have an affiliation of an independent Bible College whose faculty members and students have to measure up to the academic requirements of the university, the university giving full credit for the courses given in the Bible College. This faculty is supported by contributions from the various denominations involved, but the teaching is strictly nonsectarian.

The courses given at Missouri include Biblical Literature, Fundamental Moral and Religious Values, the Greek, Hebrew, Syriac, Arabic, Assyrian and Egyptian languages, the History of Religions, the History of the Biblical World, Church History, and the Philosophy of Religion. Special emphasis is placed on preparation for rural religious life. The faculty includes a graduate of Yale Divinity School, a graduate of Union Theological Seminary, and a Jewish teacher from the University of Chicago. Out of a total of nearly 12,000 students since 1912, members of the following communions have participated: Disciples of Christ, Methodist, Presbyterian, Baptist, Episcopal, Jewish, Roman Catholic, Congregational, Evangelical, Christian Science, and Lutheran. It is interesting to note that although the teaching is strictly nonsectarian and there is no Roman Catholic representation on the faculty or the Board of Trustees, there have been 341 Roman Catholic students since 1912.

Out of the eighty-nine institutions visited, all except twenty-six reported on the religious affiliations of their students. Of these twenty-six, twenty are publicly controlled institutions. It is undoubtedly true that the vast majority of the students at American colleges and universities have at least nominal connections with the various churches. Unfortunately, the reaction of students under the leadership of denominational chaplains indicates that a number of these nominal church members are not active in the religious groups and associations at the various universities. It is also apparent that the influence of the home churches does not enter, to any large degree, into the religious life of the university.

Figures are not available to show whether the moral breakdown has affected any considerable portion of these nominally religious students, but inasmuch as the majority of the students have religious affiliations, it would seem as if at least a number of them were affected. The failure of religious ties at home to supply an integrating philosophy and a motivating agency for morality in the life of many students is a cause of grave concern to those faculty members who realize the importance of spiritual values.

In many of the state universities of the South and in certain other parts of the country there are regularly established chairs of religion held by recognized members of the faculty. These professors of religion offer nonsectarian courses, and the intellectual level of the teaching is being raised constantly. There are such chairs of religion at the University of Georgia, the University of Florida, Florida State University, University of Oregon, Oregon State, and others. In certain other universities courses in religion are taught by clergy living in the neighborhood, most of whom do not have regular faculty standing. Unfortunately, too, the attitude of the students is to consider courses so taught, not as a means of developing an integrating philosophy of life, but rather as a convenient method for accumulating credit with the least possible expenditure of energy. In other words, in many of these institutions the courses in religion do not reflect a high academic standard, and do not command the respect of the student body. At one state university, where courses in religion are offered, a faculty committee was appointed to determine the academic standards to which these unrecognized teachers of religion must measure up before their courses were given credit. In this one institution there was only one church where the local minister qualified, and that happened to be the Church of Latter Day Saints. Another privately controlled institution offers 136 courses in religion, mostly of the two-hour credit variety. These courses are taught by a motley group of ministers of various denominations, selected with little or no attention to their educational background, their ability as teachers, or the content of the courses they offer.

Courses in religion are offered for credit at a majority of the state universities. They are available at practically all the privately controlled colleges. It would seem as if there should be a very thorough investigation of the quality of the work being done in many of these so-called religious courses. There is little evidence that where this haphazard method of teaching religion is pursued the objective of teaching a design for living is actually reached. Of the eighty-nine colleges visited, sixty give courses in religion for credit; twenty-nine do not. Out of seventy-six state universities and colleges, thirty-six have chairs of religion or departments of religion, or have the subject taught by recognized members of the faculty who have a reputation for their intellectual integrity. Sixteen state colleges and universities have courses in religion, taught by neighboring ministers, the quality of whose work should be carefully scrutinized.[24] In twenty-four state colleges and universities no courses on religion are given for credit. In the privately controlled colleges there is the same unevenness in the effectiveness of religious teaching. Some, like Yale, are making a splendid effort to maintain a high standard. Others, including a number of small denominational colleges, persist in teaching a narrow sectarianism which is shockingly lacking in scholarship. The need for sound nonsectarian religious teaching is evident in both the publicly controlled and privately controlled institutions of higher learning.

At Michigan State College a very interesting experiment is being conducted which places at the disposal of students religious values and religious knowledge, although the courses are not strictly religious in character. This plan is known as the Basic College. It consists of seven courses, six of which must be taken before the candidate is admitted to advanced standing. The President of Michigan State is entirely in sympathy with religious and moral teaching, but fears that in a state institution these courses should not be described as strictly religious. He feels that the use of the term "religion" has certain handicaps which can best be overcome by offering religious truths under another name. No attempt will be made at this point to outline all the

[24] *The Relation of Religion to Public Education*, American Council on Education, Vol. 94, April, 1947, p. 39.

courses in the Basic College of Michigan State, but there are one or two with special religious significance which should be mentioned. One of these is a course called "Effective Living." This course attempts to help each individual recognize his abilities, develop his personality, live more successfully as a member of a family,[25] and participate more intelligently in the life of his community. The material for the course is taken from psychology, sociology, philosophy, ethics, home economics, health, and recreation. One of its objectives is to develop "a vital, satisfying, and practical philosophy: getting along with one's self and with others; learning to face and to solve fundamental problems that have to do with marriage and family relations." Another course with a definite spiritual and cultural undertone is the course in "Biological Science." This is a study of life from its lowest animal form to that of man himself. It aims at an understanding of life processes, adaptation to environment, and the development of personal responsibility based on man's biological inheritance. One of the instructors in this course stated that he was seeking eagerly the best way to teach spiritual responsibility as a logical attribute of higher biological development. The course in "Literature and the Fine Arts" [26] endeavors to impress the student with the contribution to art and literature of each of the great periods, including contributions in which religion has had a part. Another course, the "History of Civilization," seeks to enrich man's knowledge of himself as a human being and to provide a more adequate background for an understanding of the present-day world. This course traces the development of man from the primitive era to our own day. It plans "to include all those interests and activities which distinguish man as a social being." This brings in modern intellectual and religious currents. If the teaching of religion is needed as a means of developing a design for living, an integrating philosophy which will determine the use a student makes of the skills he achieves in the university, and a motivating agency

[25] *Youth and the Future*, American Council on Education, 1942, p. 165.
[26] *General Education in the Humanities*, American Council on Education, 1947, p. 177 ff. Also p. 121 ff.

for morality, there is much to be said for the wide possibilities of this kind of teaching.

It does seem unfortunate to have to acknowledge even tacitly that religion has such a low reputation intellectually that it must be presented under other names and other forms in order to achieve decent recognition. The restoration of religion to academic respectability may possibly be quickened by this indirect method, but it would seem that there should be rather close co-operation between the teachers of the courses in the Basic College and the spiritual leaders of the surrounding community. The Basic College method has the advantage of presenting religion in its various relationships as the several subjects in the course unfold. However, it does have a tendency to divorce its teaching of the basic concepts of religion from any active relationship with conventional organized religion as it exists today. There is a great deal to be said for the Basic College method, but this report does not pretend to assert that it is necessarily the only answer to the need for teaching religion in the state college or state university.

Possibly because of the larger part that religion has played in the community life of the South,[27] as compared with the place of religion in the great metropolitan centers and in the newer sections of the West, there seems to be a more general and natural response to religion from students in many of the Southern universities than in some other parts of the country. There is certainly not the fear of the teaching of religion in many of the Southern states that exists in some other areas. At Virginia Military Institute, for instance, while religion is not taught as an academic subject, every student is required to attend church on Sundays, and this institution, which is a state school, contributes $100 to each clergyman of a recognized church in the community. This gives them admission without a pass to the barracks of the institution. The explanation of the appropriation is that the cadets have no pockets in their uniforms and therefore cannot contribute to the collection when attending church. At the Citadel, the mili-

[27] *Studies of Higher Education in the South,* Southern Association of Colleges and Secondary Schools, 1946, p. 33.

tary college of South Carolina, another state institution, there is church parade, and every student attends his own church every Sunday, and, more than that, every student is a member of a denominational religious group which meets on a weekday evening every week. Of course, there may be those who consider such an attitude on the part of these institutions as reactionary, but it is interesting to note that where religion has official recognition and the active support of educational leaders the students reflect the example set by those whose respect for religion is somewhat greater than their fear.

For instance, President R. F. Poole of Clemson College, South Carolina, makes the following statement:

"Seven members of the college staff are members of the Board of Stewards of the Methodist Church; ten are members of the Board of Session of the Presbyterian Church; eight are members of the Board of Deacons of the Baptist Church; and five are members of the Vestry of the Episcopal Church. The superintendents of the Church Schools of the Methodist, Baptist, and Presbyterian churches are college staff members. The church organizations and committees show twenty-five, nineteen, and fourteen staff members serving the Methodist, Presbyterian, and Baptist Churches respectively.

"The proof of the Christian values of a school can be determined by the activities of its graduates after they leave college. If I may be permitted to generalize from observation I will say that many Clemson men maintain an interest in the church and many of them are upstanding Christian workers in their home communities. For men educated primarily in technology and whose religious concepts are obtained voluntarily the good results are most commendable. . . . We are conscious of the fact that our responsibility to society demands that we educate our young men not only in agriculture and industry but in such a way that they will go out and take their places as disciplined, upright, Christian citizens." [28]

One cannot help but be impressed with the decisive action taken in Great Britain in passing the Education Act (1944),[29] with its emphasis on the teaching of religion in the secondary schools, colleges and universities of England, Wales, and Scot-

[28] *Southern Christian Advocate*, Vol. 109, No. 43, November 1, 1945.
[29] *Education in Britain*, British Information Services, I. D. 606, June, 1947.

land. As in the United States, there are both publicly controlled schools and denominational schools and colleges. There were those who advocated that all denominational schools be taken over by the public authorities. These same persons also felt that religious instruction should be nonsectarian. This was opposed by the Roman Catholics and some members of the Church of England. One point in dispute was whether the state should furnish financial support necessary to raise the standards and equipment of many church schools to equal those of the state schools and whether with such support should go an increased public control of the management and religious instruction in such aided church schools.

The act offered the church schools a fifty per cent grant toward moving to new premises, if a change of location were made necessary by a shift of population, slum clearance, or other cause. The schools which could take advantage of this offer and produce the remaining fifty per cent necessary to bring them up to state school standards retained their right to appoint teachers and to provide denominational religious instruction. Where there was only one such school for a district it was agreed that there must be nondenominational syllabus instruction available to children whose parents demanded it.

The church schools which could not raise the necessary fifty per cent are now supported entirely out of public funds. There is a special provision in such schools whereby the school management is permitted to appoint one-third of the new managing body of the school and up to one-fifth of the teachers, who must be qualified to give religious instruction according to the tenets of the controlling church. Two periods each week are devoted to instruction of children whose parents desire it. For the religious instruction of the rest of the school a nondenominational syllabus agreed upon is used.

Under the Education Act, corporate worship in schools is compulsory, religious instruction obligatory, and inspection is provided to "insure observance of daily worship and efficient religious instruction."

For the guidance of local educational authorities in England

and Wales a national basic outline of religious instruction [30] was compiled by a committee composed of Anglicans and Free Churchmen, members of Local Education Authorities, and members of the National Union of Teachers. This syllabus has three objectives: (1) to provide every child an opportunity to become familiar with the Bible; (2) to give moral and spiritual training based on the principles and standards of Christianity; (3) to show the influence of Christianity on the lives of men, on the social conditions of a country, and on the development of Western civilization. This syllabus was offered as a guide rather than as an infallible directive.

In Scotland school boards have been empowered since 1872 to provide for religious instruction. Here also there is a syllabus generally used in the schools.[31] In all centers and colleges for the training of teachers there are directors of religious instruction, appointed by the Church of Scotland; but representatives of other denominations are allowed the privilege of instructing students belonging to their Churches.

While these provisions apply primarily to the secondary level of education, it is imperative to note the emphasis placed on religion as an essential part of education in the entire secondary school system, both public and private, in Britain.

There would appear to be certain conclusions to be drawn from the consideration of religion as an academic subject in our colleges and universities. (1) While the excessive use of alcohol and sex offenses are less than there was reason to expect in a post-war period, there has been a moral breakdown culminating in cheating, lying, and stealing which is not limited to any one geographical area. (2) Along with this, there has been a noticeable increase in intellectual curiosity among students concerning religion, which is directed to the basic concepts of religion rather

[30] *A National Basic Outline of Religious Instruction*, prepared by a committee of representatives of the Joint Conference of Anglicans and Free Churchmen, the Association of Education Committees, and the National Union of Teachers. Published in 1945 by the National Union of Teachers, Hamilton House, Mabledon Place, London, W.C.1. Price 2d. (5 cents).

[31] *A Syllabus of Religious Instruction for Use in Scottish Schools*, available from the Church of Scotland Committee on the Religious Instruction of Youth, 121 George Street, Edinburgh, Scotland. Price 1/ (35 cents).

than to conventional orthodox forms and practices. (3) Courses in religion for credit are being offered in a majority of the institutions in the United States. (4) The quality of this teaching is very uneven [32] and its effectiveness is open to considerable question. (5) There is a growing opinion among faculties and administrators in favor of (a) restoring religion to intellectual respectability as a necessary part of education; and (b) having religion provide an integrated philosophy of life or design for living, as well as a motivating agency for the preservation of a decent moral code. (6) In spite of the restrictions imposed by separation of Church and State,[33] a considerable number of state colleges and universities are offering courses in nonsectarian religion for credit. (7) A strong opinion favoring inclusion of religion as a part of general education has developed, but there is considerable confusion over how to attain this objective without becoming involved with sectarianism. (8) Experiments such as the Yale plan, the University of Iowa plan, the University of Missouri plan, and the Michigan State plan, are worthy of serious study as steps toward meeting this need. (9) In view of the separation of Church and State in the United States, it is of primary and fundamental importance that in state colleges and universities at least such teaching should be along strictly nonsectarian lines.[34]

[32] *Religious Counseling of College Students,* American Council on Education, Vol. 7, April, 1943, p. 31.

[33] *The Relation of Religion to Public Education,* American Council on Education, Vol. 11, 1947, p. 23.

[34] *The Relation of Religion to Public Education,* American Council on Education, Vol. 11, 1947, p. 15.

___ 6 ___

INDUSTRIAL RELATIONS AND
WORKERS' EDUCATION IN
THE UNIVERSITIES

ONE OF THE greatest problems facing the American public is that of industrial unrest. Earlier in American history there was a period of exploitation of American labor
by entrenched capital. Like every excessive practice which carries
the pendulum so far that it is out of balance, there was bound
to be a reaction as a result of this selfish exploitation. Along with
this gradually developing reaction there has been a marked
tendency toward democratization, and a growing insistence that
the responsibility of directing government, education, and business itself should be shared by labor. Along with this, there has
been a constant demand for a wage increase for labor. The inter-
vention of the war, combined with a succession of strikes, some
just and some unjust, has led to such marked increases in the
cost of labor as to affect the national economy. Legislation restricted the operations of management and demanded a detailed
knowledge of profits, particularly through the instrument of the
income tax. No such restrictions were placed on labor organizations, and efforts to make labor as legally responsible as capital
failed again and again.

Meanwhile, the control of some of the labor unions fell into
the hands of professional organizers, agitators, business agents,
and, at times, even radicals. Labor, formerly the victim of exploitation by capital, found itself, in some instances, the victim of
exploitation by its own leaders. In the interest of fairness, public
opinion generally was sympathetic with labor's claims to greater
recognition. Efforts to improve the income and living standard

of the laboring man evoked a sympathetic response. This attitude persisted until pressure by some of the stronger unions brought about inequalities among the laboring men themselves. The stronger unions made excessive demands and because of their power obtained them. Those less favored then attempted to reach the highest scale thus obtainable. The result was an increase in cost to the average consumer until the specter of inflation began to reveal its outlines rather plainly. The "cost plus" arrangement served as an incentive to increase costs of the builder or the manufacturer at the expense of the consumer. The greater the cost, the greater the fee the contractor could claim. Meanwhile, because of the increased labor costs and the consequent increase in the cost of materials, management, in some instances, found itself with a considerably reduced income on its investment. With these increased costs, it was necessary to have more capital with which to operate. Management then to some extent succumbed to the temptation to demand more as its share, with the result that the higher price required of the public owed its increase not only to higher labor costs, but to greater demands by management. Although the wage of the average laboring man was considerably increased by this vicious circle, his cost of living was increased also. As living costs mounted, the demands of labor became more insistent.

Finally, Congress found it necessary to pass legislation regulating labor practices, which, however, was no more severe than that already passed to restrict management. Meanwhile, the strikes continued and the public found itself subjected to the activity of pressure groups, whether on the side of labor or management. These pressure groups, first apparent in the economic field, began to extend until there were such organized groups in almost every field of activity. Practically the only classes not so organized were the clergy and professional men. The teachers were organized, the social workers were organized, the municipal employees were organized, and soon the universities found themselves confronted with mounting increases in operating costs. Frequently the state appropriation was not sufficient to meet the demands made by the organizers or the more indirect increases growing out of the rise in the cost of materials, similar demands by other labor groups, and, in some instances, by management. From January to August in 1946, there were 3125 strikes in the United States, involving 3,425,000 employees, and causing the loss of 93,225,000 man days. The colleges were adversely affected in trying to meet the housing shortage and to maintain necessary services such as sanitation, public health, and heating.

Every one, whether representative of labor, management, or education was conscious of the fact that there was a serious dislocation somewhere. Labor blamed capital and capital blamed labor. The public and the universities suffered. Rival pressure groups in the great unions fought with one another, and we were confronted with what is known as jurisdictional strikes, which sometimes descended into a contest as to whether the average man would pay his tribute to one labor leader or to another. With the standardization of hours and of wages, attempts were made in some quarters to restrict even the amount of work that a workman could produce within a given period. The competitive factor which had contributed so much to American business success was denounced as a form of wage slavery. For a time, the workers were encouraged to look to Russia for an example, but the emphasis on the piece-work system under Stakhanovism reduced this sympathetic interest, and there was a strong movement in the unions to eradicate communists and those with communistic leanings. Meanwhile, the battle between capital and labor and the struggle within the labor unions themselves continued. Labor-management conferences were held, but little of practical value was accomplished, although there was a considerable overflow of oratory and of publicity in newspaper columns and editorials.

Gradually, the colleges and universities, along with the other victims of this chaotic situation, began to realize the importance of offering courses that would emphasize justice in industrial relations, protect the interest of the public, and develop intelligent leaders trained in the problems of both labor and management. For a time, management was able to secure far better talent to represent it in negotiations than was labor. Most of the labor representatives were ill-prepared men who knew only one method by which to win success for their claims, and that was the use of force entirely apart from any concept of justice. Capital, finding itself at a disadvantage, reasoned that it was justified in evading issues, compromising, and resorting to devious methods to obtain benefits. A prominent political leader once stated in my hearing that he felt it was possible for justice to prevail in labor relations, but that he doubted that either capital or labor desired it.

In the effort to meet this problem, the universities at first found themselves under the suspicion of labor. A recent book [1] suggests the representation of wage earners on the governing boards of universities. As Dr. Beck points out, in his "Men Who Control Our Universities" the majority of members of governing boards of universities are industrialists, bankers, capitalists, and professional men.

Harvard, usually rather conservative, established the Harvard Labor Fellowships. Cornell University introduced its splendid School of Industrial Relations. The University of Illinois followed the example of Cornell and entered actively into teaching in this field. The University of California also offered an extension program in industrial relations. The University of Iowa showed some activity along this line. In some instances, separate schools of industrial relations were established. In others, courses dealing with management problems and labor problems were introduced in schools of business administration or in departments of economics. The purpose of these schools and departments was to teach men the nature of the problems of both labor and management so that they would be able to represent either labor or capital, but would be primarily interested in the public welfare. There can be no satisfactory civic life without satisfied labor and management, and a reasonably satisfied public. The object of the schools is to develop an intelligent understanding of both sides of the industrial controversy and of the rights of all involved, and to have both labor and management represented at the council table by men who are equally well trained, talk the same language, do not feel that force is the only weapon to be em-

[1] *Men Who Control Our Universities*, Hubert P. Beck, 1947, Columbia University Press.

ployed, and are interested in the public welfare to the extent of bringing about increased production, a better living standard for all, improved distribution, and industrial peace.[2]

Following the introduction of these courses in university curricula, there came a demand for what is known as workers' education. This would include short courses at summer schools and courses offered by night extension services as a part of the university program. The courses in workers' education were to be inexpensive and to be arranged at hours when the workers could attend. The courses could be divided into two groups: (a) those having to do with increasing the skill of a man in his particular occupation and (b) those having to do with questions involving industrial relations, such as collective bargaining.

At the twenty-fourth annual meeting of the Association of Governing Boards of State Universities and Allied Institutions,[3] held at Providence, Rhode Island, in October, 1946, the program included a panel discussion conducted by leaders in labor education. The governing boards were interested in discovering what labor wanted of the universities and colleges. Among those on the panel were Laurence Rogin, educational director for the CIO Textile Workers Union of America; James J. Healy, director of the Trade Union Fellowships at Harvard University; Arthur A. Elder, director of the Workers Educational Service at the University of Michigan; Miss Hilda Smith, chairman of the Committee for the Extension of Labor Education and formerly dean at Bryn Mawr; and Dr. Caroline Ware, prominent economist of Vienna, Virginia, and a teacher of labor courses at American University and Howard University at Washington, D. C. These leaders were asked to explain to the members of the governing boards, representing a number of state colleges and universities, exactly what labor expected the colleges to do. It was clearly indicated early in the discussion that there was a marked difference of opinion. Schools such as the Harvard Trade Fellowships were concerned with developing highly trained leaders, thor-

[2] *Co-operation in General Education,* American Council on Education, 1947, p. 123 ff.

[3] *Proceedings, 24th Annual Meeting Association of Governing Boards,* 1946.

oughly grounded in the problems of both labor and management, who would be capable of adequately representing the public interest, the interests of labor, and the interests of capital. On the other hand, the labor union organizers who took part in the discussion were not markedly enthusiastic about schools like the Harvard Trade Union Fellowships or the Cornell School of Industrial Relations. They took the rather questionable position that labor organizers, business agents, and union leaders were already sufficiently trained and did not need the type of education thus offered. When one considers some of the persons most prominent in labor movements and the mishandling of many controversies, from the point of view of labor itself, the position of these labor organizers can scarcely stand close inspection. One of the greatest problems in settling labor disputes is that—-as evidenced in more than one instance—there has been a striking lack of acquaintance with the fundamental principles of even collective bargaining on the part of those representing labor, many of them self-appointed.

It then developed that labor organizers were primarily interested in courses like collective bargaining (under the head of workers' education) in summer schools and in the extension services. Some of them even went so far as to insist on naming the teachers of these courses, arranging the content of the courses, and having the assurance that all material presented be *ex parte*.

In the course of the discussion, a prominent member of a governing board of one of the largest state universities raised several questions. The labor leaders had based their plea for the subsidization of labor education on the ground that agricultural education was subsidized and therefore labor education should be. The university regent then asked several questions. He agreed that agriculture was subsidized, but called attention to the fact that this subsidy resulted in improved soil conditions, an increase in production, improvement in distribution, and a higher standard of living. He then asked the labor leaders whether, if labor education were similarly subsidized, the labor leaders would work to encourage "eight hours' honest work for eight hours' pay" to increase production, sadly needed in the United States at the present moment, to improve distribution, and to use the proposed courses as a means of promoting industrial peace. The answer of one labor leader was immediate. He said that in his opinion labor was not interested in any of the steps suggested by the university regent and that if such courses were introduced they would probably lead to more strikes rather than to less. It was pointed out in reply that a state college or state university exists to benefit the entire citizenry of the state and not to exploit one class of citizens at the expense of another. As a result of the discussion, there was, first, a clearly drawn line between schools such as the Harvard Trade Union Fellowships, the Cornell School of Industrial Relations, the University of Illinois, the University of Iowa, the University of Minnesota and the University of California on the one hand, and schools offering short courses under the head of workers' education in summer schools and the extension services on the other. Second, some of the labor organizers seemed to be far more interested in promoting the interests of organized labor than in establishing justice in industrial relationships and in contributing to the public welfare. Third, the regents and trustees were firmly convinced that their mission was to represent the entire citizenry of the state in publicly controlled education, and not to represent any one segment of citizenry at the expense of another.

That the labor leaders at this particular conference do not necessarily represent the mind of the entire labor movement in America is self-evident. However, the opinions they expressed are shared by many. For instance, the president of one state university was approached by the state officers of one of the great labor unions in the United States with the request that short courses be offered in workers' education on collective bargaining and similar subjects. The president, like every other university administrator concerned about this problem, welcomed the opportunity for the university to be of service. A faculty committee appointed to prepare a report on the subject brought in a favorable recommendation. The labor leaders then changed their request and made the following demands: (a) they must name the teachers who would give these courses, because they did not trust the ability of a single member of the university faculty to teach them to their satisfaction; (b) they must determine the content of the courses, from which they would omit any subject matter which they did not consider favorable to their own point of view; and (c) membership in the classes must be limited to the members of the particular unions these leaders represented. Under this system, the AFL could not sit down with the CIO, to say nothing of sitting down with the representatives of management. The reply of the regents was that in view of the fact that they were responsible for the control of university affairs, the naming of competent members of the faculty was their prerogative and that courses at the university must be available to all citizens of the state who could meet the entrance requirements. This settled the matter in this instance, but this illustration will indicate just how serious is the problem that confronts the colleges and universities in trying to give courses in what is called workers' education.

In another university, where courses in labor relations were given in the school of commerce, certain members of the faculty were known to be exceedingly friendly to the claims of labor and anxious to use the university facilities to improve industrial relations. The initiative in this instance was taken by the university itself. The representative labor leaders approached were suspicious of the motives of these faculty members, even though they were publicly known as friends of the labor movement. The result was a considerable delay in arranging the courses and a lack of enthusiastic co-operation on the part of labor leaders.

At the conference Laurence Rogin, educational director for the CIO Textile Workers Union, told the Association of Governing Boards that the eduational needs of worker groups are being met in colleges or universities "where we are able to exert political pressure." Where organized labor has been unable to exert political pressure, Rogin stated that, in his opinion, labor's educational needs had been largely unfulfilled.

He said that many people are under the impression that sufficient doses of the broadening educational process would be a cure-all for industrial strife, but he emphasized that this was not so in his opinion. He went on to point out that in some instances education may increase the danger of conflict, since it opens avenues of ideas, and "new ideas may mean unrest and unrest may mean new strikes."

The point of view of James J. Healy of the Harvard Trade Union Fellowships was entirely different. He explained that the courses offered were designed to educate leaders on the higher level of the trade union movement, as distinguished from labor schools concerned with rank-and-file instruction. He explained the effort at Harvard as an attempt to extend the same type of administrative education to trade unionists as the university long has offered men aiming at careers in business. The various international unions pay the expenses of the men entering the school, a procedure Harvard adopted because it "wanted unions to feel that they were making an investment in these men." The course of study at Harvard is for one year, and the school is largely experimental. Unfortunately, the enrollment at Harvard is limited to eighteen especially selected men. Considering the vast numbers connected with the trade union movement, this percentage of its membership is so small as to make little impression on the problem of industrial unrest, even though one grants the splendid work being done by the Harvard Trade Union Fellowships.

The official title of the Cornell School of Industrial Relations is the New York State School of Industrial and Labor Relations,[4] established in 1944 by act of the New York State Legislature. It was the first institution of its kind in the country. It has three major functions: undergraduate and graduate instruction, extension and research, and information. The purpose of the school is to provide training for those who look forward to professional careers in industrial or labor relations. The first two years of the undergraduate course include the principal social sciences, English, and public speaking, together with introductory courses in economics, labor economics, and accounting. The last two years are devoted to intensive study of the technical subjects knowledge of which is essential to effective professional service in the field of industrial and labor relations, government, industry, and labor

[4] New York State School of Industrial and Labor Relations, Cornell University Official Publication, December 1, 1946.

organizations. In many ways, the Cornell program is perhaps the most comprehensive and intensive available today. Its graduates are already being sought for government positions in the field of labor and management relations, and by industrial concerns and labor unions.

Because of limited housing and teaching facilities, the school's enrollment in September, 1946, was limited to 248 undergraduates and twelve graduate students. The Committee on Admissions has certain qualifications which they require. In addition to sound academic preparation, certain personal qualifications are listed as necessary, including ability to work co-operatively with other individuals and groups, and qualities of leadership in promoting co-operative relationships. Evidence of work experience in government, labor, or management is also listed as desirable. The New York State Legislature made an appropriation of $425,000 to operate this school in 1947, an increase of $225,000 over the appropriation for the preceding year. It has an Advisory Council, which includes the president of the university and the chairman of the Board of Trustees, the State Commissioner of Commerce, three management representatives, and six labor representatives, along with the State Industrial Commissioner and the counsel of the New York State Joint Legislative Committee on Industrial and Labor Conditions.

This school has an extension program offering courses in the field of industrial and labor relations to labor, management, government, and civic groups throughout the state. In addition, there are plans for on-campus institutes for those who cannot spend a long period of time away from home. The school does not offer any correspondence courses at the present time. It will be seen that this type of school is in marked contrast with the Harvard Trade Union Fellowships with their enrollment of eighteen students.

Reference has been made to Dr. Hubert Beck's suggestion for more labor representatives on boards of regents and trustees. It is my conviction that this labor representation can be better provided on advisory councils, such as the one connected with the School of Industrial Relations at Cornell.

The University of Illinois,[5] which is running Cornell a close second, has such an advisory committee. On it are five representatives of organized labor, five representatives of the public, and five from industry. There is also a faculty council which works with the faculty of the institute. The purpose of this school is "to foster, establish, and correlate resident instruction, research, and extension work in labor relations." It seeks to promote understanding of social and economic problems and also to provide specific services to groups directly concerned with labor and industrial relations. As at Cornell, three activities are stressed: (1) undergraduate and professional instruction, (2) extension services to civic, labor, and management groups, and (3) research and information. The school also aims to provide students with graduate training for positions with the Social Security Board, the National Labor Relations Board, the Department of Labor, including the Bureau of Labor Statistics; the Wage and Hour and Public Contracts Division, and the Conciliation Service. It also trains men for personnel work, the negotiation of collective agreements, wage and salary administration, and research and statistics.

The curriculum is divided into four parts: (a) human relations in industry, (b) labor economics (including collective bargaining), (c) labor union organization and administration and (d) personnel management.

As at Cornell and the University of California, the Institute of Labor and Industrial Relations at the University of Illinois is conceived as an agency to provide service to both labor and management. The research program is planned to meet the immediate interests of labor and management groups in the analysis of current problems of government, industry, and labor as they affect labor-management relations. This research includes an information service, which answers inquiries on questions of fact relating to any aspect of labor and industrial problems. The collection of materials on labor and industrial relations in the university library is fast becoming one of the major library resources in the country on labor and management problems.

[5] "The Institute of Labor and Industrial Relations," Phillips Bradley. *Opinion and Comment,* February, 1947, p. 7.

Research also includes the study of "unknowns in wage-price relationships in Illinois industries, the conditions of full employment, the relations of morale to productivity, the economic and social effects of industrial decentralization."

The extension services range all the way from short courses (for credit and non-credit students at various levels up to the post-graduate), correspondence courses, institutes and conferences of from one or two days to a week or more, to advisory services on individual reading, conducting forums, use of audiovisual materials, and organization of group educational programs. As in other institutions engaged in a serious consideration of the problem of labor-management relations, instead of creating a new and special division of separate study, the institute seeks to integrate existing resources on the campus with emphasis on an interdepartmental program.

The graduate professional training differs from that of some other similar enterprises, such as the New York State School of Industrial Relations, in believing that the best leaders to promote industrial understanding are professionally trained men and women at the graduate level. As at Cornell, every student is required to devote as many as six months to supervisory work in labor organizations, management offices, or shops as "internes." An instance of the work done in the extension service is a series of courses on industrial management for supervisory personnel. Publications of the institute include "Federal Labor Legislation 1946," the Hobbs Anti-racketeering Law, the Petrillo Law, the Employment Act of 1946, Social Security Act Amendments, Railroad Retirement and Unemployment Insurance Amendments, and proposed legislation. Another publication is on "Seniority and Job Security."

The University of California is another state university which is doing pioneer work in this field. Here, too, there is a community advisory committee, with one branch at Berkeley and another at Los Angeles, each section of which has a faculty advisory committee. The community advisory committee is composed of representatives of labor, industry and the general public. On it are three employers, a Roman Catholic editor, the regional attorney of the Social Security Board, a former state supreme court justice, a theological professor, the president of the Farm Bureau Federation, the director of the California State Department of Labor, and seven representatives of organized unions. These sixteen members are on the northern division branch of the community advisory committee, and there are nine on the southern division branch at Los Angeles. The southern division includes the mayor of Los Angeles, a college president, a retired railroad president, president of the Merchants and Manufacturers' Association of Los Angeles, a superior court judge, the president of the Independent Motion Picture Producers, two officers from organized labor, and a representative of the Los Angeles Building Trades Council. This institute of industrial relations is especially concerned with serving labor, management, and the general public on the Pacific Coast through collecting, analyzing and interpreting data on an impartial basis. Among the major research projects are Labor-Management Relations in Selected Industries on the Pacific Coast, Wages and Earnings on the Pacific Coast, Voluntary Arbitration of Labor Disputes on the Pacific Coast, and the Economic Significance of Wage Differentials between the Southern Part of the United States and the Pacific Coast Area. There are extensive working libraries at both Los Angeles and Berkeley. Once more, we have an interdepartmental program, which uses the facilities of the departments of Economics, Business Administration, Psychology, Political Science, History, and Engineering. Some of the many undergraduate courses are Labor Economics, Personnel Administration, Time and Motion Study, Industrial Relations, Labor Law, Constitutional Law, Tests and Measurements, Public Personnel Administration, Occupational Counseling, Industrial Psychology, Collective Bargaining and Social Insurance. There is also professional training at the graduate level.

The University of California places emphasis on community education in connection with the institute. The extension courses are designed to meet the special requirements of labor and industrial representatives, such as shop stewards, union officials, company representatives, etc., as well as of the general public. The institute sponsors occasional conferences of groups of selected community leaders on some special aspect or vital issue in the field. In addition, special two- or three-day institutes are arranged from time to time, as the need arises.

The evening classes in industrial relations and personnel management include such subjects as Industrial Relations, Techniques of Collective Bargaining, Labor Law and Legislation, Wage and Salary Administration, Collective Bargaining Systems, Labor Statistics, Human Relations in Industry, Labor Economics, Personnel Administration, Industrial Psychology, Introduction to Personnel Counseling, and Techniques of Personnel Counseling. This institute was established in 1945.

A privately controlled university which devotes attention to this field of industrial relations is the University of Southern California, located at Los Angeles. It offers a series of late afternoon and evening classes, which carry full credit, at what is known as the University College and at the Civic Center. Under the head of management, the courses include Principles of Industrial Management, Organization and Operation of a Small Industry, Personnel Relations, Industrial Relations, Personnel Administration, Motion and Time Study, Collective Bargaining, Wage Incentives, and Advanced Industrial Relations. Under Economics, a course is offered in Labor Relations. It is to be noted that the privately controlled colleges, with a few exceptions, have not been as active in trying to provide this type of instruction as the larger publicly controlled universities. When one considers that many of them do not have the interdepartmental facilities necessary to carry out a full program in this field, this is quite understandable.

The University of Michigan,[6] at Ann Arbor, established a bureau of industrial relations in 1935. Its purpose was "to promote a more adequate understanding of the field of industrial relations in so far as this could be attained by acquisition and study of current documentary literature, by pursuance of research in the field, and by the development of teaching and other serv-

[6] "The University and the Betterment of Industrial Relations," John W. Riegel, *Michigan Alumnus Quarterly Review*, February 17, 1940.

ices germane to this general function." The first task to which the bureau addressed itself was the collection of documents, reports, and other primary references in the field. At the moment, the index to this collection contains approximately 24,000 cards arranged under 250 major titles. Since the service was announced, the bureau has answered more than 4000 requests from well-known corporations, labor organizations, and individual employees, teachers, and advanced students. In 1936 the bureau began to sponsor a series of conferences for business executives on labor problems. These conferences have considered industrial relations' policy in view of current developments, labor legislation and its effects, and methods for improving labor relations between individual companies and their employees. The foremost recent conference attracted more than 500 thoughtful and serious business leaders interested in maintaining satisfactory relations with their employees. Included in the research program is a study of wage determination. A second study is The Selection and Development of Foremen. A third has to do with salary determination. Thus the bureau at Michigan has five major functions: to collect information, to offer reference service to interested parties, to aid campus instruction, to make and publish field studies, and to arrange conferences of business executives on personnel problems. Subjects considered at a recent leaders' conference included: "What is Needed to Improve Our Labor Relations," "Should Incentives for Employees be Preserved? If so, How?" "Considerations Governing the Wage Policy of a Company," "The Outlook For Labor Legislation by the New Congress," "Effective Industrial Discipline," "Problems of Management in Collective Bargaining," "Improving the Observance of Labor Contracts by Both Parties," and "How Can Better Understanding Between Employers and Managers be Brought About?" Eighty firms and corporations were represented at this conference.

The University of Michigan Extension Service [7] is unique in the conduct of its workers' education service. This is the kind of

[7] Conferences on Industrial Relations, University of Michigan, The Bureau of Industrial Relations and the University Extension Service. November, 1946; April, 1947, Saginaw.

training that many of the union leaders favor, for it is training of the working men themselves and not of leaders. The service places itself at the disposal of local unions, industrial union councils, groups of unorganized workmen or a central labor body's programs for class discussion; it also provides group firm forums, and conferences or community forums. This program was started in 1944, its cost being financed by an appropriation made by the Michigan legislature. There is a state supervisory committee on which the university, the public, and workers' organizations are each represented by two members. There is also a faculty supervisory committee. The secretary-treasurer of the Michigan Federation of Labor, AFL, and the state representative of the Michigan State CIO Council are on the supervisory committee.

In most institutions courses on industrial relations and in workers' education are given by recognized and prominent members of the faculty of the university or college. Instructors and lecturers on the Michigan workers' program are especially engaged. Some are college or public-school teachers and others are experienced union members. All have a union background or practical experience.

Classes are conducted for workmen, unions, councils, and central bodies throughout the state and in Detroit.[8] They are open to all who wish to attend and charge very small tuition fees. For individual students the cost is one dollar for a six-weeks' class (two hours each week), and $1.50 for an eight-weeks' class (two hours each week). There is a charge of twenty dollars to organizations for a six-weeks' course, and thirty dollars for an eight-weeks' course. These fees cover only a small part of the expense, the deficit being made up by grants from the state legislature. All courses are non-credit.

Among the subjects offered are Collective Bargaining, Advanced Collective Bargaining, Training for Educational Leadership, Time Study, Effective Speech for Workers, Parliamentary

[8] Conferences on Industrial Relations, University of Michigan, The Bureau of Industrial Relations and the University Extension Service. November, 1946; March, 1947; Detroit.

Procedure, Union Administration, Union Counseling, Radio Drama Workshop, Publicity Workshop, Journalism, State and Federal Labor Legislation, Health and Safety, History of the Labor Movement, Economics for Workers, Consumer Co-operatives, Social Philosophies, Contemporary Social Problems, and Home and Family Living.

The Workers' Educational Service also provides films on subjects such as unemployment compensation, consumer problems, collective bargaining, and labor history. The entire film library of the University of Michigan is at its disposal. Michigan, therefore, offers one of the finest instances of a well-rounded workers' educational program.

Another state university which has become interested in this problem is the State University of Iowa. Here there is no separate department of industrial relations. The students receive the Bachelor of Science degree in Commerce with emphasis on labor relations. This plan naturally devotes itself to the training of leaders and negotiators and does not offer a workers' educational program like that in Michigan.

The pre-commerce students take, in the main, the regular course in liberal arts. The required courses include Labor Economics, Money and Banking, Business Law, Marketing, and Business Organization and Corporation Finance. Courses concentrated on industrial relations include Personnel Management, Labor Legislation, Industrial Management, Economics Theory, Statistics and Insurance; courses in Sociology include Human Nature and Personality, and Social Control; in Engineering, Production Control, Factory Management and Time and Motion; in Psychology, Psychology of Adjustments, Psychology in Business and Industry, and Personnel Psychology; in Law, Labor Law and Arbitration; and in Political Science, Public Administration. Although this university does not engage in workers' education programs, the head of industrial relations work is frequently called on at various conferences to instruct both unions and management.

The University of Minnesota, with its Industrial Relations

Center,[9] is another outstanding institution. in this field. The center was established in 1945. It was organized to serve no special group—management, labor, or other—but to aid all through education and research. It prepares students for professional responsibility in the field of industrial relationships as employees of business firms, union members, governmental agency workers, and as private practitioners. Once again we have an interdepartmental set-up. There is a faculty committee of seven members, drawn from seven departments of the university, the resources of which are thus combined in training and research in the industrial relations field. These departments include Economics, Business Administration, Psychology, Public Administration, Engineering, Sociology, and Agricultural Economics.

The university has an advisory council, made up of a number of representative citizens of Minnesota, men who are chosen because of their interest in present-day labor relations. They are appointed by the president of the university. The council, as constituted at the moment, includes two farmers, the state's director of civil service, a newspaper editor, the director of the research division of the labor council of the CIO, two managers of employers' associations, six union officers, five business executives, and two directors of industrial relations.

The Center has a bulletin, entitled "Jobs in Industrial Relations," which outlines some of the tasks of principal positions in manpower, management, and labor leadership. The training is of several types. It includes (a) regular full-term day-school classes in a wide range of subjects for both graduates and undergraduates, (b) night school and extension courses of various lengths and (c) short courses, conferences, and institutes for those who cannot spend longer periods in regular or extension classes. Considerable attention is paid to subjects such as Labor Problems, Labor Legislation and the Psychology of Individual Differences, Personnel Management, Time and Motion Study, Personnel and Vocational Psychology and similar subjects. In addition to these regular courses, there are special lectures, short courses, and

[9] *The Industrial Relations Center of the University of Minnesota,* University of Minnesota, Minneapolis, 1947.

conferences to keep those working in the industrial relations field abreast of current developments.

Minnesota does not provide a comprehensive program in workers' education as is provided at Michigan. It is a center concerned with but one field—that of industrial relations. Within that field its facilities are equally available to workers, management, or other groups.

The research program addresses itself to such problems as discovering means of improving labor market statistics, obtaining a more realistic appraisal of the causes of labor demand and supply, and improving working conditions and employe morale.

The Industrial Relations Center at Minnesota has its own library, which includes professional journals and technical services. The library receives a large number of union papers, periodicals, pamphlets, and company house organs. It has a continuing bibliographical service to answer the numerous inquiries which come from labor, management, and the public by telephone, mail, and personal visits. It is to be noted that the courses offered at the Industrial Relations Center at Minnesota are taught by regular faculty members in seven departments, under the direction of an interdepartmental all-university faculty committee, made up of representatives of these seven departments.

Wisconsin is the great pioneer in emphasizing workers' education rather than industrial relations. The University of Wisconsin School for Workers [10] has existed twenty-three years. Today there are some fifty universities and colleges planning or already engaged in some form of workers' education. The Wisconsin theory is that the function of the university is primarily to furnish education for workers rather than to produce leaders in industrial relations, whether representing industry or labor itself. There is a strong consciousness in Wisconsin of the labor leaders' and workers' suspicion of the efforts of universities which aim at producing professionals in the field of industrial relations.

Reference already has been made to the type of school interested in graduate work in industrial relations. Such schools are

[10] *The Wisconsin Idea in Workers Education*, E. E. Schwarztrauber, The University of Wisconsin School for Workers, 1946.

the Cornell School of Labor and Industrial Relations, the Harvard Trade Union Fellowships project, and Minnesota's Industrial Relations Center. Schools dedicated to workers' education as such are best typified by the University of Wisconsin School for Workers, the University of Michigan Workers Service project, and the Rhode Island State College Extension Service for Workers. The advocates of the Wisconsin plan believe that the proponents of the labor-management or industrial relations type of school start on the assumption that labor and management are today on equal terms so far as strength and general acceptance are concerned. In Wisconsin minds, there is a grave question whether this equality exists. It is pointed out that, while the labor-management school may have the moral and financial support of industry, there has been no clear evidence that organized labor as a whole will accept schools of that type. At Wisconsin, Michigan, and Rhode Island State, organized labor, both A.F. of L. and CIO, determine the kind of programs offered. The same is true to a degree at Pennsylvania State College. West Virginia State College for Negroes and Marshall College are jointly working toward a state program of educational service for workers. The Wisconsin plan is based on the belief that organized labor wants to stabilize industrial relations, but it emphasizes that labor must determine and largely control what it wants of education before a satisfactory labor-management industrial relations level can be reached.

Schools like Cornell and the Harvard School are convinced they offer the opportunity for better understanding between labor and management. Wisconsin assumes that they already understand each other quite well. "Labor knows that management seeks low costs and high profits. Management knows that labor seeks higher wages, shorter hours, better working conditions." From this it is argued that labor and management are unequal when it comes to economic resources, and state and national and legislative and judicial support. It is evident that in the Wisconsin plan there is the underlying fear that the university may be controlled by business interests and that the aim of labor-management schools is to restrict rather than help labor. This is the same problem that was reflected at the meeting of the Association of Governing Boards at Providence.

The Wisconsin School for Workers was established in 1925. At first it consisted of a six-weeks' summer session on the university campus. For a brief period, 1937 to 1939, increased state appropriations provided extension services to workers in all industrial communities of the state. This support was withdrawn in 1939, and the school returned to its summer resident program at Madison, with such winter service to organized labor as limited staff facilities would permit.

When the school first opened, the yearly enrollment was small, ranging from thirty-four to sixty-two between 1925 and 1936. In 1945 the enrollment had increased to 425 students. The work is divided under three heads: summer resident, winter extension, and research and consultative service. At first, the program was instituted for working women only. This restriction was removed in 1938, when men were admitted. The enrollment in 1944 came from 142 industrial cities and towns distributed among thirty states, three Canadian provinces, and the island of Puerto Rico. Six federal unions and the locals of fifty-one international unions were represented at the school. The average age was thirty-seven. The average age at which these students began working was nineteen. There were 225 men and 195 women. Of the students, 394 were white and twenty-six were Negro; 293 were married, and 127 unmarried. Regarding previous education, 29 per cent had been as far as the eighth grade or less, 51 per cent had been in high school from one to four years, and 19 per cent had spent from one to four years in college. Ninety-nine per cent were union members and 95 per cent were union leaders.

The winter program makes contact with a great number of the union rank and file membership. This is done through an extension program. The courses offered assist unions in initiating and developing yearly educational programs, one- or two-day, or week-end institutes, evening meetings, forums, and discussion groups.

The school publishes a monthly news letter containing articles dealing with current labor problems. This news letter, which has wide circulation, contains an extensive labor bibliography of books and pamphlets for union libraries, local educational programs, and individual workers' studies. The school library at Madison is consulted by Wisconsin unions and by many educational institutions.

The summer session consists of programs, usually two weeks in length, and special institutes to serve special groups. Some of these are sponsored by international unions, which recruit students only from their own membership. Such are the International Ladies' Garment Workers Union, the Textile Workers Union, the International Brotherhood of Paper Makers, United Retail, Wholesale, and Department Store Employes; American Federation of State, County, and Municipal Employes; and the American Federation of Teachers. A business representatives' institute was established in 1943. The same year came the Industrial Relations Institute for Church Leadership in response to an increasing demand from the clergy in industrial communities for a greater understanding of labor's problems, and in 1944 a teachers' institute was added.

There are not only these special institutes, but general institutes open to workers, regardless of union affiliation. The courses offered include, Labor Problems, Labor Legislation, Collective Bargaining, Your Union's Money, Current World Events, Applied Workers' Education, and similar studies. The summer session for 1947 presented Workers' Education, What and Why; Union Administration Problems; Training Shop Stewards, Officers and Bargaining Committees; Union Education and Organizing, Using Departments of Labor Services, Expanding the Unions Out-of-Plant Services, Human Relations on the Job and in the Community, Recreation to Build the Union, Using the American Labor Education Service, and Mapping a Union Educational Program and Recruiting. In the afternoons there were workshops. One was on labor journalism; how to get out a shop paper and write for local papers. One was on radio; how to put on radio programs on a local station. There was one on music and skits; how to lead singing, music, and skits in union meetings. Another was on cooperatives; how to start co-ops and keep them going. There was one on visual aids; how to use movies and film strips, and how to run a projector and film strip machine.

The Industrial Relations Institute for Church Leaders [11] in 1947 offered thirteen courses. One was a series of Seminars in Labor and Industry, such as Industrial Conflict, Its Causes, and Proposed Ways Out; Pressure Groups in American Society, American Labor History, and the Structure, Function, and Administration of Unions. Two were a series of Social Action Workshops, which stressed preaching on Social Issues; methods of Building Racial Democracy, Social Action on the Local and National Level among Churches, and Techniques in Church Labor Co-operation. There were also courses on collective bargaining, principles, and practices, and on current federal and state labor legislation.

One announcement of a Wisconsin training course reads,[12]

> "Build the union by learning to:
> Get out a shop paper, write for newspapers.
> Plan and recruit for education activities.
> Lead discussions, make surveys.
> Teach classes, train leaders.
> Use community services, make a union work.
> Understand how people learn, get new ideas.
> Put on radio programs on local stations.
> Lead singing, use music in the union.
> Use movies, film strips, displays in the union.
> Set up a co-op and keep it going.
> Use government services, work with minorities."

This service at Wisconsin was for a long time unique in American educational history. It is state-supported, in some respects similar to the practice widely followed in English universities. Its example has been followed by like projects in a number of other schools. It represents an objective which distinguishes sharply between labor-management, industrial relations schools, and workers' education as such. At one summer session courses

[11] *After Black Coffee*, Robert I. Gannon, McMullen, 1947, p. 173.
[12] *Co-operation in General Education*, American Council on Education, 1947, p. 9.

were given by a Milwaukee librarian, the Assistant Director of the Georgia Workers Education Service, the Education Director of the American Federation of Hosiery Workers Union, the Director of the Labor Education Division of Roosevelt College, a social worker, and a Department of Labor representative, as well as by a few regularly employed faculty members.

Of the eighty-nine institutions visited in this study, seventy-two offer courses in industrial relations. The great majority of these are publicly controlled. It is interesting to note that of the eighty-nine institutions, only fifteen had organized unions among non-faculty workers.[13] When it comes to workers' education, there is an entirely different story. Out of eighty-nine schools, there are only sixteen which offer any considerable program in this field.

The following conclusions seem apparent: (1) Sufficient courses are offered in most of the state colleges and universities to set up an institute of industrial relations to train leaders for both business and labor. Where such institutes exist, they are largely interdepartmental. It would seem wise so to organize activity in this field as to have an institute unit in each major institution. (2) These institutes should be fully accredited, the courses preferably be taught by the university faculty, the curricula be determined by the institution, and the classes be open to all. (3) The settlement of industrial disputes depends on a working knowledge of both sides of the question. The colleges and universities of the country are in an especially favorable position to train leaders who will refuse to exploit the workers in the interests of capital, and who, on the other hand, will have a working acquaintance with methods of settling industrial disputes other than by force. (4) This type of education offers a hopeful means of exposing unscrupulous representatives of management and racketeers who dominate unions and exploit the workers themselves. (5) As for workers' education, more attention should be given to the use of summer schools, short courses, and the extension services, to promote classes in collective bargaining and related subjects. (6) Inasmuch as the state university particularly

[13] Bulletin, *University of Minnesota*, Vol. 47, No. 57, 1944, p. 27.

cannot minister to any one class at the expense of others, these courses must be taught on an impartial basis and by men who are recognized as not selfishly representing either labor or capital. (7) The author cannot agree with the Wisconsin theory that labor must determine the content of the courses and, to a large degree, name the instructors. An agricultural college, whose faculty was made up only of farmers nominated by the Grange or the Farmers Union or the Farm Bureau could easily become a center of jurisdictional disputes. Just as agriculture must take its place and at least consider that there are other branches of instruction that must be given, so in workers' education extra care must be taken to avoid the bias that may result from exclusively labor-dominated classes of instruction. (8) The regents or trustees are representatives of the entire people of a state and not of any particular class. They have, therefore, no right to delegate their authority over educational policy or procedure to any partisan group. (9)Where courses in industrial relations or in workers' education are offered, adequate representation of labor, industry, and agriculture should be provided by an advisory council which can confer with and advise the regents or trustees without usurping the powers conferred on governing boards by law.

7

ENTRANCE REQUIREMENTS

WITH the vast increase in enrollments in the colleges and universities, attention has been attracted once more to entrance requirements. Provision for returning veterans, and granting credit for military experience and for courses taken in the military service, along with the tendency of high schools to award graduating credits to those who enlisted before completing their high-school courses, has led to a very confusing situation all over the country. Institutions can be divided into three classes: (1) those so situated that they can exercise a high degree of selectivity when it comes to a choice of students to be admitted; (2) established institutions, including many of the state universities, which have certain minimum requirements and are in a position to see that those requirements are generally enforced; and (3) that group of small, weakly financed colleges whose existence depends largely on income from tuition fees, and some of which have been guilty of extreme laxity in enforcing their admission standards. When one adds to this the very liberal interpretation employed by many institutions in admitting veterans, the whole question of entrance requirements comes up for examination.

Privately controlled education has assumed that because there were no state provisions requiring them to accept students, they could exercise a much higher degree of choice than the publicly controlled colleges and universities, where the state law provides that every graduate of an accredited high school must be admitted. While this very high degree of selectivity is a prerogative of Harvard, Yale, Princeton, Vanderbilt, Stanford, and certain other colleges and universities, it is not necessarily true of every privately controlled institution in the country. As the state universities have achieved promise and have been recognized for their high academic standards, the number of students eager to enroll has made it necessary for them to employ some type of selection. This is certainly true of schools like the University of Michigan, Indiana University, the University of Wisconsin, and certain other state institutions.

"Criticism" is one of the most frequently used words in the field of education, but the use of that word does not always imply a mere emphasis on the critical method so widely advertised in the field of exact science. Institutions are critical, one of another. We are told that students must not go to this university because it is too large, or to another because the quality of its academic work is poor, or to another because it is too small and cannot afford a competent faculty, or to another because lack of adequate financial support restricts the subjects it can offer. The rivalry between institutions is not confined to the football field. Some schools are so interested in numbers that scant attention is paid to academic integrity when it comes to enforcing admission requirements. There are other schools which are deeply conscious of the importance of doing a thorough job educationally, where admission requirements are strictly enforced. In others technical provisions are stressed in an effort to make admission appear difficult. After the end of the war it looked for a time as if the state universities would be unable to accept any out-of-state students. It is interesting to note that the number of out-of-state students in the state universities is increasing, semester by semester. Some are now even making an effort to attract out-of-state students, on the ground that a student body so constituted is broader in its outlook and less provincial than one recruited from its own confines. There has been some doubt of the admission requirements set forth in certain football conferences, where a student's athletic ability has been rated more highly than his other attainments. Not only do institutions criticize one another, but there are criticisms within the institutions by the various faculties. " 'Tekoa' University has a good school of commerce but is not good for anything else." " 'Snohomish' College has a good department of English but the other departments are weak."

On one point, however, practically all the colleges and universities are in strict agreement, and that is on the quality of the work being accomplished in high schools. The Harvard Report devoted considerable space to the problem of education on the secondary school level. It pointed out the great variation between the work of high schools in suburban communities with adequate tax support as contrasted with that of small handicapped rural high schools, or of high schools in congested factory districts encumbered with enormous enrollments.

There seems to be a rather general agreement that high-school education is particularly weak in teaching English, and also in teaching the social sciences. Most of the colleges have a screening process by which students seeking admission are examined in high-school English. Courses in elementary English are required of those who are noticeably below what appears to be a speaking acquaintance with the nature or use of the English tongue. It is impossible to apply this screening process to all the subjects a student takes during his high-school course. As a student attempts to do college work, he frequently finds himself in a world absolutely strange to him because of a lack of reasonably enforced discipline at the high-school level. Of course, this is not universally true, but in institutions ranging from 3,000 to 40,000 students, there are bound to be a certain number whose experience in high school was social rather than educational. These students constitute a problem, with a result that the mortality rate at the end of the freshman year or the middle of the sophomore year is unnecessarily high. Meanwhile, really capable students, handicapped by late application for entrance, or by some other cause, are denied admission in order to make room for those who came first, even though the latter had low high-school grades as their accreditation. The loading of the high-school curriculum with subjects that do not require concentration, with the idea that high school is an end in itself, has contributed vastly to lack of proper preparation for many seeking college entrance.

The tremendous increase in high-school enrollments,[1] as indicated in the Harvard Report, along with the all too scanty appropriations on the high-school level, has meant large classes and lack of individual attention in many high schools. It has also meant that many students possess high-school diplomas who could never have passed the examinations in a small school where standards were high and the work of the students subject to close scrutiny.

The result of all these conflicting factors has led to a question by the universities whether high-school graduation in itself should be the primary consideration for college entrance. Many colleges are using the general educational development (GED) test, along with the student's transcript from his high school. Yale University has an interesting method of rating a student's high-school or secondary-school record, comparing the results of this with his GED test, and then estimating what his standing should be at the end of his freshman, sophomore, junior, and senior years, respectively. Over a period, this enables the university to determine rather closely what schools are doing good work in preparing students for Yale.

Pennsylvania State College, which has far more applications than it can normally handle, has made an interesting study of the records of students from the various high schools of the state over a ten-year period. These schools are then classified on the basis of this record, and divided, let us say, into groups known as "a" "b" "c" and "d." The graduates of high schools in the "a" and "b" groups are admitted without examination. Students from the "c" and "d" schools have to take an entrance test, and the mortality rate is fairly high. While this system avoids the matriculation of ill-prepared students from the lower group of high schools, there still remains the possibility of the admission of low-rated students from high schools in the "a" and "b" groups.

There are those who feel that there is good reason for laws which require the state college or university to accept every high-school graduate who applies. For education on the college level, however, the inequalities in high-school preparation present a

[1] See also, "Co-operation in General Education," American Council on Education, 1947, p. 11.

serious problem. One state university, where there is a great demand for admission, requires a personal interview with all students whose rating is C or below and also with their parents. It is pointed out that the records of the university indicate that unless there is some extraordinary reason for the student's low standing in high school, he has little likelihood of making a good record at the university and there is grave doubt of his ability to pass. This is in a state where the law requires the university to accept all state high-school graduates. As a result of the use of this method a considerable number of unlikely candidates for admission are discouraged.

Another factor which complicates this situation is the variation in standards of marking in different schools. In some instances there may be a passing grade of 75 per cent or its equivalent, while in other schools it may be 65 per cent or its equivalent. In some instances, the marking is more lenient than in others, irrespective of the passing grade. Most of the good private secondary schools are strict in their marking, with the result that students achieve a standard of excellence which would have a much higher rating in the public high school. At one time I delivered a commencement address at a high school in a Midwestern state. The principal proudly told me that there were a considerable number in the class with a general average of 98 per cent, and that 80 per cent of the class had a general average of over 90 per cent. My first reaction was to ask him, if possible, to keep those marks confidential and not let even the students know how high they were rated, because of the tragedy that was sure to follow when they got down to hard work on the college level. This is an extreme instance, of course, but it is an example of the great variation of standards between different types of schools.

Another problem came with the end of the war, when veterans, who had not had four years of high-school experience, sought admission to college or university. A wide latitude developed from the practice of admitting on the basis of four years of high school or *"equivalent."* Some of the "equivalent" were courses provided by the Armed Services Educational Program. There were other schools which granted accreditation merely for military service, without special instruction, and the whole question was clouded even more. Of course, many of these veterans were more mature than high-school graduates who had gone directly to college, with the result that among the better ones the power of concentration was more highly developed and habits of work adhered to more strictly. Some institutions, both publicly controlled and privately controlled, admitted veterans without the usual high-school graduation requirement. The work of these men was observed closely. It should be said that the veterans are divided into two classes: some of them are grouped among the best students in every institution, and others are a liability rather than an asset to the schools they attend. The splendid work done by the veterans admitted without a high-school diploma has led to the provision in many universities for the matriculation of those over twenty-one years of age who have not graduated from high school, but are able to demonstrate their ability to measure up to college standards. This experiment proved so successful that in some institutions arrangements were made to accept students coming directly from high school who had completed the major portion of their work toward graduation but had not yet received their diplomas. Most of these students took entrance examinations, including the General Educational Development test, and were submitted to various other tests of their aptitudes and abilities. The work of these students was then carefully observed, and it was found that many of them made surprisingly good records. The University of Missouri is at present studying a comparison of the work of students admitted without a high-school diploma with work being done by those who have graduated in the normal fashion. This study has not been under way sufficiently long to arrive at definite conclusions, but there are indications that the work of those admitted without a high-school diploma will not only compare favorably with the work of high-school graduates, but, in a number of instances, surpass it.

Connected with this question of admission requirements, there is considerable dissatisfaction in many institutions with the examination system and with conventional methods for marking the progress of students. There is a growing feeling that more attention should be given to daily work, along with less emphasis on examinations. There is also the feeling that the development of habits of study, of initiative, and of emphasis on original work should be considered. Many institutions have introduced reading courses of one kind or another. One interesting experiment is being conducted at the University of Kansas. The unique feature of this Kansas plan is that the students are given a list of significant books to be read, on which they are examined before the end of the sophomore year. There are no lectures or classroom sessions in this course. Proctors advise students once every three weeks. The interesting result has been that many of the students are working harder on this reading course, carried on entirely outside of the classrooms and with no laboratory periods, and feel that for the first time they have been treated as adults in college. The examinations passed thus far also indicate that there are certain advantages to this plan.

Another group of schools provides for the admission of students without high-school certificates, but they are listed as unclassified or special students, and not as regular students eligible for a degree. In some places, as in Michigan State, these unclassified students can attain regular standing upon proving that they are capable of carrying a full load of hours on the college level.

In many cases a differential between admission requirements for in-state and out-of-state students has been established. At the beginning of the increase in enrollments, some state colleges decided not to accept out-of-state students, and others, to accept only those of the out-of-state applicants with a rather high academic rating. In spite of this limitation, the demand of out-of-state students for admission and the proportion of them actually enrolled were maintained. In every case, in-state students received the preference. The main consideration in this connection was housing. Gradually, however, the in-state students who did not prove competent were weeded out, and their places were frequently taken by out-of-state students of higher standing. A table in the third part of this book shows the percentage of out-of-state students compared with in-state students in each institution visited.[2]

While the privately controlled colleges of high reputation enjoy a considerable freedom in the selection of students, it would be unfair to state that privately controlled colleges, as a whole, enjoy a higher degree of selectivity than the publicly controlled institutions. Some of the great state universities have been forced to employ a much higher degree of selection than others. On the other hand, many of the small, weakly financed privately controlled colleges have let down their entrance requirements because of the higher operating costs, which make tuition fees a factor in determining whether the institution can be continued or must be liquidated. Among the private institutions visited, Amherst has a scholastic aptitude and achievement test in addition to special subject and hour requirements for entrance. Amherst also considers candidates accredited through the New York State Regents' examination. The University of Southern California admits accredited high-school students from the upper half of their class who meet a fifteen-unit requirement and have good character and health. It also admits by examination. Stanford requires fifteen hours of accredited high school, and the student is supposed to have an A or B grade, and must pass the college aptitude test. Harvard and Yale are highly selective. The University of the South normally accepts high-school graduates having an average of 80. Vanderbilt has three requirements: (1) fifteen high-school units, partly prescribed; (2) position in graduating class, (3) scholastic aptitude test. This allows for a rather high degree of selectivity. The College of Wooster asks for a certificate of graduation from an accredited high school or academy, personal information, and a health certificate. Supplementary tests are optional.

When we turn from these privately controlled institutions to the state colleges and universities, we find wide variation. The only requirement in forty-nine institutions is graduation from an accredited high school or fifteen high-school units. In this group are Alabama Tech, University of Alabama, University of

[2] See Table 5.

Arizona, University of Arkansas, San Francisco State College, San Jose State College, Clemson, Colorado A. & M., Florida State University, University of Florida, Cornell, Georgia Tech, University of Georgia, Iowa A. & M., University of Kansas, Kansas State College, University of Kentucky, Louisiana State University, University of Maine, Mississippi State College, University of Mississippi, Mississippi College for Women, Montana State University, University of Nebraska, University of Nevada, University of New Mexico, University of North Dakota, Ohio State University, Oklahoma Women's College, Oklahoma A. & M., University of Oklahoma, University of Oregon, Oregon State College, Purdue, Rutgers, University of South Carolina, University of South Dakota, Southwest Louisiana Institute, University of Tennessee, Texas A. & M., University of Texas (lower quarter admitted on probation),Texas Tech, Texas College of Mines, Utah Agricultural College, University of Utah, University of Virginia, University of West Virginia, University of Wisconsin, and University of Wyoming.

Practically all these institutions admit students by examination, particularly those described as "worthy mature students," without high-school graduation. In most instances, the students thus admitted can attain regular standing by proving their ability to do college work satisfactorily.

However, there is another group of state colleges and universities which does not admit all graduates of state high schools. At the Citadel, the Military College of South Carolina, the selective process is used, and more than 50 per cent of the students are from the middle third of their high-school class or better. The University of Colorado admits the upper two thirds of high-school graduating classes without examination, and the lower third by examination. The University of Connecticut reports that normally it admits only the top quarter of state high-school graduates. Georgia Tech admits no students without high-school diploma. At the University of Illinois the lower quarter of high-school graduating classes are placed on a probationary basis. Indiana admits all graduates of accredited high schools of the state in the upper half of their classes. The lower half are required to report for conference and guidance, and, as a result, many do not ask admittance. Iowa State University discourages the lower third of all high-school graduating classes. The University of Maryland admits the top third of high-school graduates from inside the state, eliminates the lower fifth and uses a selective method for the balance. Massachusetts State University has a requirement of 80 per cent or B. Michigan State College admits only the upper third in state-accredited high-school graduating classes without examination; the second third only on express recommendation of the high-school principal, and the lower third only by written examination. The University of Michigan admits on certificate when the student has better than average grades. Minnesota takes into consideration high-school rank and aptitude tests. The University of Missouri admits the upper two-thirds of graduating classes, and the lower third are admitted on probation. At the University of New Hampshire the upper two-fifths of state high-school graduates are admitted without examination, and those below that have to pass entrance tests. At Pennsylvania State College the upper two-fifths from the top two groups of state high schools are admitted by certificates, and the remainder only by examination. At the University of Vermont students must have the recommendation of their high-school principal, rank in high-school graduating class, a satisfactory school record for the four years, and a personal interview. At Virginia Military Institute and Virginia Polytechnic Institute a high degree of selection is reported. William and Mary admits the upper half of high-school graduating classes. At the State College of Washington a rank of C in high-school work is required.

For out-of-state students the publicly controlled colleges and universities have higher entrance standards. It should be remarked here that there is practically no restriction on out-of-state students in the privately controlled institutions. At the University of Arizona non-residents must be the top third of the high-school graduating class. U.C.L.A. has scholarship requirements of B grade average for the last three years of high school, as has the University of California. At the University of Colorado only the upper fourth of out-of-state graduating classes are accepted.

At Indiana out-of-state students must be in the upper third of the high-school graduating class. Iowa A. & M. requires an out-of-state minimum of 2.5. There are higher requirements at the University of Kansas for out-of-state students. At Louisiana State University out-of-state students must be in the upper third or with C or higher average. At Michigan State only the upper third of out-of-state high-school graduating classes are admitted; at Minnesota out-of-state students must be in the upper quarter of high-school graduating classes. Montana State places scholarship restrictions on out-of-state applicants. At Nebraska they must be in the upper ten per cent, with the exception of those from adjacent states, who must be from the upper half of their classes. New Hampshire has higher requirements for out-of-state students. At Oklahoma A. & M. only the upper half of high-school graduates are accepted from out-of-state applicants; the same is true at the University of Oklahoma. At Oregon and Oregon State nonresidents are required to meet an average of 2.5, if transfers, or to be of the upper twenty per cent if they come from high school. Purdue requires that out-of-state students be from the upper two-thirds of high-school graduating classes; otherwise they are admitted by examination. At West Virginia only applicants from the upper third of high-school graduating classes are admitted from out-of-state applicants.

With the increase due to the enrollment of veterans expected to continue during the next few years, and with the additional increase due to senior high-school students who will go directly from military service to college, the problem of entrance requirements is very serious. It is undoubtedly true that some of the universities which have very large enrollments admit students who have far greater vocational aptitude than interest in academic subjects. The consequent failure of such students possibly before the end of their sophomore year, frequently results in tragedy for some of them. Many of the institutions have made a study of students entered with a C average or below C in high school. The mortality of these students in any institution of high standing is very considerable.

There is also such wide variation in the enforcement of entrance requirements that there is a grave question in the minds of many educators whether a high-school diploma is a sufficient requirement for entrance to college. The fact that many students can achieve a mere passing mark in large high-school classes without seriously applying themselves, or without assimilating any considerable information, makes the colleges skeptical about admitting all high-school graduates on the strength of their high-school experience alone. Unfortunately, the level of achievement on which success in college is based is determined, to some extent, by the work of one who can be described as an average student. There is danger, then, that where the average is low, the standards of the institution also will be low. The success of the more mature veteran students, even of those without high-school diplomas, has, in many instances, raised academic standards.

It would seem proper, therefore, to consider whether greater care should be exercised in accrediting high schools, the decision to be determined by students' college records over, perhaps, a ten-year period. In California and Colorado, for instance, the accreditation is entrusted to the state university. In the other states there are various methods of accrediting high schools. In many the standard of accreditation is low. Entrance to college without examination should be strictly limited to students of high scholastic standing during their high-school careers. It would seem desirable that the great majority of students, if not all, applying from high school should take the General Educational Development test and such other aptitude and vocational tests as might establish the quality of their work. In order to make proper provision, not only for veterans with limited resources, but for high-school students with strong vocational rather than academic inclinations, vocational centers should be set up in various urban areas, with a two-year terminal. One year of study could be devoted to a broad educational base on the college level.[3] The second year might well be devoted to strictly vocational training and the development of skills. At the end of the two-year vocational course the student would be in a position to support himself by practicing

[3] *Co-operation in General Education,* American Council on Education, 1947, p. 25.

his trade and to help relieve the present serious shortage of skilled artisans in the United States. If such a student should desire to go on and enter college after working two or three years, there should be some arrangement whereby he could secure at least one year's college credit for his work in the vocational institution or school.

Preferably, these vocational institutions should be part of the municipal or county school system and not a part of the state university system, because, under municipal or county sponsorship, they would remain loyal to the purpose for which they were intended. In some states the state university is attempting to control vocational training, much of which is not on a college level. The motive behind this effort seems to be the fear that, unless the vocational centers are made part of the university system, the appropriations granted them would be out of the control of the university. If they should become a part of the university system, experience shows that after only a short time ambitious administrators would attempt to develop these two-year institutions into four-year schools, then give them authority to grant degrees, then put them into competition with established state universities and colleges, and, finally, to privilege them to teach subjects for which they are not equipped. President Conant of Harvard has said that in America we are preparing too many men for white-collar jobs, of which there are not enough to go around, and that we should therefore move rapidly toward the establishment of vocational centers of the type described.

An interesting instance of the danger of turning two-year terminal vocational schools into full-fledged universities overnight is seen in the experience of many normal schools which only recently were offering two-year courses. Then they were expanded into four-year schools, without the power to grant degrees. The next step was for them to grant a degree in education which is an award for specialized training and a very different thing from the degree of Bachelor of Arts in universities of high standing. Soon it was demanded that these schools be empowered to award the Bachelor of Arts degree. As a result, we have seen the amazing phenomenon of a two-year normal school developing into a full-fledged four-year college, with all the degree-granting powers implied, in a period of only a few years. The present teacher shortage can no longer be blamed entirely on inadequate salaries. The shortage is due, in part, to the fact that the teachers' colleges and normal schools seem to be far more interested in educating people for everything but the teaching profession. At one very prominent teachers' college recently there were more graduates in business administration than there were in education. At another it was planned last year to start a four-year course in engineering. Another is advertising degree courses in osteopathy, optometry, theology, and agriculture. First, it was the "Twilight" normal, then, the "Twilight" teachers college; then, the "Twilight" college of education, and, finally, just "Twilight" college. Either we should stop pretending that the teachers' colleges are primarily interested in teacher training, and make all our teachers' colleges straight four-year liberal arts colleges and then strengthen the colleges of education which are part of state universities, or we should have the teachers' colleges devote themselves to the task of training educational leaders and thus help to meet the present shortage of teachers.

Entrance requirements for vocational centers or institutes as outlined should be very liberal. There are many deserving students unable to finish high school. Many of them have talents and abilities worth development. Some of the veterans who have no business being in college manage to enter because of their military service. On the other hand, there are many veterans without even a vestige of college preparation who have skills capable of being developed at a vocational center. We seem to have been quite blind to our obligation to men of this type. This is true not only of veterans; it is true of certain high-school students. In pleading for the opening of such vocational centers, one university president wisely remarked that their establishment would enable many colleges and universities to do the work they were intended to do.

Many of the good private secondary schools base their marking on examinations prepared by others than local authorities.[4] The examinations are sealed and mailed to the point where they

[4] *Studies of Higher Education in the South,* Southern Association, p. 98.

are to be taken. They are given by instructors other than members of the local faculty. Then they are sealed and returned for grading to the source from which they came. The school thus subjects both its faculty and its students to the test. In the effort to improve high-school standards and make them more uniform there is no reason why a similar system could not be adopted on a state-wide basis. At one great privately controlled university I was told that the students who had passed the New York State Regents examination proved among its best students, although they were in competition with graduates of privately controlled secondary schools. New York has such a state-wide system. The problem of admissions would be considerably simpler if a uniform system of requirements could be adopted. Furthermore, the applicant for college entrance would not only have demonstrated his ability in high school, but could be subjected to further examinations, such as General Educational Development and other aptitude and vocational tests.

Care should be taken that sentimental, artificial, social distinctions should not be encouraged by any differentiation between students who enter college and those who are admitted to vocational centers. The opportunity to enter college should always be held up as a possibility for every student at a vocational institution.

Recently tremendous attention has been given to testings and measurements. These testings and measurements are supposed to evaluate a student's intelligence and aptitudes. Many of them are a succession of "true or false" or "yes or no" queries. Some of these testings and measurements border on the absurd. Some of them have value. Jacques Barzun, in his book *Teacher in America*,[5] has a very interesting chapter on this subject which should be read by everyone interested in it. The science of testing and measuring is still in its infancy. It has a certain validity, where it is well done, in colleges which are really interested in determining abilities. In helping to settle on intelligent entrance requirements, it would seem wise to encourage the development of adequate methods of testing and measuring to be used on the

[5] *Atlantic*, Little Brown, 1945.

high-school level, possibly as early as the sophomore year. The professional testers and measurers on the college level object to this suggestion on the ground that the testing would not be sufficiently skillful. There is no good reason, however, why in the preparation for the teaching profession attention should not be given to perfecting testing and measuring methods on the high-school level. This would help to avoid many of the casualties that have taken place as a result of too strict enforcement or lack of enforcement of intelligent standards of admission.

8

CONTRIBUTION TO NATIONAL WEL-
FARE AND ECONOMY BY STATE
COLLEGES AND UNIVERSITIES

OCCASIONALLY there have been evidences of a rather smug satisfaction among some of the privately controlled colleges and universities in their attitude toward the great publicly controlled state institutions of higher learning. This attitude has not been so evident among faculties and administrators as it has been among overenthusiastic and frequently uninformed alumni. Stewart Sherman, in his book *The Genius of America* [1] has a most interesting chapter on "Education by the People," in which he presents a strong defense for publicly controlled higher education against any monopoly of culture by privately endowed educational foundations. In a democracy the preservation of independently controlled education is essential. Because of the expense involved, and the number of students desiring college training unable to gain entrance to privately controlled schools, publicly controlled higher education is a necessity. As the state colleges and universities have grown in enrollments, influence, and effectiveness, the gap between the great "name" universities of the East and the land-grant colleges and universities of the West has been bridged to some extent. No adequate picture of American higher education or of the men who control the policies of our colleges and universities can be gained by limiting one's study to the Association of American Universities. Every institution which can claim membership in that association has high rank; but, as time has gone on, institu-

[1] Scribner's, 1923.

tions not thus included have gradually achieved distinction, first in one field, and then in another. It would be utterly unfair to assume that unless an institution is a member of that association it is not maintaining as high levels of instruction or doing as fine work in research as many institutions that are so included. This applies to privately controlled as well as to publicly controlled colleges and universities. Someone recently said of the president of one of the great eastern "name" universities that he had just discovered publicly controlled higher education and was finding it very interesting.

The average taxpayer scans rather critically legislative appropriations for the support of state colleges and universities. He is deeply interested in the college or university which measures up to reasonably good standards. He is deeply concerned that the tuition be kept at such a low figure as will be within the means of any promising high-school graduate. He insists that the tax rate for education should not be any higher than is absolutely necessary. He rarely stops to think of the integrity of education itself. If low standards are characteristic of certain groups of colleges, they reflect on education as a whole. With the enormous investment in our state colleges and universities, there is every reason why their work should be as thorough and as effective as that of privately controlled institutions. Because of the recent increase in salaries for faculty members the state colleges and universities have been placed in a position where they can compete successfully with privately controlled institutions for highly skilled teachers. Meanwhile, the endowments of many of the privately controlled colleges are producing less income year by year. This, too, leads nearer to an equality in the relation between publicly controlled and privately controlled education.

Even the rivalry of public institutions within a state creates suspicion that a state university may have higher academic rank than a state college. In some states the land-grant is part of the university endowment, so that we may be said to have land-grant universities. This is true of New York State's College of Agriculture and Home Economics at Cornell. It is true of Tennessee, of the Universities of California, Arizona, Arkansas, Delaware,

Florida, Georgia, Kentucky, Maine, Massachusetts, and of some other states. In other areas the land-grant appropriations have gone to the state college rather than to the state university. There has been a tendency to describe these state colleges, with their emphasis on agriculture and mechanical arts, as "cow" colleges, and to overlook the fact that some of the best research and high intellectual levels are being supported at some of these institutions. Curiously enough, in some states—probably because it is less expensive to secure teachers of English, history and the classics than it is to secure expert scientists—state appropriations for these colleges are beginning to exceed appropriations for state universities. The emphasis on vocational training is no longer limited to the land-grant institutions. State universities which are not land-grant, and even privately controlled colleges and universities are placing more and more emphasis on preparation for special tasks in life.

It would seem as though no one had ever stopped to ask what contribution the state colleges and universities are making to our national welfare and economy. Scarcely a day passes but that research at some one of these state institutions of higher learning produces a result with an indirect, and sometimes even a direct, effect on the standard of living. In large measure state schools have been devoting their attention to the proper development and conservation of the natural resources of the areas in which they are located. A brief summary of accomplishments toward this end causes one to ask whether the contribution of these institutions is not far greater than the public realizes.

Not only has there been great service in the field of applied research, but there has been a gradual development in many of the state schools toward maintaining particularly high levels of instruction in other fields. An interesting instance of this is found in the work being done in archeology at the University of Arizona. Graduate students from the great "name" universities of the East turn to Arizona because of the excellence of its faculty in archeological research and because of the archeological deposits which are available there to an extent not generally realized elsewhere. As we make a hurried survey of the outstanding fea-

tures, both in the field of applied research and in the maintenance of high standards of teaching, it will be possible only to
touch the very high points of the various institutions. Some, of
course, display an almost unnatural modesty about their accomplishments. One president, when he was asked what was outstanding at his institution, replied, "Modesty prevents my stating the
departments in which I think ———— college excels." On the
other hand, certain colleges and universities are anything but
modest in their claims. An honest effort will be made to select
only those achievements which are notably outstanding or which
seem to be making a unique contribution. Part III of this book
has a chart [2] outlining in more detail outstanding features of
many of the institutions visited.

In attempting to evaluate very briefly and, of necessity, inadequately, the contributions of state colleges and universities to the
national economy and welfare, the tremendous services rendered
by privately controlled colleges and universities will not be forgotten. The Museum of Revolution, War and Peace at Stanford
University, the new procedures in teaching evolved from time to
time at Harvard, the work of the Sheffield Scientific School at
Yale, the high levels of instruction in many another privately
controlled institution tell their own story of usefulness. When
the citizen looks at his universities, however, his attention is
directed mainly to the state universities and state colleges. It
would be impossible to give full credit to both publicly controlled and privately controlled higher education for their contributions to the national welfare within the space of a single
volume, to say nothing of a single chapter; therefore, it must be
clearly understood that the emphasis on the contribution of the
state colleges and universities in no way implies a lack of recognition of the great accomplishments of the many privately controlled institutions.

From Maine to California and from Washington to Florida,
there is no single state college or university which is not doing
outstanding work in some way. Maine,[3] along with Wisconsin, is

[2] See Table 8.
[3] Biennial Report, President of the University of Maine, 1946.

notable for its work in pulp and paper technology. It has a national reputation in engineering, and is doing considerable research in forestry. At the University of Vermont, perhaps the
"strongest work is done in the College of Medicine and its associated curricula, such as nursing and medical technology." This
college is rather unique in that it is dedicated to the training of
general practitioners who will set up practice in a small community or perhaps in a rural environment. At the University of
Connecticut outstanding research is being conducted in the field
of animal genetics, and Connecticut has the only College of Insurance in the world, with a combination curriculum of insurance
and law. At Massachusetts State University there are more instructors in agriculture than in any other college in New England, and especially good work is being done in food technology.
In New Hampshire State University the creation of wood yeast
as a feed and the use of wood as a source for plastic materials
are featured. Rhode Island State College [4] is unique in its marine
biological laboratories on Narragansett Bay, and in its experiments in, and study of, lawn grasses for parks, cemeteries, golf
greens, playing fields, and airports.

Cornell University [5] is outstanding in so many ways that it is
difficult to single out any one. However, its engineering and
agricultural colleges are among the best schools in the United
States. Its School of Industrial and Labor Relations is attracting favorable national attention. The School of Nutrition also
has impressed scientists in this field. Pennsylvania State College [6]
is notable for its work in the petroleum refining laboratory of the
School of Chemistry and Physics. It also has an outstanding
School of Mineral Industries. At Delaware University [7] interesting work is being done in the development of plastics from the
soy bean, in jet propulsion, and in uses for waste synthetic rubber. The University of Maryland [8] has attempted to maintain an

[4] *Report of President and other Officers,* Rhode Island State College, 1945-46.
[5] *Cornell University—General Information,* 1947-48.
[6] *The Several Pursuits and Professions of Life,* Pennsylvania State College, 1945.
[7] *Going to College?* University of Delaware, Newark, Delaware, 1946.
[8] *Maryland,* Vol. 18, No. 7, Maryland Alumni Publication, Capitol Gazette, Inc.,
Annapolis, Md., June, 1947.

even balance between all departments, but its schools of Business Administration and Engineering are showing progress. William and Mary College in Virginia, second oldest educational foundation in the United States, has an outstanding Institute of Early American History, which works in co-operation with the Williamsburg Restoration (Colonial Williamsburg, Incorporated). Here also is the Virginia Fisheries Laboratory, which is supported by the Rockefeller Foundation. The University of Virginia is well known for its School of Government and also for the new Woodrow Wilson School for Foreign Service. Virginia Military Institute is best known for its work in engineering, and is a unique demonstration of a combination of military training with a sound general education. In this, it stands in marked contrast with the United States Military Academy at West Point. Virginia Polytechnic Institute is working with cedar sawdust to make laminated wood.

The University of North Carolina [9] has attracted favorable attention for its Institute of Government, and has high academic rating for maintaining exceptionally strong standards in many other departments. Growing out of its Institute for Research and Social Science are two of the most remarkable undergraduate organizations in American educational history: the Carolina Political Union and the International Relations Club. The university library has more than 500,000 volumes, and is second in its size in the southeast. Particular attention is devoted to research and information concerning the present status, problems, and immense possibilities of the South. In the Carolina Playmakers North Carolina has the first state-supported theater devoted to the development of native drama. The Medical School recently was expanded from a two-year to a four-year school. North Carolina State College has the largest School of Textiles and Textile Research in the United States. It is also outstanding in ceramic research, and has equipment worth $2,500,000 in Diesel engineering. The Woman's College of North Carolina has attracted attention for its research in nutrition and in training teachers of home economics and institutional managers. The University of South

[9] *A Ten-Year Review,* University of North Carolina, 1934-1944.

Carolina [10] has made a good record with its School of Law, while the Citadel, South Carolina, has won a fine reputation in pre-medical education. It is also outstanding in civil engineering. Clemson, like North Carolina State, is doing notable work in textiles and trying to develop penicillin and other drugs in cheese, for which local conditions are particularly favorable.

The Georgia School of Technology [11] is well known for its contributions in the engineering field, and is outstanding for its work in aeronautics. At present, its Engineering Experiment Station is specializing in food processing and wood pulp and in paint primers for yellow pine. This is the only institution in the United States with an experimental paint laboratory. Considerable work has been done, too, in thermo-dynamic studies of the properties of gases and also of flax processing, in conjunction with the TVA. On the other hand, the University of Georgia is still in its infancy in research. The emphasis at Athens is rather on high instructional levels in music and fine arts, and there is an outstanding collection of documents in the field of Southern history. Florida has two major state institutions, Florida State University and the University of Florida. Here again there is strong emphasis on broad general education. The program of the University College at Gainesville has been studied and adopted, in part or in the main, by a number of other institutions. Special attention is given to the chemistry of naval stores, and to the study of Florida [12] flora and fauna. The School of Pharmacy is one of the five outstanding graduate schools in pharmacy in the nation. The College of Engineering is working in the field of electronics, particularly in connection with storm locations and in the development of small proximity fuses. Latin American relations also receive considerable attention at Florida. An unusual service of the College of Education is a series of conferences for in-service training for county public school superintendents, and there is a project in applied economics under the Sloan Foundation to improve living conditions in Florida communities. Florida State University,

[10] *Caroliniana,* University of South Carolina, 1946.

[11] *Annual Report-Regents,* University System of Georgia, 1945-1946.

[12] *Education in Florida's Future,* Citizens Committee on Education, Tallahassee, 1946.

until recently the state woman's college, is nationally known for its work in dietetics and for exchanging internships with institutions in various parts of the country. It also has a unique internship program for training public school teachers and for students who expect to engage in state government work.

Turning back northward, Alabama Polytechnic Institute, through its College of Agriculture, is nationally and internationally known for its projects in fishing [13] and wild life. Experiments here have shown that an acre of water will produce more food from the cultivation of fish than can be raised in vegetation on the same area of land. This experiment has considerably changed the diet of underprivileged people in that locality. The University of Alabama is outstanding for inspiring the establishment of the Southern Research Institute, which corresponds in principle to the Mellon Institute,[14] for its work in pulp and paper technology, and for its work on sulphur organic compounds, in ceramics, and in the graphic and plastic arts.

The University of Kentucky is known for its improved methods of raising tobacco and for coal research, for its collections in Colonial American and Southern history, and for its work in bacteriology. Here it was recently discovered that a ton of coal can produce fourteen gallons of ethyl gasoline and still have 1300 pounds of consumable coke remaining.

The University of Tennessee has a School of Home Economics which is considered one of the four best in the United States, and its College of Engineering is nationally recognized. Unusual research is being done by some two hundred students in atomic energy, in co-operation with Oak Ridge, and also in connection with TVA.

Rutgers University,[15] in New Brunswick, New Jersey, located in the center of the chemical industry, is outstanding for chemical research. It also does original work in agriculture and in the production of new varieties of peaches and tomatoes. Special empha-

[13] *Management of Farm Fish Ponds,* Alabama Polytechnic Institute, Bulletin 254, 1947.

[14] *Bulletin,* Department of Commerce and Business Administration, University of Alabama, 1947.

[15] *Report of the President,* Rutgers University Bulletin, 22nd series 28, 1945.

sis is placed on the study of soils and on microbiology. There is a unique relationship between the School of Journalism and the State Press Association, and advanced work is offered in ceramics.

Ohio State University is doing notable work in the identification of planes by psychological methods, and has its fresh-water marine laboratory on Lake Erie. Its College of Medicine has attracted attention in hemotology and in optometry, with fundamental and advanced work in vision. The School of Aviation, in conjunction with Wright Field, offers unusual facilities.

Located in the heart of the mining area, the University of West Virginia [16] is doing unusual research in coal and coal deposits, preparing for the time when the coal industry will change its techniques. This includes the readjustment of the mode of living of many West Virginians, which looks toward the time when coal deposits will be exhausted. It also has one of the finest mineral science buildings in the United States and devotes special attention to coal liquefacation.

The University of Iowa has one of the finest medical schools in any state university. It is doing considerable creative work in art, music, the theater, and in writing. It is outsanding for work in child welfare,[17] psychology, education, hydraulics, zoology, statistics and actuarial training. Iowa State College of Agriculture and the Mechanic Arts has long been recognized for its outstanding work in agriculture [18] and engineering. Its research includes human nutrition, fermentation, advanced work in atomic energy, trends of state population, animal nutrition, veterinary pathology, and chemical engineering.

Michigan State College, with its "Basic College" course,[19] is making a great contribution to a broader general educational base. It specializes in technological research. Considerable attention has been paid to undulant fever in animals and man, the production of brucellin, and the infra-red method of combatting frost dam-

[16] *Survey of Public Education in the State of West Virginia,* George D. Strayer, 1945.

[17] *Iowa Child Welfare Research Station,* University of Iowa, Robert R. Sears, 1945.

[18] *Education in Agriculture,* The Iowa State College Bulletin, Vol. 43, No. 41, 1945.

[19] *The Basic College,* Michigan State College, Vol. 41, No. 7 Rev., 1946.

age. Its schools of Veterinary Medicine and Forestry are outstanding. The American Hotel Association is contributing to the construction of an adult education center to be operated by hotel administration students and used for annual association meetings.

Reference has already been made to the study of proper entrance requirements for college being conducted at the University of Missouri. Missouri also has an extensive plan for the establishment of vocational centers in various sections of the state, to be conducted as part of the university system. The Bible College of the university, to which reference has already been made, is also outstanding. The university has a Professional Library in Education, a fine Western historical manuscript collection, and separate libraries for the various divisions of the institution. The School of Mines and Metallurgy at Rollo, Missouri, gives special attention to petroleum geology, metallurgical engineering, ceramic engineering, research and scientific study of the fundamental and chemical principles underlying mining and metallurgical technology, and to the testing of commercial processes in co-operation with the United States Bureau of Mines. The School of Journalism is a professional school and is the oldest school devoted to education for journalism in the world.

Mississippi [20] has three institutions of higher learning for white students. At Mississippi State College [21] the Bureau of Business Research issues monthly bulletins on business trends, tax structure, insurance, banking, and developments in local industries. This work is important in connection with the establishment of new industries in the state. Its engineering research station co-operates with TVA, with special reference to strengths of materials and in wood products. Considerable attention is paid to uses of cottonseed oil, and here is the greatest experiment station for cotton in the world, with emphasis on cotton genetics and cotton fiber research. At the University of Mississippi research is carried on in petroleum geology and ceramics, and also in public health on a state-wide basis. The Bureau of Public Administration has prepared a legislative handbook for the guid-

[20] *Report from the President's Council*, 1945.
[21] *Mississippi State College—Its Objectives and Program of Work*, 1944.

ance of all legislators. Mississippi Women's College [22] is primarily a liberal arts school, with certain vocational departments. It is especially strong in music and home economics.

When Arkansas was visited, its football team was mentioned as one of its outstanding features. This was the one institution of the eighty-nine which claimed such distinction. The research at Arkansas [23] is largely devoted to agricultural subjects, but original work is being done in the Indian archeology of the West, and in regional literature and law.

Louisiana State University [24] is building a strong medical school. The university is doing excellent work in petroleum engineering and oil geology, and is famous for sugar chemistry. Considerable attention is devoted to research in sweet potato development, and studies in rural sociology are rather extensive. At Southwest Louisiana Institute [25] special attention is being given to the elimination of water hyacinth and alligator grass, two pests in this area. This school is unique in raising the literacy standard of its environment, there being a high rate of illiteracy, due to the fact that French and English had not been taught in earlier years. The institute also does good work in floriculture and home economics, especially the latter, which stresses living within a modest income and yet living moderately well.

The University of Texas has a number of splendid collections, including many rare books, a Latin American collection, and, naturally, a Texas Memorial Museum, which features the historical development of the state, its geological, and anthropological background. It is strong in the general fields of biology, chemistry, nearly all phases of mathematics, and in history. At Texas Tech there is a complete textile factory, and splendid work is being done in connection with the use of short-fiber cotton. Texas Tech has one of the finest textile research projects in the country. At Texas Mines, the scholarship of the faculty is noteworthy, and important work is being done in radio, interior deco-

[22] *Southern Association Quarterly*, February, 1939, p. 1.
[23] *University of Arkansas Annual Report*, 1945-46, Vol. 40, No. 15.
[24] *Biennial Report of the Board of Supervisors*, Louisiana State University, 1944-46.
[25] *Under All the Land—Rural Study of Lafayette Parish*, Louisiana, 1942.

rating, and design, and the undergraduate work in mining and metallurgy is attracting attention. Texas A. & M. is probably the land-grant college with the greatest emphasis on military training and discipline, along with the teaching of agriculture and the mechanical arts.

In Oklahoma [26] three state colleges and universities were visited. Oklahoma College for Women offers fine arts to young women from homes of moderate circumstances. It is strong in home economics, and its graduates are commonly spoken for in advance by large corporations paying good salaries, especially in laboratory research. It has made a splendid record for producing teachers of physical education. Oklahoma A. & M. has strong schools of agriculture, engineering, and architecture. It has a firemen's training school and is a headquarters for agricultural aviation. Its experiment station devotes particular attention to anaplasmosis research. The University of Oklahoma attracts attention for its petroleum engineering and for its school of drama. It has a fine university press. During the war it built for the Navy a spectrograph for cracking processes in oil. There is also considerable research in electronics, the study of asphalts, and in the investigation of heat transfers.

Crossing the line from Oklahoma into Kansas, we see high instructional levels being maintained at the university in chemistry, geology, and entomology. Its research in bacteriology, especially with reference to tularemia, is well known. A constructive contribution is made in engineering, especially in the use of dirt blocks not requiring machinery. There is a "Western Civilization" requirement [27] at the University of Kansas, which is not a "course" in the accepted sense of the term. It consists of a comprehensive examination based on a list of writings drawn from classical sources of Western thought as well as from current events. The students read independently, under guidance by proctors. About 800 students per semester are now enrolled for this study. The aim is to inculcate a knowledge of the tradition of western culture in general, and of the American way of life

---

[26] Third Biennial Report, State Board of Regents, 1946.
[27] *Manual for the Study of Western Civilization,* University of Kansas, 1946.

in particular.[28] Considerable emphasis is placed on the Christian idea of the worth of every human individual. Another unique feature at Kansas is a course called "Cases in Human Relationship," which is the product of a four-way experiment initiated at Harvard and embraced by Colgate, Ohio University, and Kansas. The approach to human problems is clinical in the sense that the total situation in which the given problem arises is faced in all its complexity and uniqueness rather than divided into specialized scientific courses. The case study method is employed. From the discussion of concrete cases drawn from family life, the community, military organizations, and industry, the students draw tentative generalities that may be applied to problems encountered in their own experience. Kansas State College devotes particular attention to the field of agriculture,[29] along with certain aspects of engineering. There is research in the designing of small homes, including farm homes; in the utilization of agricultural products, and in farm machinery and farm power. Engineering research is largely concerned with the durability of concrete and the quality of cements. Among the research projects are a study of factors influencing the milling and baking characteristics of wheat, and of the effect of quick-freezing on physical characteristics, palatability, and nutritional values of foods.

North Dakota is one of the smaller universities, but is unique in the teaching of Icelandic language and culture. There is also considerable research in agriculture here. South Dakota is another smaller state university devoting itself primarily to meeting the needs of a rural population, especially on the cultural side, with considerable emphasis on the fine arts.

The University of Nebraska [30] is one of the great state universities having a fine College of Dentistry and a College of Medicine. There is a splendid program of music and art education, which co-operates with the high schools of the state, and a unique program in extension, which presents various courses in

[28] *Co-operation in General Education*, American Council on Education, 1947, p. 21.

[29] *Agriculture at Kansas State College*, Vol. 30, No. 4, 1946.

[30] *Report of Nebraska Legislative Council*, Subcommittee on Colleges and Universities, 1946.

high schools under supervision of local high school staffs as a supplement to the work of the smaller state high schools. As we go farther west to Montana, we find the unique Summer Labor Institute, sponsored by a university committee and by the labor organizations of the state. In the rugged fastnesses of Wyoming,[31] special attention is given to sheep raising and wool research. There is considerable work in minerals and in the development of the natural resources of the area. At Colorado A. & M. there is a splendid School of Veterinary Medicine, and also noteworthy research in irrigation engineering and in sugar beet mechanization, and experimental work for the United States Army Signal Corps in radar. New Mexico,[32] with its sunny skies, is conspicuous for its studies in anthropology and archeology, and for its combination of three cultures, the Indian, the Spanish-American, and the Anglo-American. Spanish is a living language in this state and receives particular attention. Research work is done in connection with Los Alamos. The work in the fine arts, especially in painting, is exceptional because of the splendid artists' colonies in the immediate neighborhood.

The University of Arizona, like New Mexico, attracts graduate students from many of the privately controlled universities for advanced work in anthropology and archaeology. Considerable attention also is paid to new methods of discovering ore bodies and to the development of semitropical agriculture and to the encouragement of the citrus industry. Utah, with its great Mormon population, has two fine institutions in Utah State Agricultural College [33] and the University of Utah. At Utah State, with its fine Institute of Nutrition, the emphasis is on sheep-raising and other agricultural interests. Because of the nature of the state, special attention is paid to methods of cultivating arid soils. The University of Utah Medical School specializes in internal medicine, obstetrics, and gynecology. There is considerable work in mining ventilation, and the faculty includes world-renowned authorities in the field of mineral industries. An Insti-

[31] *University of Wyoming, Report of the President,* 1945-46.
[32] *University of New Mexico, Biennial Report,* 1945-47.
[33] *Agricultural Extension Serves Rural Utah,* Vol. 46, No. 10, 1946.

tute of Government and World Affairs recently has been established.

The University of Idaho places special stress on home economics, on the selection of consumer goods, purchasing, making and care of clothes, and choice of furniture and household equipment, and also on agriculture, which is the basic industry of the area. Its School of Forestry has attracted attention. In the State of Washington, the State College of Washington is outstanding in the field of technology, with special attention to new uses of lighter metals, such as magnesium metal. Twelve per cent of the waterpower available to produce electricity in the United States is located in this state, and special studies are made in connection with the diversified uses of cheap electric power, and with the use of water for the irrigation of vast areas.[34] The University of Washington is known because of its splendid work in connection with the Pacific Coast fishing industry. It has a fine School of Forestry. In the neighboring state of Oregon,[35] the University of Oregon has a splendid School of Architecture and a good School of Journalism. Oregon State College, which has long had an excellent reputation for its work in agriculture, is specializing in home economics and in food industries. The University of Nevada,[36] located at Reno, has a strong Physics Department, which places special emphasis on atomic development, and its Mackey School of Mines is nationally known. The University of California is famous for its advanced position in higher education. Special reference will be made in a succeeding paragraph to some of the projects being undertaken there.

There are a few schools which deserve special notice. It is rather difficult to select such schools, and the reference to them here is in no sense an intended neglect of other schools which may be doing equally good, or even better, work. However, in this survey certain institutions have attracted special attention. Among these is the University of Colorado at Boulder. At its School of Medicine, located in Denver, there are special programs

[34] *Budget Request, The State College of Washington, 1947-1949,* Pullman, Wash.
[35] *Oregon State System of Higher Education Bulletin,* Biennial Report, 1945-1946.
[36] *Report of the Regents of the University of Nevada,* 1945-46.

in the field of graduate education for training returned veteran doctors. This program has been integrated with a general health program on a state-wide basis. The School of Nursing is the only graduate school of nursing in an area including the surrounding nine states. It attracts students from various countries, many of whom are sent by the Rockefeller Foundation for the Advancement of Nursing Education. This university has been distinctive in geology, for which it is in a particularly rich area for research. Special projects include the utilization of Colorado coal for the extraction of chemicals by the hydrogenation of coal, and development of the levulose sugar process from beet products and other vegetable sugar-producing materials. Studies of all localities in Colorado are conducted by the School of Business Administration and the Bureau of Business Research. The university has investigated aviation facilities of the various towns and cities in Colorado with an eye to their physical and economic features. Special studies have been, and are being, made in close affiliation with state officers and with the legislature to determine the sources of state revenue, and to systematize the state agencies and methods of state finance.[37] Another unique feature contributed by the University of Colorado consists of studies in the management of cities and municipalities, with special attention to the building code of the state, revision of antiquated building code requirements, and the encouragement of building improvements with hitherto unused materials. Here also a unique study is being conducted in domestic heating by the utilization of solar heat. This experiment has been approved on a trial basis and is now being developed in conjunction with one of the large glass companies in the country. The work at the Medical School is attracting attention with its Division of Human Growth, which is engaged in determining the normality of development of the individual as the basis for the customary medical studies of abnormalities. There is also a Division of Industrial Medicine, which is devoted to curing and preventing chronic illnesses due to industrial causes. In co-operation with Harvard University, solar

[37] *So You're Having Troubles, Mr. Legislator?* University of Colorado, 1947. Also, *Taxation in Colorado*, Reports I, II, III, University of Colorado, 1946-47.

studies are being made at Climax, Colorado, through the corona-graph. Again, the Medical School pays special attention to psychiatric studies and the close relationship between mental and physical ills, not only from the curative, but from the educational standpoint. Over one hundred research projects are at present in operation. This school is mentioned, not because there are not other schools doing equally good work in some of the same fields, but as an indication of what a splendid contribution a state university can make toward improving living conditions for the average citizen.

The University of Illinois, with its enrollment of over 25,000, has more than 2,000 scholarships. For every dollar a student pays in fees he receives more than four dollars' worth of education. Here is to be found a betatron laboratory, and a several-hundred-million-volt betatron, one of the most important scientific instruments ever to be built at a university, opening, as it does, entirely new fields of scientific research. Especially noteworthy work is being done in the field of labor relations. The new Institute of Aeronautics co-ordinates instruction, research, and teaching in this subject, which affects half the people of the United States. The university has some of the finest museums and collections in the country, and owns its own airport of 770 acres. Its colleges are located at Urbana, Galesburg, and Chicago.

The University of Indiana has an especially strong school of medicine, which lays special stress on internal medicine, cardiology, pediatrics, ophthalmology, and radiology. Among the research courses in medicine are a federal project in the physiology of exercise, an investigation of yeast; and extensive study of the structure of endocrine glands, of ether levels in circulating blood in anesthesia, and of mercury content of body organs; an investigation into the bacteriology of gastro-intestinal tracts in infants and young children, and research in corneal radiation. There is also considerable emphasis on virus diseases, and the school has one of the largest cerebral palsy projects in the United States.

In zoology and botany the chief research project deals with the subject of genetics. A work of tremendous importance is being done in research in the sexual behavior of humans, including all levels of society. There is considerable work in nuclear physics and also in the method of developing the natural resources of Indiana. In English, study of folklore and eighteenth century literature attracts attention, while history includes a study of the West and Midwest fields. Like Yale, Indiana is strong in linguistics. Being the accrediting agency for the state high schools, the university is doing considerable work in the fields of administration in education and secondary education. The applied music work in the school of music is also on a high level. The school of law has a splendid faculty, and the department of government has been carrying on a program of publication of handbooks for the assistance of county officers. The speech and hearing clinic also deserves notice.

The University of Michigan [38] is generally recognized as one of the great outstanding institutions of the country because there are so many special features in its curricula and studies. A school of public health recently has been established, with the assistance of the Rockefeller Foundation and the W. F. Kellogg Foundation, to serve the entire Great Lakes area. Another institute has been established to develop the best methods of teaching English to foreigners, including an intensive two months' course for Latin-American visitors. The International Center for foreign students is noteworthy. There is a decentralized program in the medical school for instruction in medical specialties, in which the university co-operates with certain hospitals in Michigan cities. The work in post-graduate dentistry has a building unique of its kind, especially designed for children's dentistry. There is a solar observatory at Lake Angelus with equipment for making pictures of solar phenomena. The university has its own airport at Willow Run, and conducts research in aeronautical engineering and allied subjects. The neuropsychiatric institute is one of the finest in the United States. It furnishes treatment for patients with mental diseases, training medical personnel to care for them, and is investigating the causes and treatments of mental diseases. There is also a clinic for the study of heredity in humans. The

[38] *Status of Higher Education in Michigan*, Report to the Michigan Legislature, 1947; *The President's Report, University of Michigan*, 1944-1945.

ammonia. In physics there is research in electron and proton diffraction and in germanium semi-conductors. In mathematics there are the studies of the properties of "Peano spaces"; in pharmacy there is research in organic medicinal products, the administration of penicillin, antimalarial drugs, and in local anesthetics. Purdue has made a great contribution to transportation, no small part of which is in highway research, including studies of pavements, materials, cement, air-photo interpretations, traffic paints, traffic control and safety. A number of Purdue graduates are leading executives on American railways, and there has been outstanding work at the institution in railroad engineering. There are also studies on the lead-coating of sheet steel, the synthesis of dyes, and the hydrogenation of coal. Under electrical research come studies in television and in electric power transmission.

Another great state university that has made an enormous contribution is the University of Wisconsin.[40] This university has long emphasized its program of direct service to the people of the state. It is a program of constructive investigation and direct teaching, designed to keep the university in close contact with the citizens of all the counties. This program, which has often been called the "Wisconsin Idea," received much of its impetus from Charles R. Van Hise, who was president from 1903 to 1918. At present, twenty-six divisions of the university are devoted to this function. In many ways they profoundly influence the lives of people through health, business, industry, agriculture, and governmental relations. Examples of this direct service include almost every phase of teaching and research. In the field of medicine splendid work has been done in treatment for infantile paralysis. Considerable attention is paid to neuropsychiatry and the treatment and prevention of mental illnesses, especially through the administration of sleep-producing drugs, a method of treatment first developed in Wisconsin. A long-standing work exists in the field of syphilis, including not only treatment, but a plan of education of practical preventive value. There is considerable concentration on the study of chemical changes in the

[40] *The Biennial Report of the President, 1945-47.*

blood and in cerebro-spinal fluid examinations. Wisconsin is also famous for the discovery of Vitamins A and B, and of Vitamin D. Original work has been done in the relation of copper to anemia and the relation of nicotinic acid to pellagra in endocrinology. There is a special bequest for research in cancer, covering (1) the nature of growth processes, (2) relation of sex hormones to cancer, (3) relation of chemical agencies, especially sterols and dyes, to cancer; (4) genetic factors, (5) tissue enzymes, (6) the relation of nutrition to cancer. Among the eight laboratories in the United States devoting full time to the problems of cancer is the McArdle Memorial Institute on the Wisconsin campus. The Bureau of Business Research and Service has conducted a number of basic economic surveys of the state. These include agricultural, industrial, and resort districts, and the growth and distribution of industry in the state. The School of Commerce during the past year has held eighty-one conferences with state groups, especially "small business." Agricultural extension has managed to increase food production twenty-seven per cent in a period of seven years. The work of the university has increased milk production twenty-five per cent in five years, with the result that Wisconsin produces one-eighth of all the milk of the nation. There are many other farm services looking toward greater crop yields. The Geology Division directs its attention to research in state mineral resources and state mine evaluations. The program of child development at Wisconsin has a referral center on the campus. In engineering notable progress has been made in synthetic rubber manufacture. As at Washington State, work is being done in connection with electrical power, and the University laboratories have assisted paper mills, steel foundries, electric fence controller manufacturers, automobile plants, shipyards, lumber and forest product concerns, and other manufacturers. Reference has already been made to the splendid pioneer work of Wisconsin in workers' education. Radio broadcasting is another field in which Wisconsin has attained distinction. Along with all this scientific development, the fine arts have not been neglected, and the Summer Institute and work shops draw nearly 10,000 professional workers each year.

The University of California, with its great branch at Los Angeles, in addition to the campus at Berkeley, is outstanding for a number of reasons. Its library was recently judged by the American Library Association to be the third greatest library in the United States from the point of view of scholarly study and research. Out of a possible total of seventy-six fields of knowledge, it was classified as eminent in fifty-four. Only the library of Harvard University and the Library of Congress exceed this total. According to surveys of the American Council on Education, the faculty is one of the most eminent in the country. It includes twenty-seven members of the National Academy of Sciences. The Museum of Anthropology contains over 172,000 catalogued items; its California Indian collection ranks first in the nation; its Egyptian, second only to the Oriental Institute of Chicago; its Peruvian collection, first among university museums in the country; its Greek-Roman-Etruscan-Cypriote collection is the finest in any university in America. Other museums located here and distinguished throughout the country are the Museum of Vertebrate Zoology, the Museum of Paleontology, which ranks first in the country in western material, and the University Herbarium, preeminent in western flora and that of some sections of South America and Asia. The Radiation Laboratory is probably the best equipped and most adequately staffed laboratory for nuclear physics in the world. The invention of the cyclotron in this laboratory brought the Nobel Prize to Dr. E. O. Lawrence. It now contains three cyclotrons, including one which is by far the largest in the world, weighing 4,400 tons. The great majority of radioactive isotopes now known to science were discovered in this laboratory, as well as the trans-uranic elements, neptunium, plutonium, americium, and curium. The hydraulic laboratory, known as the Tidal Model Testing Basin, operated jointly by the U.S. Army Engineers and the University of California, is one of the most complete in the United States and the major such laboratory in the West. The Engineering Materials Testing Laboratory has many special facilities, including a four-million-pound compression testing machine and a complete laboratory for the development and testing of special concretes. Much of the testing work for the large dams in western United States and the testing of models for the San Francisco Bay bridges was done in this department of the university. Among special units, the university extension service, during the past biennium, had 158,745 class enrollments in thirty cities of California, and 36,620 correspondence course enrollments from various parts of the United States and from foreign countries. The Bureau of Public Information has the most extensive collection of pamphlets and reports concerned with local and state government in the United States. These features do not include many additional items such as the Agricultural Experiment Station and the Agricultural Extension Service, which are among the largest and most complex in the nation.

This brief summary, showing a few of the unique and outstanding features of some of our state colleges and universities, reveals the tremendous part they are playing in our national economy and welfare. Probably no single group of interests could point to such an outstanding record. Even though there has been emphasis on basic research, applied research has not had the recognition it deserves in many privately controlled institutions. The contributions to applied research in our state colleges and universities benefit the average citizen, directly and indirectly, to a degree far beyond the knowledge of the general public. The scholarship necessary to achieve these results deserves higher commendation than it has received. A catalogue of the accomplishments of the state colleges and universities, both in research and in maintenance of high levels of instruction in certain departments, presents a list unrivaled in American higher education. It is easy, in the separate states, to think only in terms of one state university and one state college; but when one tries to envision the achievements of all these state institutions, constantly carrying on intensive work that affects the life of every citizen, he begins to realize that the destiny of America is directly concerned with the adequate support of the state colleges and universities. We must see that no diversion of funds is allowed to interfere with the present great investments in these institutions, investments that should increase, rather than decrease, during the years to come. The future of higher education in a democracy, which aims to raise the level of living and of mental outreach for all individuals, must not be endangered by any consideration which would handicap or hinder the state colleges and universities in their widespread effort to serve the needs of all.

PART II

THE points covered briefly in this section were of particular interest to President Truman's Commission on Higher Education, and much of the material was referred to the Commission for its use. The subjects include (1) relations between boards and presidents, faculty, non-faculty personnel and alumni, (2) methods of financing institutions, their assets and how held, (3) administrative functions, (4) increases in tuition rates; (5) faculty salary scales and increases, (6) audio-visual aids in higher education, (7) membership of faculties in professional associations and how financed, (8) relations of the institutions to Congress.

___ 1 ___

RELATIONS BETWEEN BOARDS OF RE-GENTS AND PRESIDENTS, FACULTY, NON-FACULTY PERSONNEL, AND ALUMNI[1]

TWO principles should govern the relations between higher educational administrators and the boards of control. The first is that the board clearly understands the powers conferred upon it and sees that those powers are exercised intelligently and to the fullest extent. Throughout the country, college and university boards are responsible for the financial conduct of institutions, the selection of college and university presidents, determining educational procedures and policies, passing on faculty appointments, approving educational standards, and for seeing that politics are not allowed to interfere with the orderly conduct of the institutions. This constitutes the framework in which the president carries on his administration. The second is that the president should be held responsible for all details of administration, and boards should confine themselves to the powers reposed in them and not interfere with administrative details, unless a situation develops in which the administration shows itself incapable of conducting the institution. In such a case the governing board should have the courage and stamina either to outline policies under which the administrator can operate effectively or to request the resignation of the administrator and select in his place one in whose initiative and ability the board has confidence. Members of governing boards can make themselves a nuisance and a handicap to an institution by interfering unnecessarily in the details of administration. In organ-

[1] See Table 11 and 12.

izations as large and as complicated as the great state universities or the modern state colleges it is necessary that the president enjoy the right to exercise a certain amount of initiative. There are two types of college presidents, those who are autocratic and those who are democratic in their approach. The present trend is toward the democratic type of handling administrative problems. More than once in the history of American education, institutions have been handicapped by presidents' autocratic exercise of power. It is indeed fortunate that this type of administrator is rapidly passing from the picture and that the relation between governing boards and presidents is, more and more, one of mutual respect and confidence.

Various states have drawn up manuals [2] explicitly defining the powers of governing boards and the powers to be exercised by the presidents of the institutions. A study of these manuals reveals that the line of demarcation between board powers and the authority of presidents is being more and more clearly defined.

There is considerable variation throughout the country in the extent of power that may be exercised by presidents, irrespective of their boards. In one state, where the joint-board system exists, no president of a state institution is allowed to confer with the board in the presence of the president of any other state institution. This state also has a regulation forbidding the appearance of presidents before legislative appropriations committees, except when especially invited. This places an arbitrary power in the board and puts the president at a distinct disadvantage. It allows the board to determine, without joint conferences of all the presidents, the allocation of funds to the various institutions. It also prevents any appeal to legislative appropriations committees from the decision of the board. Under this system injustices have occurred.

In other states, especially where the separate-board system prevails, presidents undertake the chief responsibility for the presentation of their respective budgets to legislative appropriations committees. This arrangement, too, is weak, in that it places an unfair responsibility on the president. The governing board

2 See list at end of chapter.

itself should be so familiar with the budget as to be able to present it to legislative committees. If a president, through no fault of his own, is unable to persuade the legislature to grant sufficient funds to operate, the governing board should bear its full share of responsibility for the failure. In some states board members are not even in attendance when presidents are called upon to defend the proposed budgets for their institutions. There is a growing tendency to have the budget presented by board members, with the assistance and co-operation of the president and of such other administrative authorities as they may see fit to call upon.

In a majority of the states, even where the president exercises rather wide initiative, any action he takes is subject to confirmation later by the board. It is therefore exceedingly important that there should be complete understanding between the president and his governing board of the powers of the board itself, and of such administrative freedom as the president is allowed to enjoy.

In seventy-two institutions the presidents take action between meetings, subject to confirmation by the board. In seventeen institutions the president possesses much wider authority. The general policy is for the board to determine procedures and to leave matters of administrative detail to the administrative officials. Where this policy holds, it is rare that presidential actions are reversed by the board. In one privately controlled institution the president acts independently of the governing board. Another state university reports that the president is practically never overruled in matters of administration. At still another state university "the board does not confirm actions except when the president acts in an emergency." At a Western state school the president secures confirmation from the regents by phone, an exceedingly undesirable practice. In another state, where the joint board system prevails, the only check the board has on the commissioner depends on whether the board can prove any of his actions to be clearly illegal. At a great Eastern state university "only occasionally is the board called upon to confirm actions of the president."

However, in most cases the board determines the procedure, and matters of administrative detail are left to the president and his staff. It seems wise that every state should clearly define the division of authority between the governing boards and the presidents and their assistants. It might be well, also, that a study be made of the qualifications that should be required of candidates for higher educational positions. The tendency in some states to select a retired military official, or be influenced in its choice by campus politics, or be forced by pressure groups to select a candidate representing some special interest, should be studiously avoided.

When it comes to board contacts with faculty, students, and alumni, the original opinion of the author was that such contacts should be encouraged. However, a study of the conditions existing at the eighty-nine colleges and universities considered in this report leads me to revise that opinion. The less personal contact there is between board members and faculty members, non-faculty personnel, students and alumni, the better. It is of the utmost importance that board members should not be influenced by personal considerations when passing on promotions, changes in rank or salary, or new appointments. Any effort by faculty members to influence the decision of the regents for selfish reasons should be strongly resented and should react against the interest of the faculty member involved. Promotions and appointments should be definitely on the basis of merit; therefore, the more the board knows of the actual achievements of a man and the less it is guided by personal friendships, the better chance there is for a wise appointment and a strong faculty. There is a trend in some institutions today to have more faculty participation in recommendations for appointments and promotions. Dr. Beck recommends this in his report. Unfortunately, in the institutions where the faculties have considerable power in naming deans or recommending changes of rank, the procedure has not always worked well. While there is good reason for faculty consultation, the final responsibility does not rest on the faculty itself. As one president of a great university said, "If a faculty committee recommends the person to be named as dean of that particular faculty, or recommends new appointments, and it happens to be in a rather weak division or department of the institution, it is almost impossible for that department or division to become stronger as long as the faculty of that division has the power to recommend for deanships or for the higher ranks." It would seem to be a wiser plan, in order to encourage faculty co-operation, to provide a more elastic system, whereby the faculty might nominate three names for a vacancy, the administration name three, and the governing board select one of those nominated, or make an independent selection if the name of an especially outstanding man from outside the faculty should be suggested. This would give full opportunity to secure the best man available, entirely apart from personal ambition and from the not always benign influence of campus politics.

As for board contacts with non-faculty personnel, such as building service employes, engineers and electricians, it should be the duty of the governing board to hear and evaluate legitimate complaints, except that in the case of faculty members, non-faculty personnel, and students, the normal channel of approach should be through the president. Machinery for appeal should be provided if the president's office can clearly be proved to be a "dead end." However, the failure of a president's office to transmit to the board any complaint is far less frequent than are instances of grave trouble resulting from immediate, and frequently unjustified, attempts to go to the board over the head of the duly constituted authorities. Such a practice causes a tremendous amount of misunderstanding, especially when the information thus presented is inaccurate and there had been no competent investigation before the complaint was brought to the attention of the governing board.

In their enthusiasm, students are sometimes exceedingly critical of a college administration and do not bestir themselves to any extent to determine the actual facts involved. On more than one campus there has been considerable confusion because of ill-advised actions by uninformed student leaders. In a number of institutions there is no contact between board members and students whatever; in others, there is an informal relationship or very little contact. This is true of seventy-three institutions out of the eighty-nine visited. As in the case of faculty and non-faculty personnel, the board should always hear student complaints; but, once more, the normal channel of approach should be through the president after careful investigation.

In regard to alumni contacts, a few institutions have alumni representation on the board, although usually it is a minority representation. In the majority of state colleges and universities little attention is paid to whether board members are alumni or not. Too much alumni representation leads to inbreeding. The presence on the board of graduates of other institutions who have a working knowledge of education would seem to be a desirable arrangement. A strong alumni organization can be of tremendous help or a serious handicap to a university. Unfortunately, the major interest of all too many alumni is in the athletic prowess of the university's teams, rather than in the quality of its educational work. This overemphasized interest in athletics sometimes results in pressure which is hardly defensible morally. There are also alumni whose major interest is political rather than educational, and they sometimes attempt to exert political pressure to the disadvantage of the institution. As in the case of the students, the alumni are frequently the victims of rumors and misinformation, and not being in a position to know all the facts, make statements which are derogatory and unfair to the institution, its board, and its president. As a natural step in the effort to avoid misunderstandings in board and alumni relations, there is a growing tendency to have the executive secretary of the alumni association appointed by the president and confirmed by the board, and his salary paid by the institution itself. He thus becomes a member of the administrative staff and as such is in constant touch with the details of administration and can adequately present necessary facts to dissatisfied alumni, and the desires of the alumni to the board and the administration.

It would seem wise, therefore, for the contacts between board members and faculty, non-faculty personnel, students and alumni, to be limited to cases based on necessity. It is important that groups with legitimate complaints should have an avenue of approach to hearings, by invitation or request. The normal channel for suggestions and complaints should be through the president's office. However, provision should be made for appeal in case the president's office fails to function satisfactorily in this duty.

LIST OF MANUALS

1. Provisions of the Constitution and Code of the State of Alabama pertaining to the Alabama Polytechnic Institute.
2. Bylaws and Standing Orders of the Regents of the University of California.
3. College Regulations of the Citadel, Military College of South Carolina.
4. Clemson Agricultural College Bulletin, Vol. 21, No. 1, 1925.
5. Statement of Principles, Governing Duties, Responsibilities and Freedom of Regents, the President, Deans, etc. University of Colorado.
6. Laws Relating to Cornell University. 1945.
7. Constitution, Florida State University. 1945-46.
8. Education and Florida's Future. Florida Citizens Committee on Education. Tallahassee, 1947.
9. Statutes of the Georgia School of Technology, 1945.
10. Bylaws of the Board of Regents, University System of Georgia, 1944.
11. History and Government of Harvard University. May, 1946.
12. University of Illinois Statutes, 1936.
13. Regulations for the Organization of Louisiana State University. 1945.
14. University of Minnesota, Bylaws of the Board of Regents, 1939.
15. Opinion of the Supreme Court of Minnesota on Relation of University and Board of Regents, 1928.
16. Mississippi Study of Higher Education, 1945.
17. Bylaws and Rules of the Board of Regents. University of Nebraska, 1944.
18. Digest of Laws and Statutes passed by the Michigan Legislature concerning the University of Michigan.
19. A Survey of the Powers and Duties of the Board of Trustees of the University of North Carolina. 1941.
20. Third Biennial Report. Oklahoma State Regents for Higher Education. 1946.
21. Co-ordinated Control of Higher Education in Oregon, Charles D. Byrne, 1940.

22. Co-operation between Tuskegee Institute and the State of Alabama, F. D. Patterson, 1943.
23. Laws and Regulations, University of Utah, 1932.
24. Virginia Military Institute Regulations, Part 1, 1938.
25. Manual, Board of Visitors, Virginia Polytechnic Institute, 1944.
26. Acts and Joint Resolutions of the General Assembly of the Commonwealth of Virginia, Extra Session, 1945.
27. University of Wisconsin, Bylaws of the Board of Regents, 1939.
28. Yale Corporation Charter and Legislation. 1938.
29. Yale Corporation Bylaws and Regulations, 1945.

2

METHODS BY WHICH INSTITUTIONS ARE FINANCED; ASSETS AND HOW HELD[1]

THE TOTAL assets of eighty-one of the institutions visited in this study amount to $1,611,294,667. The methods by which these assets are held vary in the different states. At the privately controlled institutions the assets normally are held by a body corporate. In the state institutions, in some cases, the land, buildings, equipment, and income are held in the name of the state, while in others, title to these properties is vested in the board. There are thirty colleges and universities of those visited where all the property, endowment, and income is held by the board as a body corporate. In some cases there is a divided title, the land being held by the state and the endowment and income being held in the name of the board. In still others, such as the University of California and the University of California at Los Angeles, all the assets are held by the board itself. At the Citadel in South Carolina, everything is held by the state. In Florida, the holding corporation is the State Board of Education. At the University of Kentucky the board of trustees holds title. This is also true of Louisiana State University. At Maine ninety per cent of the buildings and lands are held by the state, ten per cent by the trustees; the endowment is in the name of the trustees, and there is a holding corporation called the University of Maine Foundation which has title to $100,000. At Indiana the major holdings are in the name of the board with the balance held by the state. In Iowa management and control of assets is under the State Board of Education. In Kansas they are held by the state. All the

[1] See Table 14.

assets of Michigan State College are in the name of the State Board of Agriculture, while at the University of Michigan title is held by the regents as a corporation. At Missouri the trustees are called curators and they hold title to all assets; while in Montana the assets are all held by the state. In Nebraska title is held by the regents as a corporation, and in Massachusetts State all assets are held by the state except a trustee endowment fund. In Mississippi the assets of all the state schools are held by the state. In North Carolina $12,000,000 in assets is held by the state and $1,200,000 by various foundations. In Oregon everything is held in the name of the state. At Rutgers, with assets of $28,000,000, $3,500,000 are held by the state and $25,000,000 in the name of a self-perpetuating board. The assets of the teachers' colleges in California are all held in the name of the state. These instances are sufficient to show that there is considerable diversity among the agencies holding the assets in the various state institutions. Of the eighty-nine visited, there are seventeen schools where the assets are held by the state and the board jointly.

Involved in any financial consideration of the colleges and universities is the method by which funds are appropriated, whether by lump sum or by what is known as "line item," whether directly to the institution or through a state office. The effectiveness of the operation of state colleges and universities can be seriously influenced by the manner in which the budget is prepared for presentation to the legislature and to the governor. There are two general methods by which this is done. One is known as the "lump-sum appropriation," which is a capital sum appropriated to be expended at the discretion of the governing board as need may arise. This allows some flexibility, in that, as the years pass, required increased expenditures can be authorized by the regents when new developments take place between legislative sessions. If money is allocated for specific objects and the material and equipment necessary for them are not available, then the money can be used for some immediate, pressing need in carrying on the work of the institution.

The other system is known as "line item." Under it every specific item must be listed for presentation to the legislature.

This goes so far as to include even postage in the various departments and divisions of the institution. Under this system funds earmarked or designated cannot be used for any purpose other than that named. It makes no allowance whatever for changes which may take place, such as the need for additional housing, the opportunity to purchase needed equipment at a favorable figure, increased faculty for departments in which there is a heavy enrollment, and for meeting similar problems. The result is that any institution which operates under the "line-item" system operates under a distinct handicap. If boards of trustees and regents are worthy of any trust and confidence at all, they should have authority to make necessary expenditures as they arise. Meeting at least monthly, in most cases, they have an intimate knowledge, along with the administration, of what expenditures are necessary and what are not. This knowledge cannot be attained by a governor or legislature in the course of a half-hour hearing once every two years. The "line-item" system apparently places a control on a board in its financial expenditures. Actually, it is outmoded, and the institutions operating under the "lump-sum" system are in position to make educational progress far more rapidly than those that are handicapped by the "line-item" arrangement. Then, too, under the "line-item" system a pressure group in a legislature can force designated appropriations for specific purposes at the expense of other more important needs of the institution.

It is interesting to note that of the eighty-nine institutions visited, eighty operate under the "lump-sum" appropriation, the others under the "line-item" system. In a few states this "lump sum" is under large heads, such as maintenance, operations, and capital outlay. It would seem wise that the states whose colleges and universities are still handicapped by the "line-item" method give careful consideration to a study of the increased effectiveness made possible by lump-sum grants.

Another factor involved in this has to do with the fees and earnings of the various institutions. In some states fees are retained by the institution, to be expended at the discretion of the board entirely independently of appropriations by the state legislature. The same is true of such earnings as come from contracts for research services and the sale of agricultural products, and from other income which is earned by the institution itself. In some other states, however, these fees and earnings have to be deducted from any appropriation granted by the state legislature. Naturally, the institution which retains the right to expend its own fees and earnings has a definite advantage over the institution where those fees and earnings are deducted from the appropriation made by the legislature. Of the colleges and universities visited, forty-six retain their fees and twenty-one do not. In one or two instances fees are reserved for building fund purposes but cannot be used without authorization by the governor.

There is considerable variation in the method by which the funds finally reach the institution after being appropriated. There is a growing tendency to appropriate directly to the institution rather than to a state treasurer or a state auditor. This is particularly true where appropriations are of the lump-sum variety rather than by the line-item method. Of the institutions visited, funds are appropriated directly to the institutions to be disbursed by them in fifty-four cases. Where the money has to come through a state auditor or a state treasurer's office, there is frequently considerable confusion and delay in completing transactions in a businesslike manner. Any institution which has had to operate under the system whereby vouchers have to be made out and sent to the state treasurer's office and approved in conformity with the line-item appropriation knows the severe handicap under which such an institution operates. It would seem wise, therefore, for institutions which do not receive their funds directly, perhaps in quarterly installments, to investigate the more efficient operation possible under direct appropriations rather than under a complicated system whereby every single item has to be approved by a clerk in an auditor's office, or in a state treasurer's office, before the expenditure can be authorized.

3

ADMINISTRATIVE FUNCTIONS[1]

I N THE ORGANIZATION of administrative functions staff assignments are fairly uniform. Finances, in most cases, are handled by the president and the business manager or treasurer. There are a few exceptions to this, such as Amherst College, privately controlled; the University of Arizona, the University of Arkansas, where there is a vice-president for finance; the University of Southern California, privately controlled, where there is a financial vice-president; the Citadel, where there is a quartermaster; Clemson, where finances are handled by the business manager and treasurer; Georgia School of Technology, the University of Georgia, Harvard, privately controlled; the University of Kentucky, Louisiana State University, University of Maine, Michigan State College, and the University of Michigan, where there is a vice-president in charge of finance. At Minnesota a vice-president is in charge of business administration. Other exceptions are the Mississippi state colleges, Missouri, where there is a vice-president in charge of business operations; University of Nebraska, New York State College for Teachers, where there is a chief account clerk; North Carolina State College, where finances are handled by the assistant controller; Pennsylvania State College, Purdue, where there is a vice-president and controller; Rhode Island State College, the University of Tennessee, Texas A. & M., University of Texas, Tuskegee, privately controlled; University of Vermont, V.M.I., V.P.I., University of Wyoming, and Yale, privately controlled.

The finances of all the others are handled by the president and the business manager. Without exception, budgets are pre-

1 See Table 11.

pared by recommendations from the departments, passed on by the president and submitted to the board for approval, and then submitted to the legislature. The usual arrangements for faculty appointments provide for conferences with department heads and deans before nominations are submitted to the governing board for approval. Non-faculty personnel policy is handled by the president's office, except in some of the larger institutions having a personnel officer or a business manager to whom this duty is assigned. Usually, academic standards are determined by the faculty, the council of deans or university senate and the president, and submitted to the board for approval. Entrance requirements are usually set by a faculty committee or academic council and administered by the registrar.

There is some variation in public relations. Some state institutions feel a hesitancy about setting up a public relations department, on the ground that a state college or university should not have to use public funds to advertise its work. Where there is no public relations officer, there is usually a news bureau which functions in somewhat the same manner. Public relations constitute one of the most important contacts a college or university can have. It is recommended therefore that colleges and universities without a functioning and effective public relations office study the situation where such offices exist, with a view to maintaining adequate public relations.

Under the head of student welfare, a definite trend can be noted. There was a time when the management of student affairs was placed in the care of a dean of men and dean of women, each possessing equal authority. The present movement is toward the establishment of a director of student affairs, with an assistant who acts as chief counsellor or dean of men, and a woman who works in the same capacity with women students. In colleges where the office of a separate dean of women has been firmly established for a number of years some difficulty has been experienced in bringing about this change. However, the general trend seems to be in this direction, and a majority of the institutions visited have already either a director, with assistants, in charge of men and women students or are planning to introduce this type of organization.

There is little difference between publicly and privately controlled institutions in the organization of administrative functions. Some of the larger universities provide for a president or chancellor, with a vice-president in charge of financial operations and an educational vice-president. The importance of public relations is leading toward the establishment of such an office with the person in charge acting as a special assistant to the president. What differences in the function of administrators exist are largely the differences due to the size of staff necessary for a very large institution as compared with a smaller one, where fewer are required for the administrative staff.

_ 4 _

INCREASES IN TUITION RATES[1]

PRESIDENT TRUMAN'S COMMISSION on Higher Education was concerned about increases in tuition, particularly in state colleges and universities, on the ground that such increases may defeat the purpose of land-grant aid to education. There is no question in anyone's mind but that, with the increased cost of living, the cost of operating institutions which have to house and feed a considerable number of students has shown a marked rise. Added to this have been necessary increases to faculty and non-faculty salaries, causing a further rise in operating costs. The number of institutions, both private and public, which have shown no increase are exceedingly few. Out of eighty-four institutions studied in regard to this aspect, there are only seven which report no increase in tuition and fees. Some of the state colleges and universities, particularly in the South, are guilty of a gentle hypocrisy in that state law forbids the collection of tuition, but provides for a matriculation fee, which, in some instances, is higher than the tuition charged in other states. The increases themselves vary considerably. There has been an especially large increase in the charge for out-of-state students. There has been a smaller, but rather general, increase, for in-state students.

There is also a definite trend toward all-inclusive fees rather than for a separate tuition fee with extra charges for health fees, student activities, student publications, athletic fees, library fees, laboratory fees, and the various other charges which formerly were added to tuition. The increases range from a slight increase of $20 a year for in-state to increases of from $30 to over $100 for

[1] See Table 16.

out-of-state students. Naturally, there are higher charges for special subjects, such as law, engineering, and medicine. In some of the privately controlled colleges, there has been no increase in the last five years, but there is a plan to increase the fees next year. In the privately controlled departments of Cornell there was an increase from $400 to $500 and in the state-controlled colleges of Cornell, the increase was from $200 to $300. At the University of Florida there was an increase of $100 for in-state students and $140 for out-of-state. At Georgia the increase was $20 for in-state and an increase of $160 for out-of-state students. At the University of Connecticut there was an increase of $12.50 for in-state and $50 for out-of-state students. There was a $25 increase for in-state at the University of Maine and a $30 increase for out-of-state students. At the University of Miami, largely a private institution, there was a 40 per cent increase in tuition from $250 to $360. At the University of New Hampshire there was a $10 increase for in-state students, and $100 increase for out-of-state. New Mexico also had a $10 a term increase for in-state, and a $25 a term increase for out-of-state students. At the University of the South, a private institution, there was a slight increase in tuition. South Carolina had a $10 per term increase for in-state students, and a $25 increase per term for out-of-state students. The University of Southern California, privately controlled, had a tuition increase of thirteen per cent for all students, making the present tuition $434 for a full program of two semesters, with law and engineering $450, and medicine, $600. Stanford had an increase from $444 annual fee to $500. Tennessee had an increase of $5 a quarter for in-state, and $30 to $75 for out-of-state students. Vanderbilt, a privately controlled institution, increased its fees about one-third in the various schools and departments. The University of Virginia had an increase of $25 for in-state students for a nine-months' session, and $50 for non-Virginians. At Virginia Military Institute the tuition was increased from $200 in 1940 to $300 in 1947. Virginia Polytechnic Institute had an increase of $10 per quarter for Virginians and $20 for out-of-state students. At Yale there has been an increase of fifty per cent in tuition fees in the past five years.

It is to be noted that the privately controlled institutions make no distinction between in-state and out-of-state students.

A study of the tables in Part III will show that the amount of increase in tuition in state colleges and universities has been considerably less than the actual costs of operation to the state and to the institution. The increases in the privately controlled colleges and universities have, of necessity, been greater than the increases in institutions dependent on public funds. Some of the states have taken advantage of the G. I. benefits in order to make a rather unreasonable increase for out-of-state students. The general conclusion is that the increases have been slight compared with actual increases in operating costs. The increases in tuition are not at all in line with the increases in faculty salaries, as will be indicated by a study of the faculty salary increases.[2]

Unless the states can continue to absorb the vast increase in operating costs, it would seem wise to consider an even further increase in fees, particularly for in-state students. No study is available of the amount contributed by the state toward the education of the individual in the state colleges and universities, but it would seem, in most instances, to be in the neighborhood of from forty-five to fifty per cent. Increased operating costs, increased enrollments, and the need for new buildings and equipment, the appropriations necessary to maintain adequate state colleges and universities, all seem to point to the need for some other source of income. A study of the tables in Part III suggest that great care should be given to consideration of the question of subsidies, whether from federal or state sources, to privately controlled and publicly controlled institutions of higher learning.

[2] See Table 17.

SALARY INCREASES SINCE PEARL HARBOR[1]

T HE PUBLIC has awakened recently to the exceedingly low level of salaries in the teaching profession. Appropriations have been made in the various states to increase salaries for teachers on the elementary and secondary school level and also on college and university faculties. This increase has been so marked as to place the state colleges and universities, for the first time, on a plane where they can compete with some of the more highly endowed institutions in securing the services of expert instructors. The increase has been general all over the country and in the institutions visited. Those which have not granted a considerable increase in salaries prove rare exceptions. The faculty increases range from a flat average percentage for all ranks of ten per cent to increases as high as forty-five per cent. The general pattern suggests a considerably higher increase for men and women in the lower ranks, the increase being graduated, so that higher salary and rank receive less increase by percentage. For instance, in one institution everyone above $3000 has been raised twenty-six per cent and everyone under $3000, thirty-two per cent. At another large state university there was, roughly, a fifty per cent increase for instructors to a thirty-three and one-third per cent increase for professors. In still another, where the increases were based on merit, there was a forty per cent increase for instructors and a twenty per cent increase for assistant professors and professors. Some other institutions gave flat cost-of-living increases. One had a flat increase of $180 and then $240, making no differ-

[1] See Table 17.

entiation among various ranks. Another large state university gave a blanket increase of ten per cent to all staff members whose annual salaries were $3000 or less, with merit increases to those above $3000. In 1945, additional increases averaging fourteen and one-half per cent were given to about ninety-five per cent of the staff on a merit basis. In September, 1946, another merit increase was given, those receiving it averaging eleven per cent to twenty-four per cent of the academic staff. The policy for 1947 was thirty per cent on the first $4000, twenty per cent on the next $1000, ten per cent on the next $1000.

At a neighboring university the increases were: heads of departments, thirty per cent; professors, thirty-seven per cent; associate professors, thirty-eight per cent; assistant professors, thirty-six per cent, and instructors, whatever was necessary to secure their services. In a Mid-western institution the increases were fourteen and three-tenths per cent for the president, twenty and three-tenths per cent for the deans, thirty-nine and three-tenths per cent for professors, sixty per cent for associate professors, sixty-six and six-tenths per cent for assistant professors, and forty-two and eight-tenths per cent for instructors. This scale is rather out of line, in that instructors did not receive a proportionate increase as compared with higher ranks. A Southern institution increased salaries ten per cent for all under $2000, seven and one-half per cent for those between $2000 and $2500, two per cent for those between $3000 and $4000, and nothing for those over $4000. To all these increases was added a flat $400 a year cost-of-living appropriation for every employe.

A column in the tables in Part III gives the average increase in salaries, covering all ranks. The instances recorded in the preceding paragraphs are to cite examples which are rather general; they show the trend to larger increases in the lower ranks and smaller increases to the higher salaried. All the above increases were granted after Pearl Harbor, and refer only to faculty members.

The cost of operations has risen notably, not only because of these faculty increases but because of increases to non-faculty personnel. Information was not secured at the various institutions on the percentage of increases granted to building-service employes, clerks, typists, and librarians. However, at one Far Western institution it is possible to compare the percentage of the non-faculty increases with the increases granted to faculty members. The average salaries paid in 1940 compared with the year 1947, with the percentage of increases, are as follows:

Faculty [1]	1940	1947	Per Cent Increase
Professor	$3578	$5222	45.9
Associate Professor	3161	4580	44.9
Assistant Professor	2526	4003	58.5
Instructor	2110	3328	57.7
Non-Faculty [2]			
Housemaids	960	2388	148.8
Janitors	1200	2388	99.0
Assistant Engineers	1380	2916	111.3
Engineers	1740	3180	82.8
Carpenters	2209	3180	44.0
Plumbers	2100	3180	51.4
Electricians	1550	3180	105.2
Clerks and Typists	1200	1920	60.0
Librarians	1692	3400	100.9

[1] Averages were developed by sampling within each classification.
[2] Averages do not include compensations paid senior employes and foremen.
This schedule shows a considerably higher general increase for non-faculty employes, a condition which probably holds largely throughout the country.

President Truman's Commission on Higher Education was particularly interested in determining whether there had been any appreciable increase in teaching-hour load which would more than compensate for the salary increases given. Almost without exception, there has been no appreciable increase since Pearl Harbor in teaching-hour load, meaning the number of hours each faculty member spends on the lecture platform or in the laboratory. However, there has been a very considerable increase in student-hour load, that is the number of students for whom the faculty member is responsible. This, of course, means more experiments to be supervised, more papers to be marked, and a resultant increase in the time required for an instructor to do this extra work. The figures submitted as the ideal arrangement of the ratio of faculty to students varies very considerably. Dr. George D. Strayer of Columbia has recently made a study of the higher educational system in one state,[2] and recommends that there should be one faculty member to every ten students. He claims that the national ratio is one faculty member to eleven students. In the state studied the ratio is actually one faculty member to 21.3 students. On the basis of about 6000 students, this institution would need 260 additional faculty members to meet the national ratio, and 313 to meet the Strayer ratio. On the basis of 7500 students, the institution would need 405 additional faculty members to meet the national ratio and 473 additional members to meet the Strayer ratio. Taking into consideration the salary increases, an average of at least thirty per cent over-all throughout the entire country, the addition of instructors on the basis suggested is almost prohibitive. There is no question but that better work is done in small classes. However, except in intensive research, it does seem as if the ratio of one faculty member to ten students is rather excessive.

This leads us to the subject of the size of classes, which are considerably larger because of increased enrollments. Many of the larger colleges and universities, unable to recruit additional competent faculty members, have as high as 1000 to 1500 students in certain lecture courses. It is argued that it is better for students to be in a class of such dimensions with a renowned "name" professor than it is for them to be divided into smaller groups under less known instructors. There are even instances in which mechanical aids, such as transcripts, radio equipment, etc., have been used to take care of abnormally large classes. Oversized groups, even when an attempt is made to break them down into sections and place them in the care of an instructor for certain periods between lectures by "name" professors, are still entirely too large for good scholarly work. The only solution of this problem will be found when additional competent teachers are available and further funds are appropriated to pay their salaries. It seems safe to assume that, as a rule, students in lecture classes of more than forty to fifty, at the most, do not receive as good instruction as those in smaller groups.

In the third part of this book are tables indicating present

[2] Budget Request, The State College of Washington, 1947-1949.

salary scales in the various institutions visited, along with the average percentage of increase in salaries for all faculty members. In order that institutions with less generous resources may not be victimized by colleges, private or public, which have funds available to pay the larger salaries, these institutions are listed by numeral rather than by name. It will be possible for the representatives of any institution to identify their own school and to gain some idea of how it compares with other schools of about the same enrollment. The divisions of the chart group institutions according to those having an enrollment of under 3000, those from 3000 to 6000, those from 6000 to 10,000 and those over 10,000. It is interesting to note that the salary scales in the section made up of colleges with an enrollment of over 10,000, are, as a rule, considerably higher than those in the group under 3000 or even between 3000 and 6000. This information should be of great value to those responsible for preparing budgets to present to appropriation committees. A geographical distribution of these colleges would also prove interesting, in that the salaries paid in certain parts of the South are somewhat lower than those paid in the Middle West and other parts of the country. A careful study of these tables will indicate to the governing boards and administrations of institutions whether their present scale is in line with that of other institutions of approximately the same enrollment.

6

AUDIO-VISUAL AIDS IN HIGHER EDUCATION

DURING the war period training films and film strips were produced in great quantities. The War Department's basic field manual, FM 21-5,[1] considered films to be "among the most valuable and most modern aids to instruction" but that they were "not designed to be the sole means of instruction in a subject." There was the same high increase in the use of visual aids in training for the naval service, the Bureau of Aeronautics, and the Army Signal Corps, which later expanded into the Army Pictorial Service.

Emergencies produce action. There has been considerable agitation for a greater use of visual aids in education in recent years. However, because of the high cost of producing films and resistance by certain teachers to the use of such aids, it was not until the war that any decisive action was taken. An American Council on Education report[2] says, "The Armed Forces during the past four years have produced more than sixfold the number of filmstrips as have ever been produced before for strictly educational purposes." These films are of value not only for technical instruction, but for morale building, and they are needed today for establishing a sound moral foundation for higher education.

The extent of the use of this material in war training, largely conducted in the colleges and universities of the country, can be estimated from the fact that over four million film showings were made before army ground and service forces in continental

[1] *United States War Department Military Training—Basic Field Manual*, Washington Government Printing Office, 1941.

[2] *Audio-Visual Aids in the Armed Services*, Miles and Spain, American Council on Education, 1947.

United States alone during the two years from July 1, 1943, to June 30, 1945. The report says, "If the Army Air Forces, Navy and overseas audiences were added to these film showings, the service probably did more than twice the amount of movie business in 1943-1945 which Hollywood had done for the entire country before the war, in comparison with the size of the potential audiences." It is to be remembered that these films were largely instructional and educational. If they have this value in time of crisis, the neglect of the use of visual aids in higher education in time of peace suggests that a valuable instrument is not being used, an instrument which could be of inestimable aid to higher education. A survey was conducted of men who had attended Class A schools where such films were used. This questionnaire was given to 794 men. Among the questions were as follows:

What do you think about the use of training films in
    your school program?

	Per cent
There were too many of them.	6
There were about the right number.	52
There were not enough of them.	42

What about the use of slides (still pictures)?

There were too many of them.	14
There were about the right number.	52
There were not enough of them.	34

What do you think about the length of time spent in
    lectures?

It was too much.	24
It was about right.	63
It was too little.	13

Do you think that the use of training films in your
    program helped you learn your job?

Yes, all or most of them were helpful.	71
Yes, about half of them were helpful.	23
No, most of them were not helpful.	6

Do you think that slides were helpful?

Yes, all or most of them were helpful.	52
Yes, about half of them were helpful.	33
No, most of them were not helpful.	15

The study of the use of films in military training supports the idea that films can and do affect emotional attitudes. Further, preparation of a class for seeing a film, with the opportunity of discussion afterward, has high educational value. There was apparent general approval of the extensive employment of visual aids, and instructors who used them believe that movies and filmstrips shorten a training time, result in greater learning, and stimulate interest and motivation. Veterans in colleges today very largely endorse a greater use of audio-visual aids than is now characteristic of civilian education.

The following statement from the summary report on the motion picture project sponsored by the American Council on Education is significant in general education: "With all the experience that has been assimilated in the evaluation of hundreds of motion pictures in general education under actual classroom conditions and in a wide variety of curriculum situations, one can only conclude that in the use of motion pictures in education the surface has hardly been scratched."

In the various institutions included in this survey, the more progressive ones are giving increased attention to the use of visual aids as an adjunct to education. These aids can never take the place of the teacher himself. There has been a certain sensitiveness among some faculty members that the wide use of visual aids would mean a reduction in the number of teachers and affect professional standing. This has been particularly true of language teachers in certain areas. Exhaustive tests conducted by the Motion Picture Association reveal that in the subjects considered, covering a wide field, the effectiveness of good teachers is markedly increased by the use of visual aids, and that the time required for learning is considerably shortened.

Governing boards should devote serious study to the use of visual aids in college and university classes.

It has been suggested that if the colleges and universities had at their disposal the vast sums available to the Army and Navy in the production and use of visual aids they would rapidly take advantage of the opportunity thus offered for improved instruction. The cost of producing educational films is exceedingly high, considering the ability of the average institution to pay for the rental or purchase of prints. Included in the budgets of the colleges and universities should be more generous appropriations for the purchase or rental of educational films, and even for the production of the films themselves. Some institutions, such as Ohio State, have already entered the production field in a limited way. The value of visual aids has been so clearly established that serious consideration should be given by governing boards and administrative authorities to their wider use in colleges and universities both publicly and privately controlled.

7

FACULTY MEMBERSHIPS IN PROFES-
SIONAL ASSOCIATIONS[1]

PRESIDENT TRUMAN'S Commission on Higher Education was also very much interested in encouraging active membership of faculty members in professional associations in their particular fields. It is of the utmost importance that a teacher keep abreast of the latest developments in his specialty. Probably the least expensive way, in terms of both money and time, to obtain this objective is for teachers to attend, with some regularity, meetings of professional associations where the latest developments in their particular fields are presented. Yet even with the salary increases granted, the average faculty member is not usually in a position where he can afford the necessary expense for attending these meetings.

Now there is an almost universal trend toward more generous provision for the attendance of faculty members at professional meetings. The general policy in most institutions is to pay the expenses of faculty members who present papers at these meetings, who go as official representatives of their institution, or who are officers of the professional organization. In some states, however, there are very definite restrictions on expenditures of this type. Only transportation expenses are allowed, perhaps with a limit on the expense incurred each day of travel. One institution reported that it had spent $5000 for this purpose during the year and seemed to feel it was doing well. Another president stated that over $35,000 had been expended for this purpose the same year and he said he did not feel that this expenditure was high enough in view of the value received. Of course, there are some faculty members who would spend the major portion of their time attending professional meetings, and there must be some restriction against the abuse of this privilege. It would seem logical for every institution to adopt a policy which at least provides that faculty members who are invited to address professional meetings, those officially designated to represent the institution, and those who are officers of associations, should be provided with adequate funds to enable them to attend, with the understanding that on their return they share what they have learned with faculty members who were not able to attend. The table in the third part of this book indicates the general practice in this regard.

8

RELATIONS OF INSTITUTIONS TO THE NATIONAL CONGRESS

LEGISLATION is introduced from time to time in Congress which is of tremendous significance to both publicly and privately controlled higher education. The privately controlled institutions have little direct contact, as such, with members of Congress. When the question of federal subsidy arises there probably will be more contact between the two. The state colleges and universities, on the other hand, have much closer relations with members of Congress. Most of them keep in rather active touch with Senators and Representatives from their own states. Practically all of the state colleges and universities are members of the American Council on Education. The state colleges belong to the Land Grant College Association. Still other institutions are active in the Association of State Universities. The American Council on Education publishes valuable bulletins [1] presenting and explaining legislation that will affect higher education. It is of great importance that active membership in the American Council and similar organizations should be maintained. A federal subsidy for higher education in the interest of military objectives has been provided for the past five years. There is a movement to have that subsidy continued. Opinion is divided as to whether it would eventually mean federal control of education. The very same principle that suggests the advantage of separate boards over the joint-board system operates in federal control of education as in control by the various states. At every session of Congress bills are introduced which affect, either

[1] Such as "Higher Education and National Affairs," American Council on Education, Washington, D. C.

directly or indirectly, the financing of higher education. These bills should be scrutinized very carefully, not merely by members of Congress, who frequently are unacquainted with the conditions that exist in some of the states most affected by such legislation, but also by members of governing boards and university administrators, who should give studious consideration to the significance of federal legislation in the area in which the institution is located. It is recommended, therefore, that time be devoted to the study of proposed legislation as a part of the regular agenda at meetings of governing boards, and that arrangements be perfected whereby information concerning proposed legislation will receive prompt consideration.

BIBLIOGRAPHY

After Black Coffee, Gannon, Robert I. (McMullen Press, 1946), pp. 3, 13, 33, 35, 36, 46, 173.
Agriculture at Kansas State College. Vol. 30, No. 4, 1946.
Agricultural Extension Serves Rural Utah. Vol. 46, No. 10, 1946.
American Association of University Professors Bulletin. Vol. 32, No. 2, p. 374.
Analysis of the Need for Facilities to Provide Adequate Higher Educational Opportunities for Veterans and for Graduates of Secondary Schools, Partch, C. E., Dean, School of Education, Rutgers University, July, 1946.
Annual Report, 1945-46. University of Arkansas. Vol. 40, No. 15.
Annual Report—Regents, 1945-46. University System of Georgia.
Area Studies in American Universities, Fenton, W. N., Amer. Council on Educ., 1947, p. 72.
Audio-Visual Aids in the Armed Services, Miles, John R., and Spain, Charles R., American Council on Education, 1947, pp. 27, 28, 55, 71, 82.

Basic College, The. Michigan State College, Vol. 41, No. 7, Revised, 1946.
Bible College of Missouri Annual Report of Board of Trustees, 1946.
Bible College of Missouri Bulletin, April, 1946, No. 4.
Biennial Report of the Board of Supervisors, Louisiana State University, 1944-46.
Biennial Report, President of the University of Maine, 1946.
Biennial Report, University of New Mexico, 1945-47.
Biennial Report, Oregon State System of Higher Education, Bulletin, 1945-46.
Biennial Report of the President, University of Wisconsin, 1945-47.
British Speeches of the Day, British Information Services, June, 1947, Vol. V, No. 5, p. 343.
Budget Request, the State College of Washington, 1947-49.
Bulletin—Department of Commerce and Business Administration, University of Alabama, 1947.
Bulletin of the University of Minnesota, President's Report for 1942-44, Vol. 47, No. 57, p. 27.
Bulletin of Purdue University—Annual Report 1944-45.

243

Caroliniana, University of South Carolina, 1946.

Communists Within the Government—the Facts and a Program. Chamber of Commerce of the United States, 1947, p. 11.

Cooperation between Tuskegee Institute and the State of Alabama, 1943.

Cooperation in General Education, American Council on Education, 1947, pp. 9, 11, 21, 25, 83ff, 123ff.

Conferences on Industrial Relations. University of Michigan, the Bureau of Industrial Relations and the University Extension Service, Nov., 1946-April, 1947, Saginaw, also Nov., 1946-Mar., 1947, Detroit.

Co-ordinated Control of Higher Education in Oregon, Byrne, C. D., Stanford University Press, 1940.

Cornell University—General Information, 1947-48.

Education in Agriculture, The Iowa State College Bulletin, 1945, Vol. 43, No. 41.

Education in Britain. British Information Services, I. D. 606, June, 1947.

Educational Record, The. American Council on Education, Vol. XVII, April, 1936, "The Control of Higher Education in America," pp. 259-272.

Educational Record, The. American Council on Education, July, 1946, pp. 370, 373, 377.

Educational Record, The. American Council on Education, January, 1947, p. 67. *Supplement No. 16—Eleventh Educational Conference,* pp. 96-97, 99, 101, 103, 105, 147, 148, 149, 150, 151.

Educational Record, The. American Council on Education, April, 1947, pp. 161, 213-215.

Faith and Fire Within Us, Jackson, Elizabeth. University of Minnesota, 1944, pp. 44-79, 91, 104.

Florida's Future in Education. Florida Citizens Committee on Education, Tallahassee, 1947.

General Education in a Free Society. Report of the Harvard Committee, 1945, pp. 16, 24, 25, 87, 104, 143-145, 174, 178, 263.

General Education in the Humanities. American Council on Education, 1947, pp. 79ff, 121ff, 177ff. App. A. B. and C., also Chapter 2.

Genius of America, The, Sherman, Stuart P., Scribners, 1923, pp. 147-168.

BIBLIOGRAPHY

245

Going to College? University of Delaware, Newark, 1946.

Guide to Colleges, Universities and Professional Schools in the United States. American Council on Education, 1945.

Higher Education and National Affairs. American Council on Education.

Industrial Relations Center of the University of Minnesota, The. University of Minnesota, Minneapolis, 1947.

Institute of Labor and Industrial Relations, The, Bradley, Phillips. Opinion and Comment, Feb., 1947, p. 7.

Iowa Child Welfare Research Station, Sears, Robert R. University of Iowa, 1945.

Louisiana State University, a Survey Report. American Council on Education, 1940, pp. 3, 4, 7, 9, 59.

Management of Farm Fish Ponds. Alabama Polytechnic Institute Bulletin 254, 1947.

Manual for the Study of Western Civilization. University of Kansas, 1946.

Maryland. Maryland Alumni Publication, Annapoils, 1947, Vol. 18, No. 7.

Men Who Control Our Universities, Beck, Hubert. Kings Crown Press, 1947.

Mississippi State College—Its Objectives and Program of Work, 1944.

National Basic Outline of Religious Instructions, A. National Union of Teachers, 1945, London.

New York State School of Industry and Labor Relations. Cornell University Official Publication, Dec. 1, 1946.

President's Report, The. University of Michigan, 1944-45.

Proceedings of the Eleventh Executives' Conference, May 22, 23, 1947. The Institute of Paper Chemistry.

Proceedings, 24th Annual Meeting. Association of Governing Boards, 1946.

Public Education and the Structure of American Society, 1946, pp. 19, 31, 35, 39. Conant, James B., Bureau of Publications, Teachers College, Columbia University, 1946.

Relation of Religion to Public Education, The—The Basic Principles. Committee on Religion and Education, April, 1947, Vol. XI, pp. 1-15, 23, 38, 39.

Religious Counseling of College Students, Merriam, Thornton W. American Council on Educational Studies, April, 1943, Vol. 7, pp. 31, 39, 42, 53-55, 57, 60-63, 65, 67, 71, 73.

Religious Foundations at the University of Minnesota. Minnesota Council of Religions, 1946-1947.

Religious Life at the State University. Bulletin of the State University of Iowa, No. 856.

Report from the President's Council, 1945, Mississippi.

Report on American Youth for Democracy. U. S. Govt. Printing Office, 1947.

Report of the Governor's Emergency Committee on Higher Education, pp. 1, 2, 3. Walker Printing Co., Montgomery, Ala., 1946.

Report of the Nebraska Legislative Council Sub-Committee on Colleges and Universities. Submitted to the Nebraska Legislative Council, Nov., 1946.

Report of the President and Other Officers, Rhode Island State College, 1945-46.

Report of the President. Rutgers University Bulletin, 22nd Series 28, 1945.

Report of the President. University of Wyoming, 1945-46.

Report of the Regents of the University of Nevada, 1945-46.

Report of Special Committee on Morals and Religion. Yale University. 1946.

Report of Survey of Public Education in the State of West Virginia, Strayer, George D. Jarrett Printing Co., 1945, pp. 1, 71, 123.

School and Society VI, Sept. 8, 1919. "Who's Who Among College Trustees," pp. 297-299.

Several Pursuits and Professions of Life, The. Pennsylvania State College, 1945.

Social Composition of Boards of Education, The. A Study in the Social Control of Public Education, Chicago, University of Chicago Press, 1927.

Southern Association Quarterly, Feb., 1939, p. 1.

Southern Christian Advocate, Vol. 109, No. 43, Nov. 1, 1945.

So You're Having Troubles, Mr. Legislator? University of Colorado, 1947.

Statistics of Land-Grant Colleges and Universities—Year Ending June 30, 1945. Bulletin No. 1, Federal Security Agency, Office of Education.

Status of Higher Education in Michigan. Report to Michigan Legislature by Council of State College Presidents, 1947, p. 1.

Story of an Idea, The. The History of the School of Religion at the State University of Iowa. University of Iowa Extension Bulletin, No. 534, 1942, p. 9.

Studies of Higher Education in the South. Southern Association of Colleges and Secondary Schools, 1946. Bulletin Nos. VI and VII, pp. 4, 16, 22, 28, 33, 56, 98, 109, 121, 123, 127, 131.

Survey of Public Education in the State of West Virginia, Strayer, George D., 1945. See: *Report of.*

Syllabus of Religious Instruction for Use in Scottish Schools, A. Church of Scotland, Committee on the Religious Instruction of Youth, Edinburgh.

Taxation in Colorado, Reports I, II, III. University of Colorado, 1946-47.

Teacher in America, Barzun, Jacques. Atlantic-Little Brown, 1945, p. 165.

Ten-Year Review, A. University of North Carolina, 1934-1944.

Third Biennial Report, State Board of Regents. Oklahoma, 1946.

Under All the Land. Rural Study of Lafayette Parish, Louisiana, 1942.

United States War Department Military Training—Basic Field Manual. U. S. Govt. Printing Office, 1941.

The University and the Betterment of Industrial Relations, Riegel, John W. Michigan Alumnus Quarterly Review, Feb. 17, 1940, Vol. 46, No. 14.

University Religious Conference of U.C.L.A. Mimeograph on "panel program."

Wisconsin Idea, The—in Workers Education—Schwarztrauber, E. E. University of Wisconsin School for Workers, 1946.

Youth and the Future. Report of American Youth Commission, American Council on Education, 1942, pp. 136-139, 165, 174, 204, 211, 225, 289.

TABLE 1

INSTITUTIONS SURVEYED IN THIS REPORT

Alabama Polytechnic Institute
Alabama, University of
Amherst College
Arizona, University of
Arkansas, University of
California, University of
California, University of, at Los Angeles
California, University of Southern
Citadel, The, Military College of
   South Carolina
Clemson Agricultural College of
   South Carolina
Colorado Agricultural and Mechanical
   College
Colorado, University of
Connecticut, University of
Cornell University
Delaware, University of
Florida State University
Florida, University of
Georgia, Board of Regents of the
   University System of
Georgia School of Technology
Georgia, University of
Harvard University
Idaho, University of
Illinois, University of
Indiana University
Iowa State College of Agriculture and
   Mechanical Arts
Iowa, State University of
Kansas State College
Kansas, University of
Kentucky, University of
Louisiana State University
Louisiana, Southwestern Institute
Maine, University of
Maryland, University of
Massachusetts, University of
Miami, University of
Michigan State College
Michigan, University of
Minnesota, University of
Mississippi State College
Mississippi State College for Women
Mississippi, University of
Missouri, University of
Montana, State University
Nebraska, University

Nevada, University of
New Hampshire, University of
New Mexico, University of
New York State College for Teachers
North Carolina State College of
   Agriculture and Engineering
North Carolina, Women's College of the
   University of
North Dakota, University of
Ohio State University
Oklahoma Agricultural and Mechanical
   College
Oklahoma College for Women
Oklahoma, University of
Oregon State College
Oregon State System of Higher Education
Oregon, University of
Pennsylvania State College
Purdue University
Rhode Island State College
Rutgers University
San Francisco State College
San Jose State College
South Carolina, University of
South Dakota, University of
South, University of the
Stanford University
Tennessee, University of
Texas, Agricultural and Mechanical
   College of
Texas College of Mines and Metallurgy
Texas Technological College
Texas, University of
Tuskegee Institute
Utah State Agricultural College
Utah, University of
Vanderbilt University
Vermont, University of
Virginia Military Institute
Virginia Polytechnic Institute
Virginia, University of
Washington, State College of
Washington, University of
West Virginia University
William and Mary, College of
Wisconsin, University of
Wooster, College of
Wyoming, University of
Yale University

TABLE 2

SAMPLE QUESTIONNAIRE
Employed for institution personally surveyed in this study.

ASSOCIATION OF GOVERNING BOARDS OF STATE UNIVERSITIES
AND ALLIED INSTITUTIONS

Instructions: Please make your answers as complete and specific as possible.
Additional comments may be written on page four or on an attachment. Information received by this questionnaire will be used for the purpose of study and
analysis, and no information of a confidential nature from an institution will
be specifically identified in any publication of the results of this study.

Institution_____

Pre-War Enrollment_____Present Enrollment_____

Number of Board members_____Single or Joint State Board?_____

Separate College or University Board?____How are Board members selected?_____

_____What basic qualifications are required, if any?_____

_____

How many Board members are college graduates?____Are there any geographical restrictions in the selection of regents?_____

How are vacancies filled?_____

Length of term on Board_____

Are terms staggered and how?_____

How is Board organized? (Rotation in office, Committees, etc.)_____

_____

How frequently does Board meet?_____

FUNCTION OF BOARD

What chief responsibilities are assumed by the Board (e.g. Does it determine education-

al procedure and policy? Does it approve or prescribe academic standards? Does it

pass on faculty and administrative appointments? Is its function primarily political?)

_____

What are the total number of institutions of higher education in your state, both public

and private, and how are they governed?_____

How many junior colleges and how supported?_____

Is Board frequently called upon to confirm actions taken by President on his own initia-

TABLE 2 (continued)

tive? Explain._____

How much freedom does the Board give to the President in the administration of the institution?_____

Does Board have close contact with faculty, student body, and employees? Explain.

_____

How is your alumni secretary elected and by whom is he financed?_____

_____

FINANCES

Are funds available for use by Board at their own discretion? _____ What portion?

_____Are your funds a lump sum appropriation or line item?_____

_____Are funds appropriated directly to institution or through a State Office?

_____Is the money disbursed through a state office or by the institution directly?_____Does institution have freedom

for expenditure of appropriated funds?_____Of fees?_____

_____What assistance is given by Board in procurement of funds? Legislative appropriation?_____

_____

Approximate percentage of individual gifts and endowments to total budget_____

What are your total assets and how are they divided as regards lands, buildings, equipment, endowment, current assets, scholarship funds, etc?_____

_____

ADMINISTRATION

In organization of administrative functions, what staff appointment has primary responsibility for the following? Finances_____Budgets_____

Appointments of faculty_____Personnel Policy_____

Academic Standards_____Entrance Requirements_____

Public Relations_____Student Welfare_____

What increases in tuition fees have been made during the past five years, for in-state

students?_____ For-out-of-state students?_____

TABLE 2 (continued)

Are these fees all-inclusive, covering matriculation, library, athletic fee, student publications, etc.?_____

What is the range of salaries in the following ranks? Instructor_____

Asst. Prof._____Assoc. Prof._____Prof._____

Head of Department_____Deans_____Top administrative personnel____

_____President's salary_____

What is the percentage of increase in faculty salaries by ranks since Pearl Harbor?___

_____

Has there been any appreciable increase in teaching hour load?_____

In student hour load?_____

What is the size of your largest class?_____Does a close relationship exist

between your institution and other State and private institutions?_____

Explain_____

Are faculty members active in state, regional, and national associations, and does institution finance attendance at such meetings?_____

Have there been any active controversies in your institution with regard to academic

freedom within the past five years?_____Explain_____

Has there been any subversive teaching or activity in your institution which has attracted public attention in the past five years?_____If so, please describe briefly in few

sentences_____

Has your institution any requirement in American History or American Government for

all graduates?_____

Does your Board or institution have any systematic means by which members of Congress are kept informed of needs of higher education in your state?_____

_____

Is your Board satisfied with the institution's present method of presenting the needs of

higher education to the State Legislature?_____If not, what recommendations for improvement?_____

What percentage of your students are state residents?_____Out-of-state?_____

TABLE 2 (continued)

What is the religious breakdown among students by percentages? (Roman Catholic,

Jewish, Protestant, No preference)_____

Have you a University Chapel?_____

What courses are offered in Religion for credit and taught by whom?_____

_____

What denominational groups are active on your campus?_____

Are your non-faculty employees organized into unions?_____

What courses are offered in Industrial Relations?_____

What courses are offered in Workers' Education, such as Collective Bargaining, in Sum-

mer School or in the Extension Service?_____

What are your entrance requirements?_____

What percentage of those enrolled graduate?_____

What is your institution outstanding for (1) in research, or (2) in maintaining particular-

ly high levels of instruction in certain fields?_____

_____

_____

Please discuss any major problems you feel may exist in higher education, particularly

in regard to influence and activity of top administrators and Boards of Regents and

Trustees_____

_____

_____

TABLE 3

CONTROVERSIES

Institution	Academic	Subversive	Requirement in American History and Government
Alabama Polytechnic Institute	None	None	Amer. Hist. required first year; also Amer. Govt. in some professional curricula. Amer. Econ. Backgrounds, Polit. Sci., Natl. and State Local Govt. required in some courses.
Alabama, Univ. of	None	None	No requirement. Numerous electives.
Amherst College	Minor complaints	None	American Problems will be required of all sophomores beginning in 1948.
Arizona, Univ. of	None	None	Requirement in Liberal Arts departments. Wide field of electives.
Arkansas, Univ. of	None	None	State law requires Amer. Hist. for graduation. Numerous electives offered.
California, Univ. of	Not within Institution	Radical activities in Hollywood Writers Mobilization led to rule. No one advocating overthrow of government by force enrolled or employed.	Require knowledge of Amer. Institutes and History by examination or courses for B.A. degree.
California, Univ. of, at Los Angeles	Same as California, University of		
California, Univ. of Southern	None	One student was found to be a Russian spy.	General History of Civilization, one year of American Civilization and Institutes. Numerous electives.
Citadel, The	None	None	Required: two years Hist. of U. S., Amer. Parties and Politics. Survey of Amer. Govt. Others elective.
Clemson Agric. College	None	None Intensely loyal	Amer. Hist. and Amer. Govt. required of nearly all. Others elective.
Colorado A. & M.	None	None	Numerous electives; some departments require.
Colorado, Univ. of	Three instances	No public charge	No requirement. Numerous electives.
Connecticut, Univ. of	None		Requirement in Amer. Lit., Amer. Govt., Amer. Econ. Numerous electives.
Cornell Univ.	None	Accused of Communism 1941-42, due use of Russian teachers.	Some departments require. Numerous electives.
Delaware Univ. of	None		Numerous electives.
Florida State University	None	None	Two years required in Soc. Sci. includes Amer. Econ., Polit. and Soc. Backgrounds. Generous electives.

TABLE 3 (continued)

CONTROVERSIES

Institution	Academic	Subversive	Requirement in American History and Government.
Florida, Univ. of	None	None	One year required in Amer. Institutes. Usual electives.
Georgia School of Technology	None	None	Constitution of Georgia. No over-all requirement. Electives somewhat limited.
Georgia, Univ. of	None	None	Constitution of Georgia and U. S. Amer. Hist. required in Liberal Arts.
Harvard Univ.	None	None	All courses are elective.
Idaho, Univ. of	None	None	Not specifically required.
Illinois, Univ. of	None	None	No general requirement; electives offered.
Indiana Univ.	None of any significance	One instance. Investigation revealed no evidence.	No requirement. Generous electives.
Iowa State A. & M.	None	None	Amer. Govt. required; not satisfied with typical course in Govt.
Iowa, State Univ. of	None. Movement toward greater self government by faculty.	None	No requirement. Generous electives.
Kansas State College	None	None	Inclusive course in Govt. required in College of Arts and Sciences.
Kansas, Univ. of	None	None	Working knowledge of Amer. Govt. required. Generous electives.
Kentucky, Univ. of	None	None	Numerous electives offered.
Louisiana State Univ.	Some "Academic Freedom" difficulties.		Numerous electives offered.
Louisiana, Southwestern Institute	None	None. Active AAUP chapter on campus.	Requirement in History and Polit. Sci. majors. Others elective.
Maine, Univ. of	Nothing important	None	U.S. Hist. required of Soc. Sci. majors. Numerous electives.
Maryland, Univ. of	None	None	Amer. Civilization Program required in three brances of university.
Massachusets, Univ. of	None	None	Require course in either Amer. Govt., Hist. of the U.S., or State & Local Govt. Others elective.
Miami, Univ. of	None	None	Departments require Hist., Govt., etc., and wide range of electives offered.
Michigan State Coll.	None	None. Some AYD activities.	Basic requirements in Social Sci. and Hist. of Civilization.
Michigan, Univ. of	None. By-laws provide dismissal or demotion procedure, so likelihood of complaints reduced.	None	None required. Generous electives.

TABLE 3 (continued)

CONTROVERSIES

Institution	Academic	Subversive	Requirement in American History and Government
Minnesota, Univ. of	None	None. Small AYD chapter.	None required. Generous electives.
Mississippi State Coll.	None	None	Amer. Govt. required in most departments.
Mississippi State Coll. for Women	None	None	Amer. Govt. or Fundamentals of Econ. required. Numerous electives.
Mississippi Univ. of	None	None	None required. Generous electives.
Missouri, Univ. of	Yes. Failure to reappoint Prof. of Speech. Institution now listed "censored administration" by AAUP.	None	Electives.
Montana State Univ.	None		Required as part of major sequence in the Social Sciences.
Nebraska, Univ. of	None	None	None required. Generous electives.
Nevada, Univ. of	None		Electives offered.
New Hampshire, Univ. of	None	None. One instance seven or eight years ago.	Electives offered.
New Mexico, Univ. of	None		Covered in required Soc. Sci. and English courses.
N. Y. State College for Teachers	None	None	Not required.
N. C. State Coll. of A. and E.	None	None	Amer. Hist. and Citizenship required for non-military students.
N.C., Women's Coll. of the Univ. of	None	None	Elective.
North Dakota, Univ. of	None	No. Only instance criticism of reference textbooks.	Generous electives.
Ohio State Univ.	None	No. A vague incidents. AYD discontinued.	Amer. Hist. required. Generous electives.
Oklahoma A. and M.	None	None.	Amer. Hist. and Amer. Govt. required. Generous electives.
Oklahoma Coll. for Women	None	None	Amer. Hist. and Amer. Govt. required. Generous electives.
Oklahoma, Univ. of	None	None	Amer. Hist. and Amer. Govt. required. Generous electives.
Oregon State College	No. New faculty organized in 1944.		Elective.
Oregon State System	None		Encourages courses in Citizenship, etc.

TABLE 3 (continued)

CONTROVERSIES

Institution	Academic	Subversive	Requirement in American History and Government
Oregon, Univ. of	None		Elective except for History majors.
Pennsylvania State Coll.	None	No. Occasional problems within faculty.	Elective.
Purdue Univ.	None	None	Elective.
R. I. State College	None	None	Required in certain curricula. Elective in others.
Rutgers Univ.	None	None	Amer. Hist. and Amer. Govt. required. Others elective.
San Francisco State Coll.	Not for years		Amer. Constitutions, Amer. Hist., Ideals and Institutions required. Others required for majors. Various electives.
San Jose State College	None		Same as San Francisco State College.
South Carolina, Univ. of	None	None	Required course in Polit. Sci. covers duties in citizenship.
S.D., Univ. of	None	None	Generous electives.
South, Univ. of	None	No. Considerable latitude in expression of economic and social ideas.	Required courses in Hist., Govt., or Econ., include material in American Backgrounds.
Stanford Univ.	None	None	Require survey course in Amer. Civilization for every B. A. Numerous electives.
Tenn.,Univ. of	None		Electives.
Texas A.& M.	None		
Texas Coll. of Mines	None	None	Amer. Democracy and Texas Govt. required. Other electives.
Texas Technological Coll.	None	Not for ten years	Course in Amer. Govt. and Texas Constitution required. Other electives.
Texas, Univ. of	Yes		Amer. Hist., Amer. Govt., and Constitution of Texas required.
Tuskegee Inst.	None	None	Nine quarter-credits required.
Utah State Agri. Coll.	None	No. AYD not successful.	Electives.
Utah, Univ. of	None	No. AYD died out.	Not required. Amer. Hist. required of all high school graduates.
Vanderbilt Univ.	None	None	Soc. Sci. required. Others elective.
Vermont, Univ. of	None	None	Require either Amer. Govt. or Amer. Hist. as a matter of distribution.
Virginia Military Institute	No. One treatise on Negro question.	None	Required in Liberal Arts courses.
Virginia Polytechnic Inst.	None	None	Elective, except in Schools of Business Administration and Agriculture.
Virginia, Univ. of	None		

TABLE 3 (continued)

CONTROVERSIES

Institution	Academic	Subversive	Requirement in American History and Government
Washington, State College of	None	None	Electives.
Washington, Univ. of	None	None	
West Virginia Univ.	None	None	Recommended that six hours of Amer. Hist. be required.
William and Mary, College of	None	No. One case of conscientious objector.	"Do teach" Amer. Hist., Amer. Lit., and Economics and Government.
Wisconsin, Univ. of	Two cases, one doubtful.	Rumors	Generous electives.
Wooster, College of	None	None	Elective.
Wyoming, Univ. of	None	None	Amer. Govt. required. Others elective.
Yale Univ.	None		Outstanding courses in each. "American Studies" offered with unusual library resources.

TABLE 4

RELIGION

Institution	Courses for Credit	Univ. Chapel	Denominational Groups Active
Alabama Poly. Institute	Credit is given as elective.	No	Yes
Alabama, Univ. of	English Bible, Biblical Archeology, Sources of Religious Experience, Eng. Old Testament, Life and Teachings of Paul, New Testament Greek, English New Testament, Prophets and New Testament in Acts and Selected Epistles, Jewish History, Hebrew and Judaism. Others by local clergy.	No	Yes. Wesley, Westminster, Canterbury, Hillel, Newman, Baptist, Lutheran.
Amherst College	Life and Teachings of Jesus, Christianity in First Century, Bible: Its Literature and Teaching, Religion and Literature.		
Arizona, Univ. of	History of Religion, Comparative Religions, Philosophy of Religion, etc.	No	Yes. Westminster, Mowian, Episcopalian, Newman, Baptist.
Arkansas, Univ. of	Old Testament Prophets, Life of Christ, Life and Letters of Paul, Literature of Old Testament, Literature of New Testament. Taught by local ministers.	No	Gamma Delta (Luth.), Bapt., Canterbury, Newman, Wesley, Westminster.
California, Univ. of	Religion can be offered as major or taken as minor.	No	Yes
California, Univ. of at Los Angeles	About 90 courses offered. Can be taken as minor only.	No	Yes
California, Univ. of	115 courses advertised in Religion of which 36 offered in 1947. Denominational courses offered by local clergy on Judaism, Roman Catholic Church and Program, Eastern Orthodox Church and Program, Mormon Church and Program, Epis. Church and Program, four Roman Catholic courses, but only one for each of other churches. Also courses in Christian Life, History of Christian Ethics, Growth of Protestantism, Living Religions of the World, Religion and the Modern Mind, etc.	No	Yes
Citadel, The	Philosophy of Religion.	Yes	Newman, Presb., Student Christian Association.
Clemson Agric. College	Courses taught by local clergy as assigned by college. Old Testament, New Testament, Life of Christ, Comparative Religions.	No	Newman, Canterbury, Brandeis, YMCA.
Colorado A. and M.			Canterbury, Newman, Student Christian Assn., Lutheran.

TABLE 4 (continued)

RELIGION

Institution	Courses for Credit	Univ. Chapel	Denominational Groups Active
Colorado, Univ. of	India and China Religions, Contemporary Religious Ethics, Modern Trends in Religions of Various Cultures, Life and Thought of Jesus, Theories of Religions Living, Religion and Social Ethics, Religion in Western Culture, Studies in Religious Literature, Sci., Philosophy and Religion Since the Renaissance, Nature, Man and God, Contemporary American Philosophy of Religion, Problems in Philosophy of Relig.	No	Methodist, Canterbury, Newman.
Connecticut, Univ. of	Courses in non-sectarian religion offered for credit by member of faculty.	No	
Cornell Univ.	Ethics, Philosophy of Religion, History of Religion, Advanced Philosophy of Religion. Taught by faculty.	Yes	
Delaware, Univ. of	Philosophy of Religion	Yes	
Florida State Univ.	Old Testament, New Testament, The Bible, Religious Education, Christian Culture, Religions of the World, Contemporary Religious Beliefs, Philosophy of Relig.	No	Yes. Newman, Wesley, Westminister, Hillel Bapt. Student Union, Christian Science, Episcopal Center.
Florida, Univ. of	Religious Foundations of Modern Life, Problems in Religious Philosophy, Old Testament, Career of Jesus, Comparative Religion.	No	Newman, Hillel, Weed Hall (Epis.), Wesley, Bapt. Student Union, Presb. Center, Luth. and Christian Science.
Georgia School of Technology	No Courses.	No	YMCA, Newman, Baptist Student Union, Wesley.
Georgia, Univ. of	History of Religions, Old Testament, Literature, New Testament Literature, The Prophetic Movement, The Teachings of Jesus.	Yes	Newman, Bapt. Student Union, Wesley, Presb., Episcopal, Hillel.
Harvard Univ.	Has Divinity School.	Yes	
Idaho, Univ. of	Three religious institutes adjacent to campus offer courses accepted for credit at university.	No	
Illinois, Univ. of	Philosophy, Moral Ideas of Practice, Philosophy of Religion, Literary Study of the Bible.	No	Hillel, Newman, Wesley.
Indiana Univ.	No fixed courses in religion. It is taught as an aspect of civilization in various departments.	No	Hillel, Meth., Presb., Lutheran, Christian, Newman, Canterbury, Christian Sci., Inter-Varsity group.
Iowa State A. & M.	Introduction to Bible, Christianity. Past and Present, Religions of Mankind, Old Testament, Social and Ethical Teachings of New Testament, Meaning and Purpose Of Life, History of Philosophical Quest, Philosophy of Religion.	No	Baptist, Methodist, Presb., Episcopal, Roman Catholic, Lutheran, Christian, Congregational.

TABLE 4 (continued)

RELIGION

Institution	Courses for Credit	Univ. Chapel	Denominational Groups Active
Iowa, State Univ. of	Hebrew Languages, Advanced Hebrew, Christian Origins, Jewish History and Literature, The Protestant Faith, The Catholic Church and Civilization, Catholic Church since 1500 A.D., Cath. Church and Society, Life Motives, Living Religions of Mankind, Little Known Religious Groups in America, New Testament History and Literature, Teachings of New Testament, Seminar on Inter-Faith Relationships, Readings in Relig., Seminar in Old Testament, Research in Religion. A degree is granted with religion as a major.	No	Hillel, Newman, YWCA, YMCA, Canterbury, Roger Williams Fellowship, Gamma Delta, National Assn. of Lutheran Students, Wesley, Westminster.
Kansas State College	English Bible, History of Religion; some courses by local clergy certified for credit.	No	Baptist, Christian, Luth., R. C., Meth., Congre., U. Presb., Church of Christ. Scientist, Presb., Epis., Free Meth., Ch. of Christ, Ch. of Nazarene, Assembly of God.
Kansas, Univ. of	English Bible, Hebrew History II, Life and Teachings of Jesus, Beginnings of Christianity, Old Testament Literature II, Survey of New Testament, Social Teachings of Jesus, Prophecy and the Prophets, New Testament and Modern Thought, History of World's Living Religions.	Yes	Wesley, Newman, Hillel, Westminster Fellowship, Roger Williams Foundation, Theta Epsilon, Youth Fellowship, Kappa Phi, Kappa Beta, Jewish Student Union, Gamma Delta, Presb., Meth.
Kentucky, Univ. of	Religion and Culture, Cultural Process and Hebrew Christian Religions, Great Religions of the World, Literature of the Bible.	No, but one is approved.	
Louisiana State Univ.	No courses at present.	No	Newman, Canterbury, Wesley, Presb., Jewish, Baptist.
Louisiana, Southwestern Institute	No courses for credit.	No	R.C., Bapt., Meth., Epis., Presb.
Maine, Univ. of	Religion in Modern Life	No	Showing growth in strength.
Maryland, Univ. of	No courses for credit. R.C. chaplain has offered to give three hours a week to course on religion.	No	Hillel, Newman, Canterbury, Westminster, Meth. Strong clubs.
Massachusetts, Univ. of	Introduction to English Bible, Nature & Destiny of Man, A Christian Interpretation.	No	
Miami, Univ. of	Bible as Literature, Comparative Study of Religions, Religious Biography. Not major courses.	No, but planned.	Newman, Meth. Student League, Christian Science, Congregational, Christian League, Canterbury, Luth., YMCA and YWCA.

TABLE 4 (continued)

RELIGION

Institutions	Courses for Credit	Univ. Chapel	Denominational Groups Active
Michigan State College	Society of Religion, Knowledge of the Arts, Introduction to Christianity, Philosophy of Christianity, Ethics of Christianity, Modern Social Problems of Christianity, Religion in Modern Life, Life and Teachings of Jesus, Educational Work of the Church. Students limited to eight credits toward graduation in Relig. Education.	No, but one to be built.	Epis., Christian Sci., Luth., R.C., Jewish, Peoples Ch.
Michigan, Univ. of	Non-sectarian courses. No limit on number student may take.	No	Hillel, Newman, Christian Science, United Lutheran Assn., Wesley, Westminster, Roger Williams Guild, St. Mary's Chapel, Pilgrim Hall (Cong.)
Minnesota, Univ. of	Pre-theological training in several departments. History of Religion, Psychology of Religion, Philosophy of Religion, Religion as a Social Institution; two English courses on Bible as Literature.	Yes	Very Active.
Mississippi State Coll.	Biblical Literature.	No	R.C., Epis., Presb., Meth., Baptist.
Mississippi State Coll. for Women	Ethical Teachings of Jesus, Poetry of Old Testament, Life of Jesus Christ, Life and Letters of Paul, Old Testament History, etc. by members of the faculty.	Yes	Meth., Bapt., Presb., Newman and Christian Church.
Mississippi, Univ. of	None for credit.	Yes	Church of Christ, Jewish, R.C., Presb., Bapt., Epis., Methodist.
Missouri, Univ. of	History of Religion, Introduction, Language and Literature, Philosophy of Religion.		
Montana State Univ.	Basic Values of Religion, Church in the World Today, Workshop in Human Relations, given by affiliated School of Relig.	No	Meth., Presb., Congregationalist, Luth., R.C.
Nebraska, Univ. of	Old Testament Ideals, New Testament Ideals, Christian Philosphy Prior to Reformation, Philosophy of Religion, Philosophy and Psychology of Relig.	No	Newman, Westminster, Wesley, Baptist, Lutheran, Jewish.
Nevada, Univ. of	Introduction to Religion, Philosophy of Religions. Taught by faculty.	No	Newman, Episcopal, Congregational.
New Hampshire, Univ. of	None for credit.	No	Congregational, R.C., Jewish.
New Mexico, Univ. of	None for credit.	Yes	R.C., Bapt., Hillel, Christian Science.

TABLE 4 (continued)

RELIGION

Institutions	Courses for Credit	Univ. Chapel	Denominational Groups Active
N. Y. State Coll. for Teachers	None		Hillel, Newman, Canterbury, Student Christian Assn., Christian Science, Inter-varsity Christian Fellowship, Lutheran.
N.C. State Coll. of A. and E.	Six courses in religion offered by the Prof. of Ethics and Religion.	No	Student Christian Assn., Bapt., Presb., Epis., Meth., R.C., Jewish.
N.C., Women's Coll. of the Univ. of	English Department offers Literature Course on Bible.	No	Active.
North Dakota, Univ. of	Has School of Religion with numerous courses.		Yes
Ohio State Univ.	English Bible, Designs for Living, Religious Questions, Meaning of Human Life, Philosophy in Religions of Far East, Philosophy of Religion, Metaphysics of Personality Values.	No	Hillel, Newman, Wesley, Westminster, Lutheran Student Assn., Christian Sci., Inter-varsity Christian Fellowship, YMCA, YWCA.
Oklahoma A. and M.	Courses taught by local clergy, when approved and accepted for credit.	No, but plans one.	Newman, Bapt. S.U., Wesley, Westminster, YWCA, YMCA.
Oklahoma Coll. for Women	Courses offered by clergy accepted for credit in religious education.	No, but plans one.	R. C., Meth., Christian, Epis., Bapt., Presb., YWCA.
Oklahoma, Univ. of	Courses taught by local clergy, when approved, are accepted for credit.	No	Hillel, Newman, Wesley, Westminster, Bapt. S. U.
Oregon State College	New Testaments, Prophets and Their Message, Bible as Literature, Principles of Religion, Leadership, Philosophy of Religion.		
Oregon, Univ. of	Faculty teaches Religious Foundations of Western Civilization, Bible, Philosophy of Religion, Religion of Classical Antiquity, Judaism and Christianity, Oriental Religions.	No	Newman, Wesley, Westminster, Hillel, Bapt., YMCA, YWCA.
Pennsylvania State Coll.	Considering establishment Chair of Religion.	No	Hillel, Wesley, Newman, Student Christian Assn.
Purdue Univ.	Two courses in English Bible as Lit. Student pastors offer Concepts of Religion, Backgrounds of Religion.		Canterbury, Christian Sci., Hillel, Inter-Faith Council, Newman, Purdue Christian Foundation, Univer. Luth. Assembly, Wesley, Westminster.
R. I. State College		No	Newman, Student Fellowship, Canterbury.
Rutgers Univ.	Courses for credit taught by University chaplain. Also offers course in Introduction to the Bible.	Yes	Newman, Hillel, Christian Science, Lutheran, Protestant Fellowship, Rutgers Bible Fellowship.
San Francisco State Coll.	Philosophy of Religion, Comparative Religion, Bible and Contemporary Life.	No	Newman, Student Christian Association, Hillel.

TABLE 4 (continued)

RELIGION

Institutions	Courses for Credit	Univ. Chapel	Denominational Groups Active
San Jose State College	Bible as Literature, Psychology of Religion, Literature and Religion.	No	Canterbury, Wesley, Westminster, Hillel, Newman, Student Christian Assn.
South Carolina, Univ. of	Historic Basis of Old Testament, N.T., Biblical Archeology, Modern Sunday School Teaching, Literary Forms in Bible. Has Department of Religion.	Yes	Hillel, YMCA, YWCA, Bapt. Student Union, Canterbury, Carolina Christian Service Club, Newman, Wesley, Westminster.
South Dakota, Univ. of	Old Testament, New Testament, History offers Reformation and Protestantism., Philosophy of Religion, Ethics.	No	Newman, Student Christian Assn., Canterbury, Luth., Bapt., Congregational. Also Faculty Committee.
South, Univ. of	Old Testament, New Testament, Church History, Comparative Religions. Full year of either Bible or Philosophy required.	Yes	None on campus.
Stanford Univ.	Comparative Religions and Christianity and Heretics. Courses under Philosophy.	Yes	Very active, not on campus.
Tennessee, Univ. of	School of Religion not organic part of University, but given full credit for courses.	No	R.C., Jewish, Protestant,
Texas A. & M.	No information given.		
Texas Coll. of Mines	Ethics, Philosophy of Life, Ethics of Human Relationships.	No	Newman, Bapt. Student Union, Methodist, Presb.
Texas Technological College	Offered off-campus for credit: Hebrew History, New Testament History, Contemporary Religious Problems, The Prophets, and Teachings of Jesus.	No	Baptist, Methodist, Christian.
Texas, Univ. of	Credit allowed for courses in religion and religious education, when approved by faculty. No department or chair of religion.	No	Newman, Wesley, Christian Science, Bapt. Student Union, Canterbury, Christian Youth Fellowship, Hillel, Luth., Presb., Inter-varsity Christian Fellowship.
Tuskegee Inst.	None		
Utah State Agricultural College	Given on non-sectarian basis for credit. Comparative Religion, History of Religion, Bible Literature.	No	L.D.S., R.C., Epis., Presb.
Utah, Univ. of	English Bible as Literature, Philosophy of Religion. L.D.S. Institute of Religion offers non-credit courses.	No	Newman, Jewish, Hillel, L.D.S., University Fellowship House.
Vanderbilt Univ.	Old Testament, New Testament Biblical Literature, Philosophy of Religion, Religion and Psychology. Has Graduate School of Religion.	Yes	Student Christian Assn., Canterbury, Westminster, Wesley.
Vermont, Univ. of	Assistant Prof. of Religion gives courses for credit.	Yes	
Virginia Military Institute	None	No	

TABLE 4 (continued)

RELIGION

Institutions	Courses for Credit	Univ. Chapel	Denominational Groups Active
Virginia Poly-Technic Institute	None	No	Newman, Student Christian Assn.
Virginia, Univ. of	Courses given for credit to about 200 students.	Yes	Newman, Hillel, off-campus.
Washington, State Col. of	None	No	
Washington, Univ. of	None	No	
West Virginia Univ.	Philosophy Department offers Hist. of Religion.	No	Newman, Canterbury, Wesley, Westminster, Hillel, Baptist.
William and Mary Coll. of	None	Yes	
Wisconsin, Univ. of	None	No	Luth., Congregational, Meth., Presb., Jewish, R.C., Bapt., YMCA, YWCA, Epis.
Wooster, Coll. of	14 courses in Department of Religion, plus Philosophy of Religion, History of Christian Thought, Psychology of Religion, Department of Religion has four members	Yes	Largely Presbyterian.
Wyoming, Univ. of	None given on campus.	No	L.D.S., Wesley, Canterbury, Newman, Roger Williams.
Yale Univ.	Yes. Variety offered.	Yes	Hillel, R.C.

TABLE 5

STUDENT POPULATION

INSTITUTION	In-state %	Out-of state %	RELIGIOUS PREFERENCE Protest- ant %	Roman Cath. %	Jewish %	No Pref. %
Alabama Polytechnic Institute	83	17	89	3	1	7
Alabama, Univ. of	88	12	78	.23	.17	20
Amherst College	20	80				
Arizona, Univ. of						
Arkansas, Univ. of	92	8	63	1.7	.07	35
California, University of	70	30	No census			
California, Univ. of, at Los Angeles	74	26	67	15	18	
California, Univ. of Southern			65	10	20	5
Citadel, The	33-1/3	66-2/3	82	12	6	
Clemson Agric. College	85	15	96-2/3	3	.33	
Colorado A. & M.	66	34	67	11-1/3	.003	21
Colorado, Univ. of	65	35	75	11	3	10
Connecticut, Univ. of	99.9	.1	63	25	12	
Cornell Univ.	63	37	60	16	14	10
Delaware, Univ. of	82	18	69	20	7	2
Florida State Univ.	99.7	.3	90	7	3	
Florida, Univ. of	94	6	85.8	8.9	5.3	
Georgia School of Technology	52	48	52	5	2	41
Georgia, Univ. of	93	7	85	3	2	10
Harvard Univ.	35	65	No record			
Idaho, Univ. of	86	14				
Illinois, Univ. of	84	16	62-1/2	16-2/3	12-1/2	8-1/3
Indiana Univ.	86	14	70	14-1/2	7.4	8.1
Iowa State A. & M.	85	15	80	9	3	8
Iowa, State Univ. of	75	25	75	15	4	6
Kansas State College	91	9	81	7		12
Kansas, Univ. of	74	26	86	6	.8	7
Kentucky, Univ. of	87	13	88	7	1	4
Louisiana State Univ.	84	16	65.7	31.4	2.9	
Louisiana, Southwestern Institute	95	5	34.5	65	5	
Maine, Univ. of	88	12	75	21	3	1
Maryland, Univ. of	83*	17	69	15	11	5
Massachusetts, Univ. of	99	1	49	31	18	2
Miami, Univ. of	65	35	52	18	30	
Michigan State Coll.	85.5	14.5	Not available - majority Protestant			
Michigan, Univ. of	67	33	74.8	16	9.1	.1
Minnesota, Univ. of	85.6	14.4	Not available			
Mississippi State Coll.	97	3	94	5	1	
Mississippi State Coll. for Women	94	6				
Mississippi, Univ. of	90	10	93.2	6	.8	
Missouri, Univ. of	72	28	58	9	5	28
Montana State Univ.	86	14	No record kept			
Nebraska, Univ. of	86	14	85.9	8.1	2.5	3.5
Nevada, Univ. of	70	30	38	21	.9	40

*Includes District of Columbia

TABLE 5 (continued)

STUDENT POPULATION

INSTITUTION	RELIGIOUS PREFERENCE					
	In-state	Out-of state	Protest-ant	Roman Cath.	Jewish	No. Pref.
	%	%	%	%	%	%
New Hampshire, Univ. of	77	23	67	28	5	
New Mexico, Univ. of	72	28	No official religious registration			
N. Y. State Coll. for Teachers	100	0	No record kept			
N.C. State Coll. of A. and E.	80.4	19.6	95	3	2	
N.C., Women's Coll. of the Univ. of	86	14	92.44	2.07	2.85	2.64
North Dakota, Univ. of	85	15	76.2	19.4	.5	3.8
Ohio State Univ.	91	9	61.3	10.7	6.6	21.2
Oklahoma A. and M.	86.5	13.5	89.5	4.5	1.5	4.5
Oklahoma Coll. for Women	86	14	91	5	.24	2.1
Oklahoma, Univ. of	80	20	81	6.6	2	10.4
Oregon State College	89.4	10.6	73.5	8.7	1.6	16.3
Oregon, Univ. of	80	20	68	10		22
Pennsylvania State Coll.	91	9	66	21	10	2.4
Purdue Univ.	65	35	72.2	15.4	3.8	8.6
R. I. State College	90.4	9.6	52	38	9	1
Rutgers University	95	5	25.5	28.1	38.5	7.9
San Francisco State Coll.	96.5	3.5	No census			
San Jose State Coll.	96.6	3.4	No census			
South Carolina, Univ. of	95	5	80	15	5	
South Dakota, Univ. of	81	19	72	19	1	8
South, Univ. of	26	74	97.4	2		.6
Stanford University	70	30				
Tennessee, Univ. of	85	15	91	2	1	5
Texas A. and M.	94	6	No census			
Texas College of Mines	90	10	65	33	2	
Texas Technological College	96	4	96.9	3	.1	
Texas, Univ. of	95	5	80	9	3	8
Tuskegee Inst.	39	61	71.6	4.2		24.2
Utah State Agric. Coll.	85	15	(80% L.D.S., balance divided among others)			
Utah, Univ. of	90	10	84.4	4.2	.32	10.65
Vanderbilt Univ.	60	40	Overwhelmingly Protestant			
Vermont, Univ. of	75	25	66	27	6.5	.4
Virginia Military Inst.	53	47	90	9	1	
Virginia Polytechnic Inst.	76	24	88.5	6.5	5	
Virginia, Univ. of	50	50			8.5	
Washington State College of	82.6	17.4	Not available			
Washington, Univ. of	90	10	53	9	2	36
West Virginia Univ.	93	7	94	3	3	
William and Mary College of	70	30	89	8	3	
Wisconsin, Univ. of	81	19	Not available			
Wooster, Coll. of	55	45	90	4	1	5
Wyoming, Univ. of	83	17	77.32	11.93	.35	10.20
Yale University	20	80	80	9	9	

TABLE 6

INDUSTRIAL RELATIONS

Institution	Unionized	Courses in Industrial Relations	Courses in Workers' Education
Alabama Polytechnic Institute	No	Industrial Relations, Industrial Management, Production Control, Natural Resources of South, etc.	No
Alabama, Univ. of	Carpenters and painters	American Economic History, Economic Problems and Policies, Industrialization of South, Economic Analysis, Public Service Companies, Introduction to Industrial Management, Labor Problems, Industrial Management, Time and Motion Study, Personnel Management, Industrial Relations, Labor Law and Legislation.	No
Amherst College	No	Always have at least one course.	No
Arizona, Univ. of	No	Labor Problems, Labor Relations, courses in Management for engineers and miners and in Bus. Adm.	Short courses in summer school and in extension and correspondence classes.
Arkansas, Univ. of	No	Labor Problems, Labor Legislation in College of Bus. Adm., Labor Law in Law School.	No
California, Univ. of	Some employees unionized but university is open shop.	Institute of Industrial Relations with Advisory Com. made up of prominent industrial and labor leaders. Courses in Labor Economics, Personnel Adm., Time and Motion Study, Industrial Relations, Labor Law.	Short courses at night and in summer school on Collective Bargaining, Labor Law, Labor Statistics, etc.
Calif. Univ. of, at Los Angeles	Same as California, University of.		
California, Univ. of Southern	No	Under Economics--Labor Relations, Labor Legislation, Economic Reform, and Seminar on Labor and Industrial Relations.	Summer School has course in Labor Relations.
Citadel, The	No	Labor Problems required for Bus. Administration.	No
Clemson Agric. Coll.	No	Plant Management in Textile School and Labor Problems in Economics.	
Colorado A. & M.	No	Economics-Bus. Law, Bus. Adm., Principles of Cooperation, Labor Economics, Sociology-Community Organization, Contemporary Social Trends.	Summer courses stress training teachers of vocational education. Study of Organized Labor, Study of Apprenticeship, Employer-Employee Relations. Shop Organization and Control Methods.

TABLE 6 (continued)

INDUSTRIAL RELATIONS

Institution	Union-ized	Courses in Industrial Relations	Courses in Workers Education
Colorado, Univ. of	Bldg. and Service employees organized. Individual workers belong local unions.	Personnel Management Problems in Personnel Management, Business Organization and Management, Government Regulation of Business, Production Management, Industrial Management, Labor Economics.	Labor Problems, Labor Legislation, Labor Law. Has Institute of Labor Relations under University Bureau of State & Community Service.
Connecticut, Univ. of	Campus workers have Company Employees Assn.	Has Institute of Labor Relations, offers major for undergraduate degree; also non-credit courses and research.	Labor Management Institute held summer meetings in 1945. Courses planned for near future.
Cornell Univ.	Teachers Union weak; building service employees AFL.	School of Industrial Labor offers courses in labor problems.	Courses for personnel workers and farmers.
Delaware, Univ. of	No	Industrial Relations, Labor Problems and Management in Department of Economics and Bus. Adm.	No
Florida State Univ.	No	Industrial Relations, Personnel Administration, Comparative Economic Systems, History and Development of Economic Thought, Economic Order.	No
Florida, Univ. of	No	Job Evaluation; Specifications, Engineering Relations and Industrial Safety; Human Engineering; Motion and Time Study; Management Training; Machine Technology in American Life; Labor Economics; Personnel Management; Government in Relation to Labor; Government Control of Business; Problems in Economic Security, etc.	Short courses.
Georgia School of Technology	No	Introduction to Industrial Management Problems, Personnel Management, Organization for Production, Production Control, Factory Planning, Production Problems, Motion and Time Study.	Short courses: Organization of Trade Education, Foremanship Conferences, Methods of Shop Demonstration, Indus. Plant Surveys, Shop Organization, Trade Analysis, Retail Lumber Dealers Course, Radio Broadcasting.
Georgia, Univ. of	No	Industrial Management, Business Law, Labor Problems, Personnel Adm. Comparative Economic Systems, Economics of American Industry, American Economic History.	No

TABLE 6 (continued)

INDUSTRIAL RELATIONS

Institution	Union-ized	Courses in Industrial Relations	Courses in Workers' Education
Harvard Univ.	Type-setters AFL Co. Union, Harvard Univ. Employee Relations Assn.	Variety of courses offered In-dus. Relations and Labor Prob-lems, conducted by Law School, Bus. School, Faculty of Arts & Sciences.	No summer school for workers education.
Idaho, Univ. of	No	Courses under Business and Eco-nomics relative to this subject.	No summer school courses in workers' education.
Illinois, Univ. of	Some individ-ual work-ers be-long to unions. No AFL branch.	Institute of Industrial Labor Re-lations offers Industrial Organ-ization and Administration, Hu-man Relations in Industry, In-dustrial Economics, Techniques of Supervision, Personnel Adm., Industrial and Personnel Rela-tions, Industrial Management.	Collective Bargaining, Job Evaluation, Recreation, Political and Civil Rights, The Labor Movement, Iron and Man. Numerous Exten-sion courses are offered.
Indiana, Univ.	3 power plant workers. AFT branch. Some in-dividual employ-ees be-long to unions.	School of Bus: Corporation Fin-ance, Principles of Management, Problems in Employee Relations, Business Law, Personnel Adjust-ment to Business, Office Manage-ment, Problems in Industrial & Personnel Management, etc.	Two series of courses by university faculty-- one by AFL and one for CIO.
Iowa State A. & M.	No	Under General Engineering: In-dustrial Organization, Employee Methods and Employee Develop-ment, Safety Engineering, Prin-ciples of Personnel Supervision, Time and Motion Study, Indus-trial Engineering, Factory Per-sonnel.	Engineering Extension Ser-vice: Techniques of Teach-ing Trades, Foundations of Industrial Education, Prob-lems of Industrial Educa-tion.
Iowa, State Univ. of	Not large mem-bership.	Labor Economics, Money & Banking, Business Law, Market-ing, Business Organization and Corporation Finance, Personnel Management, Labor Legislation, Industrial Management, Econom-ic Theory, Statistics, Insurance.	No
Kansas State College	No	Numerous courses in Industrial Relations offered in School of Arts & Science.	Labor courses under Econ-omics, Sociology, Psychol-ogy and Education.

TABLE 6 (continued)

INDUSTRIAL RELATIONS

Institution	Union-ized	Courses in Industrial Relations	Courses in Workers' Education
Kansas, Univ. of	No Under State Civil Service.	General Requirements in Human Relations, Social Restrictions of Post-War World, Collective Bargaining, Social Disorganization, Labor Economics, Personnel Management, Economic Systems, Imperfect Competition, Production Management, Office Management, Industrial Training and Supervision, Labor Law.	Employer-employee Relations and Collective Bargaining.
Kentucky, Univ. of	No	Labor Problems, Labor Legislation, Business Organization, Problems in Management, Industrial Relations.	No courses, but AFL requested several years ago that university give courses on Labor Problems.
Louisiana State Univ.	No	Labor Problems, Social Movements, Personnel Management.	Discussing course on Labor and Industry by State Federation of Labor with help of university.
Louisiana, Southwestern Institute	No	Labor Problems, Industrial Management, Modern Industry Commercial Society, Personnel Mgmt.	No
Maine, Univ. of	No	Courses in Economics and Bus. Administration.	Only regular courses in Economics and Bus. Adm.
Maryland, Univ. of		Courses under Bus. Adm.	No Special classes.
Massachusetts Univ. of	No	Industrial Relations, Labor Problems and Management Problems, Economics of Business and Industry, Economics of Consumption, Business and Consumer Assn., Current Economic Problems, etc.	No
Miami, Univ. of	No	Economics of Labor, Government and Economic Life, Income and Wealth, Economic Planning, Political Parties and Pressure Groups, Legislative Principles and Problems, Principles of Business, Personnel Management, Industrial Management.	No courses in Workers' Education as such.
Michigan State College	Some non-faculty belong local unions.	Problems of Labor and Industry, Business Organization and Management, Office Management, Business Law, Labor Economics, State in Relation to Labor, Cooperative Business Management, Personnel Management, Economics of Social Security, Wages, Industrial Disputes.	Practically no provision.
Michigan, Univ. of	Individual workers belong local unions.	Given in School of Bus. Adm.	Through Extension Service.

TABLE 6 (continued)

INDUSTRIAL RELATIONS

Institution	Union-ized	Courses in Industrial Relations	Courses in Workers' Education
Minnesota, Univ. of	Non-faculty highly organized. A major problem.	Labor and Socialistic Movement; Labor Legislation and Social Insurance, Psychology in Personnel Work, Vocational Psychology, Senior Topics. Others at Industrial Relations Center.	Through Extension Service
Mississippi State Coll.	No	Labor Relations, Personnel Management.	No
Mississippi State Coll. for Women	No	Only general courses in Economics, Sociology and Political Science.	No
Mississippi, Univ. of	No	Labor Problems, Post-War Economics, Industrial Management, Personnel Management, Industrial Relations.	No
Missouri, Univ. of	No	Personnel Management, Industrial Management, Labor Problems, Labor Legislation, Industrial Psychology, Administration Law.	No
Montana State Univ.	Carpenters, janitors and truck drivers. Local AFT also.	Economics 114, Industrial Relations, after 6 credits in Labor Economics.	A Labor Institute sponsored jointly by a university committee and labor organizations of the state.
Nebraska, Univ. of	No	Current Labor Problems, Government in Relations to Labor, Industrial Management, Personnel and Labor Relations.	No
Nevada, Univ. of	No	Labor and Management, Labor Economics, Business Cycles, Industrial Mangement, Personnel Management, Administration of Business, Fundamentals of Business Organization.	No
New Hampshire, Univ. of	No. Veterans' housing delayed by unions.	Personnel Organization and Administration, Job Analysis and Wage Administration, Industrial Office Organization and Management, Industrial Supervision and Foremanship, Human Relations in Industry, Labor Relations, Industrial Relations, Industrial Organization and Management, etc.	
New Mexico, Univ. of	No	Labor Problems and various courses in Business Administration.	No
N. Y. State Coll. for Teachers	No. Has Civil service assn.	Has relative courses under Sociology and Economics.	No

TABLE 6 (continued)

INDUSTRIAL RELATIONS

Institution	Union-ized	Courses in Industrial Relations	Courses in Workers' Education
N.C. State Coll. of A. and E.	Bldg. Service employees	No courses.	No
N.C., Women's Coll. of the Univ. of	No	Labor Problems.	No
North Dakota, Univ. of	Bldg. Service employees. Some workers at vocational schools.	Labor Problems, Business Management, Economic Development, Economic Problems, Principles and Problems of Economics, Principles of Bus. Adm., Personnel Administration, Contemporary Social Problems, Social Security Problems.	Short courses for agricultural workers only at Agricultural College.
Ohio State Univ.	Small Bldg. Service. AFL; some craft unions. Small AFT.	Offers 23 varied courses.	No
Oklahoma A. and M.	No	Various courses offered.	No
Oklahoma Coll. for Women	No	Labor Movements and Problems, Corporation Finance, Business Law, Economic Society.	No
Oklahoma, Univ. of	No	Business Organization and Management, Management of Small Business Enterprises, Personnel Management, State in Relation to Business, Industrial Management, Industrial Supervision, Time and Motion Study, Problems in Business Administration, Labor Economics, Industrial Combinations, Economic Systems, Labor Economics, Economic Progress.	No
Oregon State College	Non-faculty employees are on State Civil Service; skilled workers union.		Yes
Oregon, Univ. of	Non-faculty AFL.	A four-hour course in Labor Problems and Labor Organizations.	No
Pennsylvania State Coll.	Some maintenance employees AFL.	Courses offered under Industrial Engineering and Industrial Psychology.	Summer courses.

TABLE 6 (continued)

INDUSTRIAL RELATIONS

Institution	Union-ized	Courses in Industrial Relations	Courses in Workers' Education
Purdue Univ.	No. Efforts made to organize.	Industrial Personnel Administration, Industrial Management, Industrial Relations, Production Planning, Production Control, Industrial Safety, Personnel and Industrial Relations, Wage Administration, Wage Incentives, Management Seminar, Advanced Management Problems, Labor Economics, Labor Law, Business Law, Advanced Labor Economics, Current Economic Problems, American Industry and its Place in World Economy, Contemporary Economic Thought, Psychology of Industrial Training, Seminar in Industrial Training, Field Problems in Industrial Psychology.	Extension courses in Economics of Industry, Legislation Affecting Industrial Relations, Labor Problems, Industrial Safety, Human Relations for Supervisors, Wage Policy, Personnel Management.
R. I. State College	No	Economics of Labor, Labor Legislation.	Extension courses.
Rutgers Univ.	No	28 varied courses offered.	Extension Division conducts annual Labor Institute and Industrial Conference.
San Francisco State Coll.	No	Labor Problems, American Standards of Living, Personnel Administration, Social Control.	No
San Jose State College	No	Labor Economics, Government and Labor Disputes, Labor Relations.	No
South Carolina, Univ. of	No	One course in Labor Problems.	No
South Dakota, Univ. of	No. Has chapter AAUP.	2 courses in Labor Problems, 2 in Industrial Management, also Business Law, Government and Business, Current Economic Problems.	No
South , Univ.of	No	Labor Relations.	No
Stanford Univ.	Only employees of University Press.	Division of Industrial Relations in Graduate School, courses on Principles and Policies of Industrial Relations, National Labor Relations Act, Executive Control, Occupational Hygiene, Time and Motion Study, etc.	Faculty members hold extra-curricular conferences with management and labor leaders.
Tennessee, Univ. of	No	No	No
Texas A. and M.	No	Under Economics and in Management Engineering.	No
Texas Coll. of Mines	No	Personnel Management, Labor Problems.	No

TABLE 6 (continued)

INDUSTRIAL RELATOINS

Institution	Unionized	Courses in Industrial Relations	Courses in Workers' Education
Texas Technological College	No. Community not cordial to organized labor.	Labor Economics, Economic Systems, Development of Economic Doctrines, Current Economic Problems, Industrial Management and Personnel Administration.	No
Texas, Univ. of	No	Personnel Management, Collective Bargaining, Current Problems in Industrial Management, Seminar in Labor, Government Public Personnel Administration Development and Relationships.	Has year-round program by itinerant faculty, giving courses in special skills to foremen for relay to workers. 19 handbooks prepared in special branches.
Tuskegee Institute		Variety of courses under Industrial Education and under Management; also vocational courses covering many fields.	School of Mechanical Industry offers vocational courses.
Utah State Agri. Coll.	No	International Economic Relations, Corporation Concentration and Public Policy, Current Economic Problems, Personnel Management, Labor Economics.	No
Utah, Univ. of	No	Personnel Administration, Indus. Organization of Management, Labor Problems.	
Vanderbilt Univ.	No	Labor Problems and Labor Relations, Problems of Unemployment, American Government in Business.	No
Vermont, Univ. of	Bldg. Service employees. Four teachers in AFL.	Industrial Relations, Labor Problems, Management Problems. Have had two courses in evening extension on labor Relations with both labor and management's points of view.	
Virginia Military Institute	No difficulties.	No special courses.	No
Virginia Poly-Technic Institute	No	No	No
Virginia, Univ. of	Hospital employees CIO. No strikes.	Courses under Economics from a conservative point of view.	
Washington, State Coll. of	Bldg. Service partially organized.	Personnel Administration.	Labor Economics and Problems, Labor Legislation.
Washington, Univ. of	No	Institute of Labor Economics is organizing a full curriculum.	Extension courses in this field offered by Institute of Labor Economics.
West Virginia Univ.	No	Labor Relations, Management, and Public Relations.	Courses for miners and mine supervisors.

TABLE 6 (continued)

INDUSTRIAL RELATIONS

Institution	Union- ized	Courses in Industrial Relations	Courses in Workers Education
William and Mary College of	No. State employ- ees not permit- ted to organize.	Courses under Business Admin- istration Economics, Government, Psychology.	No
Wisconsin, Univ. of	Non-fac- ulty be- long loc- al un- ions. 100 members in AFT.	Numerous courses. Wisconsin was pioneer in this field; carries on extensive work. Has com- mittee on Industrial Relations to integrate courses.	Courses given by Extension Service throughout the state.
Wooster, Coll. of	No	Labor Problems.	No
Wyoming, Univ. of	No	Labor, Labor Relations, Indus- trial Relations, Personnel Man- agement, Business Administration Problems, Business Ethics, Busi- ness Law, Elementaries of Busi- ness Administration.	Plans under consideration.
Yale Univ.	Mainten- ance em- ployees CIO. Had 1-day strike.	Has center for study of Prob- lems in Labor and Management.	Courses taught by faculty in Yale classrooms and labs. administered by New Haven College.

TABLE 7

ENTRANCE REQUIREMENTS

Institution	Requirements
Alabama Polytechnic Institute	Graduate of accredited high school or 15 Carnegie units.
Alabama, University of	Graduate of accredited high school with 15 Carnegie units. Admits students over 20 on examination.
Amherst College	Eight to 11 units of the following: English, 4 years (3); Elementary Algebra (1); Intermediate Algebra, (1); Plane Geometry (1); Greek, Latin, French or German, minimum (2); in addition, a scholastic aptitude test and achievement test. Candidates accredited by N. Y. State Regents' examinations will be considered.
Arizona, Univ. of	Graduate of accredited high school and resident of state. Non-residents must be top third of class. Turning away three students for every one taken.
Arkansas, Univ. of	High school diploma; except that non-graduate with 15 acceptable units admitted on special recommendation.
California, University of	Graduate of accredited high school within certain subject requirements, or 15 units, both subject to scholarship requirement of B grade average for last three years. University is authority for accrediting high schools.
California, Univ. of, at Los Angeles	Same as California, University of.
California, University of Southern	Diploma from accredited high school with 15 unit requirement, upper half of high school class and good character and health. (Also by examination.)
Citadel, The	Standard. May use selective process to admit. More than 50% of students from middle third of high school class or better.
Clemson Agric. College	South Carolina high school diploma. No other selectivity. Mortality about 25% first year.
Colorado A. and M.	Graduate from accredited Colorado high school with 15 credits, or by entrance test. Non-residents must be eligible to land-grant institution where high school work was done. Students over 25 admitted on probation for one quarter and if they maintain 2.0 average are given equal standing.
Colorado, Univ. of	Graduate of accredited high school with 15 selected units from upper 2/3 of class, lower 1/3 being admitted by examination. Out-of-state from upper quarter of graduating class. Worthy mature students admitted on examination as special students until maintain 2.0 average for 4 years and present equivalent of entrance requirement; then may be graduated from College of Arts and Sciences.
Connecticut, University of	Normally only top quarter of state high school graduates.
Cornell University	High school graduate with 15 units in specified subjects, or by examination; also certificate of character and certain health requirements.
Delaware, University of	Graduate of accredited high school with 15 acceptable units, or by examination; credentials to indicate sound moral character, good health, etc. Out-of-state students must present outstanding scholastic records.
Florida State University	Diploma from an accredited high school, units selected from certain groups. Also by examination. Also mature adult specials.
Florida, University of	Graduation from high school; by examination.
Georgia School of Technology	High school diploma with 15 units, including 2 in Algebra, 1 in Plane Geometry, and 1 in Physics. No students admitted without diploma.

TABLE 7 (continued)

ENTRANCE REQUIREMENTS

Institution	Requirements
Georgia, University of	Certificate of graduation from accredited high school entrance examination provided the applicant has not been in an accredited high school the previous year; by qualifying as a mature adult special student.
Harvard Univ.	Highly selective.
Idaho, University of	Graduate of accredited high school with 15 acceptable units, or of senior 3-year high school with 12 units; non-graduates with required units on special recommendation; veterans over 19; mature students as specials.
Illinois, University of	Graduate of accredited high school by certificate; lower fourth on probationary basis. Worthy mature students without diploma admitted as "unclassified." (can attain advanced standing after satisfactorily completing two years of under-graduate work).
Indiana University	All graduates of accredited Indiana high schools in upper half of graduating classes and all graduate veterans admitted to Jr. Division without condition. Lower half required to report for conference and guidance. Out-of-state in upper third of class admitted. Worthy mature students without diploma admitted as special students and can obtain regular standing by doing satisfactory work.
Iowa State A. and M.	All graduates of high scnool with 15 units. In-state minimum 1.75; out-of-state minimum 2.5. Worthy mature students without diploma admitted as special students for first year.
Iowa, State University of	Accepts all high school graduates but discourages lower third; or by examinations and recommendations.
Kansas State College	Diploma from any accredited Kansas high school or academy. Some special units out of 15 required for non-graduates. Veterans may make up requirements after enrollment. Out-of-state students must have principal's recommendation.
Kansas, University of	Diploma from any accredited Kansas high school. Some special units. Out-of-state requires higher selectivity. Worthy mature students admitted without diploma but not advanced to regular standing until worth proven.
Kentucky, University of	Graduate of accredited high school with 15 units; otherwise by examination.
Louisiana State University	Accredited high school diploma for state citizens, or with 15 Carnegie units. Entrance by examination rare. Out-of-state must be upper third or with "C" or better average.
Louisiana, Southwestern Institute	Diploma from accredited high school. Mature and worthy students provisionally.
Maine, Univ. of	Graduate of accredited high school; otherwise by examination.
Maryland, University of	Top third of high school graduates from out-of-state; from in-state eliminates lower fifth and selects from the balance.
Massachusetts, University of	80% or "B" or by examination.
Miami, Univ. of	15 units and graduation from an accredited high school, excluding low ranking graduates. In rare cases, adults without diploma.
Michigan State College	Upper third of high school (Michigan accredited) admitted without examination. Second third only upon express recommendation of principals; lower third only by written examination. Non-accredited graduates by examination. Out-of-state must be upper third.
Michigan, University of	Graduate of accredited high school with required subject matter admitted on certificate when better than average grades. Others have opportunity for indicating their ability.

TABLE 7 (continued)

ENTRANCE REQUIREMENTS

Institution	Requirements
Minnesota, University of	Graduate of accredited Minnesota high schools by certificate, by aptitude test or by high school rank. Out-of-area students must be upper quarter if veterans or upper tenth if non-veterans.
Mississippi State College	15 units from properly accredited secondary school. High school diploma not accepted unless supported by 15 units. Students over 21 by GED test.
Mississippi State Coll. for Women	15 earned units in properly accredited secondary school. Mature students admitted as special students until they have met entrance requirements.
Mississippi, University of	High school diploma from all state high schools. Students over 21 without diploma. Out-of-state requirements same.
Missouri, University of	(A) By certificate; (B) by examination; (C) part by certificate and part by examination; (D) veterans by examination.
Montana State University	All graduates of Montana high schools eligible. Scholarship restrictions on out-of-state applicants.
Nebraska, University of	Graduate of accredited high school with 15 Carnegie units. Out-of-state must be upper 10%; adjacent states, upper half. Admits adults as students at large.
Nevada, University of	High school diploma. Turned away 1000 qualified students in 1946.
New Hampshire, University of	Upper 2/5 of state high school graduates. Below that on examination. Higher requirement for out-of-state students.
New Mexico, University of	High school diploma from accredited high school. Non-graduates and veterans by GED test. Turned away one out of three in 1947.
N. Y. State Coll. for Teachers	Selective, by Board of Regents. 16 units of secondary school work or college entrance examination.
N.C. State Coll. of A. and E.	Standard.
N.C., Women's Coll. of the University of	Normally "C" grade.
North Dakota, University of	High school graduate with 15 specific units. Mature worthy students by examination.
Ohio State University	All graduates of accredited high schools with 15 specific units. Mature worthy students by examination.
Oklahoma A. and M.	Graduation from accredited high school. Out-of-state from upper half. Mature students as specials.
Oklahoma Coll. for Women	Graduation from accredited high school or 15 units, including certain specified units.
Oklahoma, University of	Graduation from accredited high school with certain specified subjects. Out-of-state from upper half. Mature students as specials.
Oregon State College	Graduation from standard high school with 16 specified units. Out-of-state may be held for additional requirements demonstrating superior ability. Mature students as specials.
Oregon, University of	High school diploma for Oregon residents. Non-residents required to meet average of 2.75 if transfer, or upper 20% if coming from high school.
Pennsylvania State College	Selective process. Some schools only by examination; upper 2/5 from most.
Purdue University	15 units of secondary school work including specified units. Graduates of Indiana accredited high schools admitted without examination. Non-accredited on examination. Out-of-state from upper two-thirds. Otherwise by examination. Some admitted as "unclassified."
R. I. State College	Certificate of graduation from secondary school with relatively high rank; or by examination.

TABLE 7 (continued)

ENTRANCE REQUIREMENTS

Institution	Requirements
Rutgers University	Graduate of accredited secondary school with some specified subjects; or by examination.
San Francisco State College	High school diploma.
San Jose State College	High school diploma.
South Carolina, University	Standard. High school diploma entitles to enrollment.
S. D., Univ. of	Graduate of accredited high school with 15 specified units. Otherwise by examination. Students over 21 without diploma, without examination as "special" students can attain regular standing within one year by satisfying requirements.
South, Univ. of	Normally a high school average of 80.
Stanford University	15 hours accredited high school with grades of "A" or "B" and college aptitude test. Accepted 3000 out of 8000 applicants in 1946.
Tennessee, University	High school graduation or equivalent. Uses GED test for non-graduates. Students over 21 admitted without standing. Turned away 1000 qualified students in 1945 due to lack of room.
Texas A. and M.	Graduation from accredited high school with 15 units and certain specified subjects. Lower quarter admitted on probation. Admission on special approval for mature students without high school diploma -- may take examination to obtain admission units.
Texas College of Mines	Diploma from accredited high school, or individual approval of mature students.
Texas Technological College	Diploma from accredited high school with minimum of 15 specific units. No one refused except for housing limitations.
Texas, University of	Graduation from accredited high school with 15 units and certain specified subjects. Lower quarter admitted on probation. Admission on special approval for mature students without high school diploma -- may take examination to obtain admission units.
Tuskegee Institute	15 high school units. Graduates by certificate from accredited schools; non-accredited by examination.
Utah State Agricultural College	15 units of work from standard high school. Accepts mature students and veterans without high school diploma -- credit depends on examinations.
Utah, Univ. of	15 approved Carnegie units, or college GED test.
Vanderbilt University	(A) 15 units partly prescribed; (B) position in graduating class; (C) scholastic aptitude test. These three form basis for selectivity.
Vermont, University of	Composite requirements consisting of recommendation of high school principal, rank in class, school record, test, and personal interview. Special and unclassified students admitted also. Persons who are qualified for regular admission may enroll in certain studies.
Virginia Military Institute	Standard. High degree of selection.
Virginia Polytechnic Institute	Standard. High degree of selection.
Virginia, University of	Four year high school course successfully completed (accredited) with 15 entrance units; or by examination.
Washington, State College of	Grade point 2.00 or "C" average.
Washington, University of	Graduate of accredited high school with 2.5 average and 15 units partly specified. Some provision for non-graduates by special examinations.
West Virginia University	High school diploma for West Virginia students. Out-of-state, upper third. Class at present upper fifth.

TABLE 7 (continued)

ENTRANCE REQUIREMENTS

Institution	Requirements
William & Mary, College of	Standard. Upper half.
Wisconsin, University of	Graduates of accredited Wisconsin high schools with 16 units, 9 of which are specified. Otherwise by examination. Veterans by satisfactory evidence of readiness. Mature students without high school diploma as specials, may become regulars on dean's recommendation.
Wooster, College of	Certificate of graduation from accredited high school or academy, personal information, health certificate. Supplementary tests optional.
Wyoming, University of	High school diploma with 15 accredited hours. Non-graduates not admitted except veterans as special students; also mature students as unclassified and special students.
Yale University	Record and examination. Only in exceptional cases will students be admitted without high school diploma.

TABLE 8

OUTSTANDING FEATURES

Institution	Outstanding Features
Alabama Polytechnic Institute	Agriculture in the field of Agronomy. Nationally and internationally known projects in fishing and wildlife. Outstanding animal nutrition work. New uses for sweet potatoes. Architecture.
Alabama, University of	Inspired establishment of Southern Research Institute in Birmingham corresponding in principle to Mellon Institute. Pulp and paper technology. Special work in Chemistry on sulphur organic compounds. Ceramics in the field of shales and raw materials. Nutrition. Southern Association of Science and Industry to improve Southern education.
Amherst College	"Modesty prevents my stating the points and departments in which I think Amherst excels." (from report)
Arizona, University of	Anthropology including ethnology. Mining minerology and geology - new methods of discovering ore bodies. Semi-tropical agriculture in citrus and vegetables. Best work in archaeology in the United States.
Arkansas, University of	Research in Entomology, agricultural crops, food nutritions, Indian archaeology of the Midwest, regional literature, law. Instruction in engineering, football.
California, University of	See page 183.
California, Univ. of, at Los Angeles	See page 183.
California, University of Southern	General educational program in lower division called General Studies. Also School of Social Work and School of Library Science. School of Education a dominant school in state. Strong School of Philosophy. Physical and occupational therapy.
Citadel, The	Civil Engineering. Noteworthy in Business Administration and Political Science. High enrollment in pre-medical course. Military training not given at expense of academic education.
Clemson Agric. College	Soil Science and dairying. Textiles and methods of production. Trying to develop penicillin and other drugs in cheese due to particularly favorable local conditions. Good agricultural extension service. Research in canning, quick-freezing and refrigeration.
Colorado A. and M.	Veterinary Medicine, Forestry. Research in Irrigation Engineering, Agronomy, Sugar Beet Mechanization and Veterinary Surgery. Doing experimental work for U. S. Army Signal Corps in radar.
Colorado, University of	See page 176.
Connecticut, University of	Research in animal genetics and animal disease with reference to poultry and dairy cattle. Has College of Insurance with combination curriculum of law and insurance.
Cornell University	School of Chemical Engineering, Colleges of Agriculture, Home Economics and Veterinary Medicine, New York State School of Industrial and Labor Relations, School of Nutrition. Combines practical and liberal education.
Delaware, University of	Pioneered in foreign study -- provides one year's supervised study abroad for undergraduate students with full credit toward the American baccalaureate degree.
Florida State University	Dietetics, exchange internships. Programs for training teachers. Library science. Applied arts such as commercial art. Department of Government. Requires foreign language for graduation. Pre-Columbian Museum of Art and Archaeology. 900 acre dairy farm. Model dining hall. Stresses internships and placement of students.
Florida, University of	See page 167.

TABLE 8 (continued)

OUTSTANDING FEATURES

Institution	Outstanding Features
Georgia School of Technology	Aeronautical engineering, architecture and cooperative engineering. Food processing and wood pulp, paint primers for yellow pine, experimental paint farm, thermodynamic studies of the properties of gases and flax processing. Original economic studies of various areas of the state. Peanuts.
Georgia, University of	Plant pathology, particularly on tomato diseases, sweet potato diseases and corn breeding. Agricultural Engineering, particularly on farm houses and rural electrification. Zoology in the field of parisitic diseases. Strong departments of Music and Fine Arts, Southern History (outstanding collection of documents in this field), Zoology, Agricultural Engineering.
Harvard University	"I do not feel competent to suggest that there is anything 'unique or original" about Harvard. Nor would I care to be quoted officially in an estimate of the departments which I would consider 'the strongest in the University.' " (from report)
Idaho, University of	Special stress in Home Economics, on the selection of consumer goods, purchasing, making and care of clothes, and selection of furniture and household equipment; and also on agriculture, which is the basic industry of the area. Its School of Forestry has attracted attention.
Illinois, University of	See page 177.
Indiana Univ.	See page 178.
Iowa State A. and M.	State's center for science and technology. Research in farm crops (oats, corn, soybeans), animal nutrition, dairy processing, dairy bacteriology, plant genetics, plant pathology, agricultural engineering, human nutrition, fermentation (bacteriology), atomic energy (metallurgy), veterinary pathology, statistics on sampling processes, chemical engineering in the processing of agricultural by-products, highway safety, state taxation, trends of state population, farm plans, agricultural climatology and insect control.
Iowa, State University of	Child Welfare, Psychology, Education, Hydraulics, Fine Arts (particularly creative work in art, music and theater), Literature (creative writing), Zoology, Statistics and Actuarial Training.
Kansas State College	See page 172.
Kansas, University of	High instruction level in chemistry, geology, entomology. Research in bacteriology, especially tularemia; geology, especially paleontology; human anatomy; engineering (work with dirt blocks not requiring machinery); mathematics and chemistry. Strong staff in chemical engineering. Research Foundation promoting industrial research. Bureaus of Business Research and Governmental Research very active. Natural History Museum and Entological Museum outstanding.
Kentucky, University of	Agriculture, especially in fields of soils, tobacco and animal industry. Strong Colleges of Engineering, Education and Commerce, Law. Research in American and Southern History, State Government and Taxation, Bacteriology, Archaeology and Anthropology, Coal research.
Louisiana State University	Famous for sugar chemistry and engineering. Also petroleum engineering and oil geology. Outstanding in fighting sugar cane diseases, especially sugar cane borer. Also in research in sweet potato development. Studies in rural population and rural sociology highly developed. Medical school well equipped. Schools of Geology and Chemistry nationally recognized.
Louisiana, Southwestern Institute	Agriculture. Special work in elimination of water hyacinth and alligator grass, two pests in streams. Unique in raising literacy standard, illiteracy due to French and English not being taught for years. Good in Floriculture and Home Economics.

TABLE 8 (continued)

OUTSTANDING FEATURES

Institution	Outstanding Features
Maine, University of	Pulp and paper technology. National reputation in engineering. Research in forestry, food processing. Has department to assist small industries with technical problems.
Maryland, University of	Schools in Business Administration, Agriculture, Engineering and Arts and Sciences all good. Attempts to maintain balance between all departments so no one school notably stronger.
Massachusetts, University of	Chemistry, Entomology, Landscape Gardening, Food Technology, and Science in general. Emphasis on agriculture.
Miami, University of	Sciences, Inter-American Relations and Music. Has plans for special work in tropical marine zoology and botany, tropical engineering, medicine, veterinary science, horticulture, agriculture, forestry, inter-American studies, international trade, foreign affairs, and fine arts. Extensive research in zoology and botany. Expanding in chemistry and engineering. Sociological studies beginning by experiment in teaching of American Democracy in high schools now underway.
Michigan State College	Technological research. Undulant fever in animals and man, the production of brucellin, development of the infra-red method of combatting frost damage, studies in nutrition with relation to soil properties. Outstanding School of Veterinary Medicine and School of Forestry, curricula in hotel administration and police administration. American Hotel Association contributing to construction of an adult education center to be operated by hotel administration students and used as meeting place for annual association meetings.
Michigan, University of	See page 178.
Minnesota, University of	See page 179.
Mississippi State College	Bureau of Business Research which issues monthly bulletin on business trends, tax structure, insurance, banking and developments in local industries. Also Engineering Research Station which cooperates with TVA with special reference to strengths of materials and in wood products. School of Science emphasizes entomology and insect control, especially termites, basic research and application on livestock and crops. Professor of Entomology is State Entomologist; Professor of Chemistry is State Chemist. Usages of cottonseed oil. Greatest cotton experiment station in world with emphasis on cotton genetics and cotton fiber research. Unique study in pastures and cattle feeding. Crossing of sorghum and Johnson grass. Techniques in artifical insemination, especially of dairy cattle. Strong organic chemistry, work with fine chemical library. Graduate work in Department of Entomology. Outstanding in agricultural economics and agronomy.
Mississippi State College for Women	Primarily a liberal arts college with certain vocational departments. Gives B.A. and B.S. degrees. Music and Home Economics strong. Extra-curricular activities aim at citizen development.
Mississippi, University of	Most distinctive work in research in petroleum geology and ceramics. Also research in public health on State program. Faculty research not emphasized in early days, but effort being made to remedy this. Bureau of Public Administration being used to improve county and community tax, court, and administrative systems, and have prepared legislative handbook for guidance of all legislators. Physics Department and English Department do very well.
Missouri, University of	See page 170.
Montana State University	Summer Labor Institute, sponsored jointly by a university committee and the labor organizations of the state.

TABLE 8 (continued)

OUTSTANDING FEATURES

Institution	Outstanding Features
Nebraska, University of	College of Dentistry, College of Medicine. Work in vertebrate pale-ontology; Great Plains archaeology; plant ecology, Agriculture, especially in various breeds of corn, wheat, potato diseases, dairy husbandry. Music and art education connected with high school work. Department of Chemistry. Unique program in University Extension presenting courses in high schools under supervision of local high school staff as a supplement to the smaller state high schools.
Nevada, University of	Strong Physics Departments with seven physicists in Atomic development. Mackey School of Mines well known.
New Hampshire, University of	Research in wood industries, creation of wood yeast as feed and use of wood as source for plastic material. Agriculture devoted to local needs, especially poultry and dairying.
New Mexico, University of	Anthropology and archaeology; Spanish, which is living language in the state; Art, particularly painting, due to art colonies in neighborhood; International Affairs, Chemistry and Physics in connection with Los Alamos laboratory, also geology. Give Masters degrees in 27 fields and Doctors degrees in five.
N. Y. State Coll. for Teachers	Institution set apart for preparation of teachers of academic subjects in the Junior-Senior high schools of New York State. No courses in elementary education. Also prepares high school teachers in the field of Business Education and for high school librarians.
N. C. State Coll. of A. and E.	Largest school of Textiles and textile research in the United States. $2,500,000 in equipment for Diesel Engineering. Ceramics research, agronomy and animal industry strong fields.
N. C., Women's Coll. of the University of	Research in nutrition and teacher training for Home Economics. Also trains institutional managers and home demonstration agents. Good Physical Education Department which prepares for college teaching. Also strong Music Department.
North Dakota, University of	Norse languages and culture including Icelandic; Bituminous products research; food processing research. Work in paint chemistry; plant breeders have established high quality hard-grained spring wheat; varieties of flax and of vegetables; development of special cheeses; Veterinary Department outstanding contributions to animal disease research.
Ohio State University of	Chemistry, Entomology, Electrical Engineering, Ceramics, College of Education (including Psychology), some phases of Liberal Arts, some areas in Medicine, Professor Hoyt Sherman's work in Fine Arts, Professor Samuel Renshaw's identification of planes in Psychology. Fresh Water Marine Laboratory on Lake Erie, Educational Opportunities Service, College of Medicine in Hemotology and some lines of experimental surgery, good Dental Schools, Optometry and fundamental and advanced work in vision. Petroleum research, School of Aviation (contracts for leading special problems in Aviation Research); Romance Languages from the standpoint of talking rather than reading; good Department of Russian.
Oklahoma A. and M.	Schools of Agriculture and Engineering, particularly Department of Animal Husbandry, School of Architecture, Industrial and Technical Engineering, Firemanship Training School, Hotel Management Training, short courses in field of Agriculture and Industry; Experiment Station, particularly anaplasmosis research; Agricultural Aviation (National Flying Farmers organization was organized and has its national headquarters on college campus, sponsored by college); Research Foundation.

TABLE 8 (continued)

OUTSTANDING FEATURES

Institution	Outstanding Features
Oklahoma Coll. for Women	Offers fine arts to young women from homes of moderate circumstances. Strong in home economics. Good in science. Graduates commonly spoken for in advance at good salaries with large corporations especially in laboratory work (research). Large enrollment in Physical Education and graduates making good records not only in teaching Physical Education but in promoting summer camps, camp fire work, etc.
Oklahoma, University of	Outstanding for Petroleum Engineering, School of Drama. Are now erecting a building for technical research for which university has a foundation. Outstanding University Press (new $100,000 building for Press); outstanding collections are Phillips Collection for Southwestern history, Art, Archaeological; University built a spectograph during the war for Navy for cracking processes in oil. Considerable research for private industry by contract in electronics, chemical and physical studies of certain asphalts, investigation of heat transfer and corrosion, processing of aldehydes, alcohols and mixtures thereof.
Oregon State College	Home Economics, Food Industries.
Oregon, University of	Schools of Architecture and Allied Arts, Journalism, Music and Medical School in Portland.
Pennsylvania State College	Strongest schools and departments are Chemistry, Physics, Engineering. From state point of view, Agriculture and Mineral Industries, strong and important. Had short courses for steel workers, during summer with good results.
Purdue Univ.	See page 181.
R. I. State College	Marine Biological Laboratory on Narragansett Bay; turf experiments of the Agricultural Experiment Station; research in poultry pathology (cause of blackhead disease of turkeys and methods of control); research on the storage and refrigeration of orchard fruits.
Rutgers University	Work in soils, introduction of new varieties of peaches and tomatoes, in microbiology, in ceramics, in the relation of the School of Journalism to the State Press Association, the organization of student life at the College for Women.
San Francisco State College	Primarily a liberal arts college, but gives emphasis to teacher training.
San Jose State College	Oldest public college on west coast. Offers pre-medical course, ideal arrangement with city schools in teacher-training, cadet training. Starting four-year engineering school. Fine system of records.
South Carolina, University of	Development of sense of honor in students as men. Has Student Honor Committee. School of Education and Law School excellent.
S. D., Univ. of	See page 174.
South, University of	Has clung tenaciously to a liberal arts curriculum. Feature long association with and ownership by the Episcopal Church which colors entire life of institution. Has close relationship between faculty and students, nearly every faculty member being "at home" to students each Sunday night. Excellent pre-medical course and pre-professional business course.
Stanford University	Graduate School of Business; strong in electrical engineering; geology, mining and petroleum, mineral sciences, good School of Education, outstanding work in polio research in Chemistry. Developing linear accelerator for atom smashing experiments.
Tennessee, University of	School of Home Economics considered one of best four in the United States. College of Engineering nationally recognized. Graduate students working in atomic field at Oak Ridge.
Texas A. and M.	See page 172.

TABLE 8 (continued)

OUTSTANDING FEATURES

Institution	Outstanding Features
Texas Coll. of Mines	Aims to be a sound undergraduate college and to do an outstanding job in teaching. Scholarship of faculty noteworthy. Doing outstanding work in radio; also unusual work in interior decorating and designing. Undergraduate work in Mining and Metallurgy noteworthy.
Texas Technological Coll.	Textile Engineering and Research, Animal Husbandry, Home Economics, especially in field of clothing, Petroleum Geology, cotton research.
Texas, University of	General field of biology, especially genetics; chemistry, nearly all phases of mathematics, history. Has Rare Books Collection (includes Stark, Wrenn, and Aitken Libraries); Garcia Library, Latin-American in content; Reaugh collections; Texas Memorial Museum, exhibits featuring the historical development of the State, its geological and anthropological backgrounds.
Tuskegee Institute	Negro college whose graduates have rendered significant services all over the world. Service has been rendered to the South and the nation by work in agriculture, industrial education, health and business.
Utah State Agricultural College	Work in irrigation, management of arid soils, fruit cultivation, especially peaches, apples; range phase of forestry; dairying, sheep raising, horticulture, poultry; also Institute of Nutrition; crop breeding and development of smut-resistant wheat, sugar beet research, tomato and celery diseases. Dr. Harris, president of Utah State Agricultural College was head of the mission to Greece in May, 1946 for the study of agriculture and related subjects and also of economic problems of Greece such as trade, transportation, water power, fiscal and tax policy; also member of mission to seven Arab nations commissioned by State Department and United States Department of Agriculture.
Utah, University of	Medicine, particularly internal medicine, obstetrics and gynecology, pharmacology, physiology, pediatrics, bacteriology. Also mining ventilation. Faculty includes world-renowned authorities in the field of mineral industries, including ceramics, chemistry (textile fabrics), fine arts (sculpture). Recently established Institutes of Government, World Affairs and has Bureaus of Economic Research and Educational Research to expand fields of social sciences.
Vanderbilt University	Aim is to provide a good Arts education; has pre-professional courses in rare instances. Schools of Medicine and Nursing outstanding.
Vermont, University of	Two and four-year courses in education. Exceptionally good in training doctors for Vermont and neighboring states. Has plans to make medical college a center for effective public health program including local nursing homes, hospitals, etc., throughout the state. Research in connection with maple syrup and methods of producing and perfecting tree production. Emphasis on dairying, especially milk production.
Virginia Military Institute	Engineering (B.S. and B.A.). Good pre-medical course and special attention to chemical engineering. Basis is sound general education rather than over-emphasis on military science.
Virginia Polytechnic Institute	Chemical Engineering, particularly in graduate school. Working with cedar sawdust to make laminated wood. Research in animal diseases and parasites.
Virginia, University of	Good School of Government and is organizing a Woodrow Wilson School of Foreign Service. Law and Medical Schools good; also a small but good Engineering School.
Washington, State College of	See page 175.

TABLE 8 (continued)

OUTSTANDING FEATURES

Institution	Outstanding Features
Washington, University of	Anatomy, Business Research, Chemistry and Chemical Engineering, Creative writing, Drama, Far Eastern Institute, Fisheries, Foreign languages, Forestry and Forest Products, Geology, Governmental Research, History, Microbiology, Nursing, Pathology, Physiology, Political Science, Psychology, Sociology.
West Virginia University	Research in coal deposits, preparing for time when coal industry changes its technique. Finest mineral industry building in United States. University houses the State Geological Survey, testing laboratories of State Road Commission, laboratory of United States Bureau of Mines with special attention to coal liquefication.
William and Mary, College of	Institute of Early American History jointly supported by the College and the Williamsburg Restoration. Also Virginia Fisheries Laboratory. Hampton Roads Area studies supported by Rockefeller Foundation.
Wisconsin, University of	See page 181.
Wooster, College of	Gives a program of independent study in the major field as the culmination of a liberal arts program. Prepares men for business, the learned professions. Faculty research most distinguished in field of sciences.
Wyoming, University of	Wool, poison plans, sheep raising, work in minerals, Wyoming history, range and wild life program, geology, botany, Rocky Mountain Herbarium, Zoology, and natural resources. Has Research Institute, Educational program of University closely tied in with state needs and possibilities.
Yale University	Coordination of studies of science and humanities. Center of study of linguistics. Important work in Institute of International Studies.

TABLE 9

ORGANIZATION OF BOARDS

Institution	How Organized	Meetings
Alabama Polytechnic Institute	Governor is chairman; vice chairman elected by Board; Executive Committee of 5 members; Budget Committee of 3; special committees as needed. Governor is active chairman.	Annually, first Monday in June; others on special call, usually about 3 meetings.
Alabama, University of	Governor is ex-officio president of Board. 2 trustees elected from Congressional District in which university is located, one from each of remaining 8 Congressional Districts.	2 annual meetings: 1 June 1, other about December 1. Special meetings on 7 days' notice.
Amherst College	Chairman, Secretary, Executive Committee, Standing Committee. Committees are: Finance, Budget, Instruction, Buildings and Grounds, Honorary Degrees, Folger Library, Eastman Foundation.	4 times a year.
Arizona, University of	Committees are Executive Committee for university and 2 state colleges, Finance, Committee on Educational Relations, Committee on Agriculture, Special Building and Land Committee and Special Survey Committee.	On call of chairman, usually 5 times a year.
Arkansas, University of	Chairman, elected annually, appoints committees. Standing committees: Personnel, Research, Athletics, Agriculture, Buildings, Grounds and Hospital, Legal.	At commencement and on call. About once a month.
California, University of	Chairman elected. Standing committees: Agriculture, Audit, Development and Endowments, Finance and Business Management, Grounds and Buildings, Lick Observatory, San Francisco Schools and Institutions, Southern California Schools, College and Institutions, Teacher Training Institutions. No executive committee.	Once a month. Finance Committee meets once a week, sometimes oftener.
California, Univ. of, at Los Angeles	Same as California, University of.	
California, University of Southern	Executive Committee does not function actively. Finance Committee, Building & Grounds, Investment, Honorary Degrees.	Finance Committee meets monthly; others occasionally.
Citadel, The	Executive Committee of 3 members. No other standing committees. Special committees appointed as required.	Twice a year and on call. Usually 4 times a year.
Clemson Agric. College	Standing committees: Executive Committee of 7, Agriculture Committee of 6, Fertilizer Committee of 6, Finance Committee of 5.	March, June, October, and on call. Executive Committee meets between Board meetings.
Colorado A. and M.	In April of alternate years, President and Vice-president elected from membership, also a Secretary and a Treasurer from non-members, all for 2-year terms. No committees specified. By tradition, 1 member elected to serve with executives as Executive Committee; Sometimes a Finance Committee is named.	Two annual and 1 biennial meetings fixed. Others at intervals of from 1 month to 6 weeks at discretion of Board.
Colorado, University of	University president is ex-officio chairman. Standing Committees: Executive, Auditing, Buildings and Grounds, Finance, Faculty Relations, Official Relations & Legislation, Medical Education and Conduct of Hospital. This is a constitutional board.	By statute twice a year; actually once a month with frequent Executive Committee meetings.

TABLE 9 (continued)

ORGANIZATION OF BOARDS

Institution	How Organized	Meetings
Connecticut, University of	Board acts as a whole. Occasionally special committees are appointed.	Each month except August and October.
Cornell University	5 Standing Committees appointed annually: Executive, Investment, Buildings and Grounds, Planning and Development, Law.	4 times a year.
Delaware, University of	Officers elected annually - President, Vice-president, Secretary and Treasurer; also Standing Committees as Executive, Agriculture, Arts and Sciences, Education, Engraving, Finance, Buildings and Grounds.	Twice yearly and on call.
Florida State University	Chairman, vice-chairman, secretary (employed no chancellor). One committee for each institution.	Monthly and on call.
Florida, University of	Board elects its chairman, vice-chairman, and a paid secretary. No chancellor. Committee for each institution.	At least once a month.
Georgia Board	Chairman, vice-chairman, chancellor, executive secretary, director of budgets, treas. The latter four are non-members. Standing and special committees appointed by chairman. Chancellor chief executive officer. No executive committee. Committees are: Education, Finance, Law & Organization, Buildings and Grounds, Agriculture. Special Committees as needed.	Monthly.
Georgia School of Technology	Same as Georgia Board.	
Georgia, University of	Same as Georgia Board.	
Harvard University	More than a score of committees organized under Board of Overseers, these empowered to inspect various departments of instruction and administration and report to the Board as a whole. Reports published for private circulation.	Corporation fortnightly; overseers one annual meeting and six other stated meetings a year; also on call.
Idaho, Univ. of	Rotate in office by custom.	9 or 10 times a year.
Illinois, University of	Board elects own officers. Rotation in office not practiced. 10 standing committees: Executive, Agriculture, Alumni, Athletic Activities, Buildings & Grounds, Chicago Department, Civil Service and Employees, Finance, General Policy, Patents, Student Welfare and Activities. Ex-officio members have vote. Secretary is a paid employee. Treasurer elected by board and not a paid employee. A public corporation and a statutory board.	Monthly and on call.
Indiana University	Acts as unit, under chairman, except Executive Committee acts between meetings. President of Board elected for undetermined term. University president at meetings but not member.	By statute once a year; and on call, average once a month.
Iowa State A. & M.	Chairman elected by vote of board. Rotation at will. Standing Committees: Faculty, Building and Business. Separate Finance Committee for full-time service.	Once each month.
Iowa, State University of	No rotation of officers. Board elects its officers for two-year period. Two committees of members: Faculty and Building and Business Committee Finance Committee appointed of non-members on salary. Institutional president non-member.	By statute 4 times a year; in practice, once a month.

TABLE 9 (continued)

ORGANIZATION OF BOARD

Institution	How Organized	Meetings
Kansas State College	Chairman rotated among members for one-year term; special committees appointed; constitutional board; president of college non-member.	Monthly; special meetings on call.
Kansas, University of	Statutory chairman elected annually, reasonable rotation in chairmanship; full-time paid secretary and university president not members. Standing Committees: Housing, Book Store, Retirement, Legislative, Oil Lease, Radio, Duplication of Work, Physical Education. Special committees on annual and legislative budgets, on special problems and projects.	Monthly with occasional exceptions. Special meetings on call.
Kentucky, University of	Governor is active chairman; Executive Committee elected by members. Vice-chairman presides at Executive Committee meetings. Special committees appointed as needed.	4 times a year. Executive Committee monthly and on call.
Louisiana State University	Rotation in office; standing committees carry on between meetings, reporting to Board all recommendations. Committee membership appointed by Board chairman for 2 year term. Standing Committees are: Finance, Buildings and Grounds, Faculty and Studies, Agriculture, and Extra-curricular and Athletic and Student Affairs.	4 regular meetings a year; special meetings on call, usually 2 additional.
Louisiana, Southwestern Institute	Chairman elected by members. Committees: Finance, Building, Education, Insurance, Legal, Legislative, Spastic Work.	Every other month, subject to call, usually 8 times a year.
Maine, University of	President and clerk elected annually by Board. Standing Committees: Executive, Finance, Physical Plant, Educational Policy, Honorary Degrees, also advisory committees on Agriculture and Technology.	About once a month.
Maryland, University of	4 Standing Committees: Budget, Building, Agriculture and Endowments. No Executive Committee.	Monthly and on call.
Massachusetts, University of	President, chairman of Board and committees elected by Board, annualy. Governor, an ex-officio member, usually elected president Executive Committee. Active. Also Finance, Faculty, Extension, Experiment Station, Legislative.	2 stated meetings a year, with numerous special meetings.
Miami, University of	Chairman, vice-chairman elected by Board. Standing Committees appointed by chairman: Executive, Finance, Membership. Special committees appointed as needed. Secretary of university is Board secretary; President is member, Vice-president is not. Mayor of Coral Gables and member of City Commission elected to Board because of financial support.	Annually and on call, usually 6 to 8 times a year.
Michigan State College	Chariman elected for 2-year term; committees appointed by chairman. Most action taken as Committee of the Whole. Superintendent of Public Instruction, Ex-officio, has vote. College president does not. Secretary is a paid employee, so is Treasurer.	Once a month and on call.

TABLE 9 (continued)

ORGANIZATION OF BOARDS

Institution	How Organized	Meetings
Michigan, University	President of university presiding officer. 3 Standing Committees: Educational Policies, Finance and Property, University Relations; Emergency Committee consists of chairmen of 3 Standing Committees and has power to take action when necessary. Secretary of Board is a paid university employee.	Monthly and on Call.
Minnesota, University of	Chancellor of university is President of Board, but has no vote. Standing Committees: Executive and Finance, Physical Plant, Investments, Budget; Special committees appointed as needed. Board elects own chairman, first and second vice-president, a secretary, assistant secretary, and a treasurer. No rotation in office. Secretary is a paid employee.	Normally 13 times a year. At least once a month except August.
Mississippi State College	Board elects one of its members president for period of one year or until successor is elected and elects a non-member as executive secretary, who maintains an office in Jackson, Mississippi. Special committees are recommended in the by-laws of the Board, among those recommended being Finance, Athletic, Agriculture, and Education.	January and June. Custom is once a month.
Mississippi State Coll. for Women	Citizens of Mississippi, one from each Congressional District, one from each Supreme Court District, and two from state at large. Board fills temporary vacancies. Eligible for reappointment. Standing committees are: Budget, Buildings, Athletics and special committees as need requires.	January and June. Custom is once a month.
Mississippi, University of	President elected annually from membership; appointed committees (athletics, building, budget, etc.) Special committees as need requires.	Monthly.
Missouri, University of	Full Board, Executive Board of 3, Exec. Committee of Mines and Metallurgy.	By statute, twice a year. In practice, at least once a month.
Montana State Univ.	Governor is ex-officio chairman; Superintendent of Public Instruction is ex-officio secretary.	Quarterly and on call.
Nebraska, University of	Rotation in election of president. Secretary is university Comptroller and non-member. Standing committees are: Executive, Finance, Professional Education and Research, Student and Public Relations, General Education, Property. President is always chairman of Executive Committee and each member is chairman of one committee and member of 3 committees.	By law twice a year and on call, average monthly.
Nevada, University of	Chairman elected by Board each 2 years. He appoints following committees: Property, Instruction, Library, Student Welfare. Executive Committee composed of chairman and one other member elected by Board.	Regularly 4 times a year. Oftener if necessary.
New Hampshire University of	Executive Committee. Special committees appointed as needed. Standing committees are: Executive, Finance, Personnel, Property, and Agricultural Affairs.	Monthly.
New Mexico, University of	President, Vice-President, Secretary. No rotation. No committees.	About every 6 weeks.

TABLE 9 (continued)

ORGANIZATION OF BOARDS

Institution	How organized	Meetings
N. Y. State Coll. for Teachers	No special committees; somewhat advisory in character.	4 times a year.
N.C. State Coll. of A. and E.	Executive Committee. Visiting Committee to each of 3 institutions once a year. Trustee committee on advanced Honorary Degrees. Executive Committee of 12 has full interim authority.	January or June. Executive Committee meets on call, usually 6 times a year.
N.C., Women's Coll. of the University of	Same as North Carolina State College of A. and E.	
North Dakota, University of	Board elects president for a term of 1 year. Rotation in office. Board appoints a State Commissioner of Higher Education. He serves as Executive Secretary to Board. No standing committees, but special committees as needed. Constitutional Board.	On call, about 10 times a year.
Ohio State University	Chairman each year is member whose term expires that year. No standing committees. Board acts as Committee of the Whole. Special committees sometimes appointed. Statutory board. Paid secretary not a member. Generally bi-partisan.	Regularly each month; special meetings on call.
Oklahoma A. and M.	Rotation in office. Board has finance and Building Committees; others as needed.	Regular monthly meetings. Some special. Fifteen in 1946.
Oklahoma College for Women	No standing committees of Board. Ex-officio member, State Superintendent is chairman.	Usually 7 or 8 times a year. Fixed Commencement meeting.
Oklahoma, University of	President elected so that each member serves as such once during term. No standing committees; appointed as need arises.	Monthly and on call. 21 meetings in 1946.
Oregon State College	Elects officers, President, Vice-President. President appoints committees: Building, Curriculum, Experiment Station, Finance.	Every six weeks.
Oregon State System	Board has President and Vice-President and one member of Executive Committee elected by Board each year. Secretary is appointed by Board from staff. Executive Committee functions between meetings.	8 meetings a year.
Oregon, University of	See Oregon State System.	
Pennsylvania State College	Officers and Executive Committee elected annually. Committees appointed by president of Board. Committees are: Architecture, Business and Finance, Buildings & Grounds, Education and Student, Staff Welfare,	Minimum, twice annually. Executive Committee 7 times annually and on call.
Purdue University	President, Vice-President, Secretary and Treasurer elected at annual meeting in October of odd years by ballot. May elect Assistant Secretary and Assistant Treasurer. Standing committees are: Executive and Finance, (Pres. and 2 members appointed by him); Physical Plant & Equipment (appointed by President); Investment (Pres. and Treas., Pres. of university and two Board members); Committee terms 2 years. Other committees as deemed necessary.	Minimum, 4 per year. Special meetings as necessary.

TABLE 9 (continued)

ORGANIZATION OF BOARDS

Institution	How Organized	Meetings
R. I. State College	Chairman, vice-chairman and secretary elected annually. No sub-committees; Board functions as a whole.	Monthly except July and August. Special meetings on call.
Rutgers University	President of university is chairman of Board; Executive Committee acts for Board between meetings; others have delegated powers.	Quarterly.
San Francisco State College	Elect chairman and act as committee of the whole nearly always. No standing committees, but can be created by the Board.	4 times a year and subject to call.
San Jose State College	Same as San Francisco State College.	
South Carolina, University of	Executive Committee (6), Finance, Buildings and Grounds, Student Affairs, Student Health, University Activities, Athletics, Honorary Degrees. Governor is chairman of Board.	Twice a year, plus 2 or 3 special meetings. Executive Committee meets on call.
S.D., Univ. of	President of university is non-member. Board elects own chairman and secretary. No rotation in office. Separate standing committees for each of 9 institutions under joint board. Special Committees appointed as needed.	Two fixed meetings a year; in practice once a month.
South, University of	Board of Regents acts as Executive Committee of Board of Trustees and elects own chairman. Chairman of Trustees is chancellor of university, elected by trustees. No definite term.	Trustees once a year. Regents quarterly and on call.
Stanford University	Committees on Finance, Academic Affairs, Buildings and Grounds, Rules, Nominations, Planning and Development. Board elects own president.	Once a month.
Tennessee, University of	Elects annually a chairman of the Board. An advisory committee appointed for each college. Also Executive Committee carries on interim functions.	Twice a year, usually December and August. Executive Committee on call, sometimes once a week.
Texas A. and M.	Board elects a president and appoints new committees each two years following appointment of new members.	6 times a year and on call.
Texas College of Mines	Reorganized each odd year. Executive and 16 other standing committees. All active.	Monthly except in summer. Committees meet prior to Board.
Texas Technological College	President, Secretary. Committees are: Executive, Building, Social Affairs, Finance, Legislative. Also special committees on Agriculture, Minerals, and Textiles.	3 fixed meetings and on call. Usually 8 times a year.
Texas, University of	Elects own chairman when 3 new members come on Board. Standing committees appointed by chairman: Athletics, Auditing, Budget, Buildings and Grounds, College of Mines, Complaints and Grievances, Executive, Finance, Land, Legislative, Library, McDonald Observatory, Visiting Medical and Dental Branches, Museum, Public and Student Relations, Lease of University Lands.	Once a month, December and August. Sometimes omitted. Also on special call.

TABLE 9 (continued)

ORGANIZATION OF BOARDS

Institution	How Organized	Meetings
Tuskegee Institute	Officers are: Chairman, vice-chairman, and a secretary, who are elected annually for 1 year. Secretary may or may not be trustee. Committees are: Executive and Finance.	Twice a year - October and April.
Utah State Agricultural College	Chairman selected by Board. Secretary appointed, non-member. Committees are: Executive, Agriculture, Engraving and Mechanical Arts, Home Economics, Commerce, Arts and Sciences, Education and Summer Session, Experiment Station, Extension Division, Faculty and Course of Study, Livestock, Buildings and Grounds, Heat, Power, and Light, Branch Agricultural College, Legislative and Finance, Student Affairs, Alumni, Faculty Relations, Policy and Procedure.	Monthly and on call. Executive Committee meets infrequently.
Utah, University of	Chairman, Vice-chairman, second vice-chairman, Secretary, Assistant Secretary, Treasurer. (latter 3 non-participating). Term of office 2 years. Standing committees appointed by chairman.	Monthly and on call.
Vanderbilt University	Executive Committee (8) operates between meetings. Finance Committee (5). Special committees from time to time.	Twice a year -- February and June. Executive Committee meets on call.
Vermont, University of	Officers and committees elected annually except chairman (president, ex-officio). Committees are Executive, Investment, Auditing, Education, Agriculture, Medicine, Engraving, Arts and Education, Buildings and Grounds. Special committees appointed annually on budget. Scholarship, etc. as needed.	6 times a year. Committees meet on call.
Virginia Military Institute	By committees (11). Committees meet on call.	Twice a year and on call.
Virginia Polytechnic Institute	Executive Committee (5) elected by Board. All other committees appointed by Rector, approved by Board.	Quarterly. Executive Committee about 8 times a year. Others on call.
Virginia, University of	Board elects own chairman and he is called the Rector of the university. Executive Committee has power between meetings of Board. Committees are: Finance, Buildings and Grounds, and one on Mary Washington College. Special committees as required.	Once a month.
Washington, State College of	By annual internal election of officers, rotation.	Once a month.
Washington, University of	Self-governing. No fixed rotation. Committees appointed by President of Board for 1 year.	Once a month, or oftener.
West Virginia University	President, Vice-President, and appointed Executive Secretary, paid, who is also Vice-President and Controller. Board acts as a unit. Study and advice from committees. Special committees appointed as needed.	Average over 6 meetings a year, and on call.
William and Mary, College of	One-third rotate each term. Standing committees are: Executive, Finance, Buildings and Grounds, Athletic. Executive Committee principally for emergencies.	Three per year and on call. Committees meet on call.

TABLE 9 (continued)

ORGANIZATION OF BOARDS

Institution	How Organized	Meetings
Wisconsin, University of	President, Vice-President and Secretary elected annually. President appoints committees. No rotation in office. Paid Secretary, non-member. Standing committees are: Executive, Finance, Education, Welfare and Student Life. Special committees are: Construction Development, Personnel, Regent-Faculty, Regent-Alumni, Regent-Visitors.	Each month and on call.
Wooster, College of	Elected chairman and vice-chairman; committees elected on nomination of Board. President of college is member. Secretary paid. Standing committees are: Administration, Buildings and Grounds, Faculty Relations, Finance, Financial Development, Library, Nominations.	3 times a year.
Wyoming, University of	Board elects chairman. No rotation in office; elects own Secretary, non-member. Standing committees are: Executive and Finance, Physical Plant and Equipment. Constitutional board.	On call as needed, 6 or 8 times a year.
Yale University	Permanent officers, deans and directors elected by ballot. President of university, ex-officio member of Board. Other officers, Provost, Secretary. Treasurer. Standing committees are: Prudential, Finance, Educational Policy, Library and Museums, Architectural Plan, Honorary Degrees, Buildings and Grounds. Committees also elected. President is chairman of Prudential Committee.	Twice a month except during summer.

TABLE 10

SELECTION AND COMPOSITION OF BOARDS

Institution	Kind	No.	Ex-officio	Qualifications	How Named	Vacancies & Eligibility	Term Yrs.	College Grads.
Alabama Polytechnic	single	12	2	1 from each Congressional district; 2 from home Congressional district.	Appointed by Governor, approved by senate.	Filled by Governor with interim appointments; eligible for reappointment.	12 (s)*	11
Alabama, Univ. of	single	12	2	Resident citizen from Congressional district.	Self-perpetuating, confirmed by senate.	Eligible to succeed themselves.	12 (s)	12
Amherst College	single	18	2	Non-formulated. Mainly outstanding alumni.	6 by vote of alumni, rest self-perpetuating.		Life, except alumni trustees.	10
Arizona, Univ. of	joint	10	2	College graduates.	Appointed by governor, approved by senate.	Eligible for reappointment.	8	10
Arkansas, Univ. of	single	10	0	3 alumni; rest by Congressional district.	Appointed by governor, approved by senate.	Filled by governor.	10 (s)	8
California, Univ. of	single	24	8		Appointed by governor, approved by senate.	Eligible for reappointment.	16	22
California, Univ. of, at Los Angeles	Same as California, University of.							
California Univ. of Southern	single	30			Self-perpetuating.	Eligible for reelection	3 (s)	19
Citadel, The	single	13	5	Alumni	7 elected by General Assembly; 1 by Alumni Assn.	Eligible for reelection.	6	13

* (s) staggered

TABLE 10 (continued)

SELECTION AND COMPOSITION OF BOARDS

Institution	Kind	No.	Ex-off-icio	Qualifications	How Named	Vacancies & Eligibility	Term Yrs.	College Grads.
Clemson Agric. College	single	13			7 self-perpetuating; 6 elected by Gen. Assembly.	Eligible for re-election.	4 (s) life	11
Colorado A. and M.	single	10	2	Half, practical farmers.	Appointed by governor, approved by senate.	Board fills interim vacancies; eligible to succeed themselves.	8	7
Colorado, Univ. of	single	6	1	State residents.	Popular vote.	Governor fills interim vacancies; eligible to succeed themselves.	6 (s)	6
Connecticut, Univ. of	single	13	3	Alumni must be out of college 10 yrs.	9 appointed by governor, 2 elected by alumni.		5	12
Cornell Univ.	single	45	11	3 labor, 3 agric. 3 industry.	18 by Board; 5 by governor, 10 by alumni, 1 life member.		5 except 1 (labor)	31
Delaware, Univ. of	single	32	4	1 skilled in mechanic arts; at least 5 from each county.	8 by governor; 20 self-perpetuating.	Interim vacancies same. Not eligible for reappointment.	6 (s)	32
Florida State Univ.	joint	5	0	Out of county.	Appointed by governor.	Eligible for re-appointment.	4 (s)	4
Florida, Univ. of	joint	5		Out of county.	appointed by governor.	Eligible for re-appointment.	4 (s)	4
Georgia Board	joint	15	0		Nominated by governor, confirmed by senate.	Interim vacancies by Board; eligible for re-appointment.	7 (s)	12

TABLE 10 (continued)

SELECTION AND COMPOSITION OF BOARDS

Institution	Kind	No.	Ex-off-icio	Qualifications	How Named	Vacancies & Eligibility	Term Yrs.	College Grads.
Georgia School of Technology	Same as Georgia Board.							
Georgia, Univ. of	Same as Georgia Board.							
Harvard Univ.	2 boards	39	2		5 self-perpet-uating; 30 elected by grads.	Eligible for re-appointment aft-er 1 year in-terval.	6	39
Idaho, Univ. of	single	5		Members of State Board of Education.		Rotate in office by custom.	5	
Illinois, Univ. of	single	11	2	Citizens.	Popular vote.	Filled by gov-ernor, eligible for reappoint-ment.	6 (s)	11
Indiana Univ.	single	8	0	State citizens, only 1 from a county, except Monroe.	3 by alumni elections; 5 elected by State Board of Education, approved by governor.	Filled by State Board and gov-ernor. Eligible for reappoint-ment.	3 (s) (alumni)	6
Iowa State A. and M.	joint	9	0	Bi-partisan.	Appointed by governor, ap-proved by senate.	Filled by gov-ernor, eligible for reappoint-ment.	6 (s)	8
Iowa, State Univ. of	Same as Iowa State A. and M.							
Kansas State College	joint	9	0	Competent state citizens; bi-par-tisan.	Appointed by governor, ap-proved by senate	Filled by gov-ernor, eligible for reappoint-ment.	4 (s)	7
Kansas, Univ. of	Same as Kansas State College.							
Kentucky, Univ. of	single	15	3	Distinguished citizens.	Appointed by governor.	Eligible for re-appointment.	6	10

TABLE 10 (continued)

SELECTION AND COMPOSITION OF BOARDS

Institution	Kind	No.	Ex-officio	Qualifications	How Named	Vacancies & Eligibility	Term Yrs.	College Grads.
Louisiana State Univ.	single	14	1	Not university employees.	By governor with consent of senate.	Eligible for re-appointment.	14 (s)	7
Louisiana, Southwestern Institute	joint	11		State residents.	8 by popular vote; 3 appointed from Public Service Commission District, approved by senate.	Eligible for re-appointment.	6 (elect.) 4 (appt.)	10
Maine, Univ. of	single	9	1	State residents 21-70.	Appointed by governor, approved by Council.		7 3 (alumni)	7
Maryland, Univ. of	single	11	0	2 must be members of certain organizations.	Appointed by governor and approved by senate.	Eligible for re-appointment.	9	8
Massachusetts, Univ. of	single	18	4	None specific.	Appointed by governor.	Eligible for re-appointment.	7 (s)	15
Miami, Univ. of	single	30		Reputable.	Self-perpetuating.	Eligible for re-election.	3	17
Michigan State College	single	8	2	Usual state office.	Popular vote.	Filled by governor, eligible for reelection.	6 (s)	3
Michigan, Univ. of	single	10	2	Usual state office.	Popular vote.	Eligible for re-election.	8 (s)	10
Minnesota, Univ. of	single	12	0	By Congressional district.	Elected by Legislature.	Filled by governor; eligible for reappointment.	6 (s)	10
Mississippi State Coll.	joint	15	0	1 from each Congressional district, 1 from each Superior Court district, 2 state at large.	Appointed by governor, approved by senate.	Filled by Board; eligible for re-appointment.	12 (s)	13

TABLE 10 (continued)

SELECTION AND COMPOSITION OF BOARDS

Institution	Kind	No.	Ex-off-icio	Qualifications	How Named	Vacancies & Eligibility	Term Yrs.	College Grads.
Mississippi State College for Women	Same as Mississippi State College.							
Mississippi, Univ. of	Same as Mississippi State College.							
Missouri, Univ. of	single	9	3	State Citizens, by-partisan.	Appointed by governor, approved by senate.		6 (s)	
Montana State Univ.	joint	11	3	Bi-partisan, equal division of Congressional district.	Appointed by governor, approved by senate.	By governor.	8	7
Nebraska, Univ. of	single	6	0	1 from each Congressional district.	Popular vote.	Eligible for re-election.	6	5
Nevada, Univ. of	single	5		Usual state office.	Popular vote.	Interim filled by governor.	4 (s)	5
New Hampshire, Univ. of	single	13		Bi-partisan.	10 appointed by governor, 2 elected by alumni.	Eligible for re-appointment.	4	7
New Mexico, Univ. of	single	5	2	1 vicinity resident.	Appointed by governor, approved by senate.	Eligible for re-appointment.	4	5
N. Y. State Coll. for Teachers	neither	7		Influential and successful citizens.	By State Board of Regents.	Eligible for re-appointment.	7	
N.C. State Coll. of A. and E.	joint	105	7	None specified.	Elected by legislature.	Eligible for re-appointment.	8	Majority.
N.C., Women's Coll. of the Univ. of	Same as North Carolina State College A. and E.							
North Dakota, Univ. of	joint	7	0		Appointed by governor, approved by senate.	Eligible for re-appointment.	7 (s)	5

TABLE 10 (continued)

SELECTION AND COMPOSITION OF BOARDS

Institution	Kind	No.	Ex-off-icio	Qualifications	How Named	Vacancies & Eligibility	Term Yrs.	Col-lege Grads.
Ohio State Univ.	single	7	1	State Citizen.	Appointed by governor, approved by senate.	Eligible for re-appointment.	7 (s)	7
Oklahoma A. and M.	single	9	1	By Congress-ional district.	Appointed by governor, ap-proved by senate.	Filled by gov-ernor, elig-ible for reap-pointment.	8 (s)	4
Oklahoma Coll. for Women	single	5	1	State citizen.	Appointed by governor, ap-proved by senate.	Eligible for re-appointment.	5 (s)	5
Oklahoma, Univ. of	single	7	0	No sectarian or partisan test allowed.	Appointed by governor, ap-proved by senate.	Eligible for re-appointment.	7 (s)	6
Oregon State College	joint	9		Non-resident of college com-munity, only 1 alumnus.	Appointed by governor, ap-proved by senate.	Eligible for re-appointment.	9 (s)	8
Oregon State System	Same as Oregon State College.							
Oregon, Univ. of	Same as Oregon State College.							
Pennsylvania State Coll.	single	32	4	Alumni mem-bers, by grad-uates of 3 years. Not members any other coll-ege board or faculty.	9 by alumni; 12 by county delegates, 6 by governor.		3	23
Purdue Univ.	single	9		3 resident, alumni (1 Agricultural-ist), 2 agricul-turalists, 2 in-dustrialists, 2 citizens of char-acter and dis-tinction (1 woman).	Appointed by governor.	Filled by gov-ernor except alumnus. Eli-gible for reap-pointment.	3 (s)	7

TABLE 10 (continued)

SELECTION AND COMPOSITION OF BOARDS

Institution	Kind	No.	Ex-officio	Qualifications	How Named	Vacancies & Eligibility	Term Yrs.	College Grads.
R. I. State College	joint	7	1	No other public office.	4 appointed by governor, 2 elected by alumni.	Interim vacancies filled same way.	3 (elect.) 7 (apptd.)	7
Rutgers Univ.	single	58	11		Appointed by governor, and approved by senate.		5	
San Francisco State Coll.	single	10	2	State Department of Education.	Appointed by governor and approved by senate.	Eligible for reappointment.	4	4
San Jose State College	Same as San Francisco State College (single board for all state teachers' colleges).							
South Carolina, Univ. of	single	18	4	1 each Judicial district.	Elected by legislature.	Eligible for reappointment.	4	17
South Dakota, Univ. of	joint	5	0	Non-resident of university county.	Appointed by governor and approved by senate.	Eligible for reappointment.	6 (s)	2
South, Univ. of	single (regents)	16		By diocese, plus 6 elected by alumni.	Elected by Board of Trustees, a body of 91.	Eligible for reappointment.	3	16
Stanford, Univ.	single	15		None stipulated.	Self-perpetuating.	Eligible for re-election.	10	15
Tennessee, Univ. of	single	18	4	1 from each Congressional district; 2 from Memphis; 2 from Knoxville. Interested in higher education.	Appointed by governor.	Eligible for reappointment.	14 (s)	15
Texas A. and M.	single	9		State citizens.	Appointed by governor and approved by senate.		6 (s)	7

TABLE 10 (continued)

SELECTION AND COMPOSITION OF BOARDS

Institution	Kind	No.	Ex-officio	Qualifications	How Named	Vacancies & Eligibility	Term Yrs.	College Grads.
Texas College of Mines	joint	9	0		Appointed by governor and approved by senate.	Eligible for re-appointment.	6 (s)	9
Texas Techno-logical Coll.	single	9	0	State citizens.	Appointed by governor and approved by senate.	Eligible for re-appointment.	6	9
Texas, Univ. of	Same as Texas College of Mines - joint board for University of Texas, Texas Medical School, Texas College of Mines.							
Tuskegee Inst.	single	17-25		None specified.	Up to 19 self-perpetuating; balance ap-pointed.		3 (s)	all but 1
Utah State Agric. Coll.	single	14	2	Bi-partisan.	Appointed by governor and approved by senate.	Filled by gov-ernor, eligible for reappoint-ment.	4 (s)	7
Utah, Univ. of	single	15	3	State residents.	Appointed by governor and approved by senate.	Filled by gov-ernor, eligible for reappoint-ment.	4 (s)	12
Vanderbilt Univ.	single	33		None specified.	Self-perpet-uating.	Eligible for re-appointment.	8 (s)	33
Vermont, Univ. of	single	20	2	None specified.	9 self-perp-etuating, 9 elected by General Ass-embly.	Eligible for re-election after 1 year interval	6	17
Virgiaia Mil-itary Inst.	single	13	2	Good citizens.	Appointed by governor.	Eligible for re-appointment in alternate terms.	4	11
Virginia Poly-technic Inst.	single	15	2	State citizens.	Appointed by governor.	Not more than 2 terms.	4	12

TABLE 10 (continued)

SELECTION AND COMPOSITION OF BOARDS

Institution	Kind	No.	Ex-officio	Qualifications	How Named	Vacancies & Eligibility	Term Yrs.	College Grads.
Virginia, Univ. of	single	14	1	8 alumni.	Appointed by governor and approved by senate.	Not more than 2 terms until lapse of 1 term.	4	13
Washington, State Coll. of	single	5			Appointed by governor and approved by senate.	Filled by governor.	6	3
Washington, Univ. of	single	7		State citizens.	Appointed by governor and approved by senate.	Filled by governor.	6 (s)	6
West Virginia Univ.	single	7	0	Bi-partisan; 3 alumni; by Congressional district.	Appointed by governor and approved by senate.	Eligible for reappointment.	4	6
William and Mary, Coll. of	single	11	1	6 alumni.	Appointed by governor and approved by Gen. Assembly.	One immediate reelection permitted; then eligible again after 4 years.	4	10
Wisconsin, Univ. of	single	10	1	State citizens, not more than 2 per county.	Appointed by governor and approved by senate.	Filled by governor, eligible for reappointment.	9 (s)	5
Wooster, Coll. of	single	30			Self-perpetuating, approved by Synod of Ohio.	Eligible for reelection.	3 (s)	25
Wyoming, Univ. of	single	12	3	State citizens, by-partisan, not more than 1 per county.	Appointed by governor and approved by senate.	Filled by governor.	6 (s)	

TABLE 10 (continued)

SELECTION AND COMPOSITION OF BOARDS

Institution	Kind	No.	Ex-officio	Qualifications	How Named	Vacancies & Eligibility	Term Yrs.	College Grads.
Yale Univ.	single	19		6 Fellows must be 1st degree of 5 years standing; 10 successors have none specified.	10 self-perpetuating, 6 elected by alumni.		to age of 68	19

TABLE 11

RELATIONS BETWEEN PRESIDENTS AND BOARDS

The general practice followed in most institutions is for the Board to prescribe general policies, but leave details of administration to the president and the administrative staff. Institutions which deviate from this general procedure are listed below, with details given with reference to their manner of procedure.

Institution	Administrative Procedure
Alabama, University of	President does not take action on matters of major importance unless first authorized by Board or Board's Executive Committee.
Arkansas, University of	Plan is to give new president extensive authority. Actions, however, subject to confirmation by Board.
California, University of	Wide latitude but little occasion to act on own, due to frequent Board meetings.
California, University of Southern	President exercises wide control and acts independently of the Board.
Colorado A. and M.	In matters of appointment, president takes action between meetings. On matters out of ordinary, president confers with executive committee by phone or mail before acting, obtain confirmation at next meeting.
Cornell Univ.	President acts on own initiative when speedy action is essential.
Delaware, University of	President is practically never over-ruled in matters of administration.
Georgia School of Technology	Other than expenditure of funds and election of faculty and staff members, Board does not generally require president to secure its authorization.
Maryland, University of	Board does not confirm actions except when president acts in emergency.
Montana State University	Normally matters of broad policy, such as the Board makes its concern, are taken to Board before action is taken. In general policies, the Board expects president to administer the institution.
Nevada, University of	Custom of president to call by phone each regent and to discuss with each one any action which must be taken of a policy-making nature, which will be ratified at next meeting.
North Dakota, University of	Board must confirm all expenditures of more than $300 per item. Commissioner makes decision on recommendation of president which is eventually referred to Board for record. Commissioner has wide powers and only subject to revise in case of illegality.
Pennsylvania State College	Board sometimes called upon to confirm actions taken by president. Executive Committee acts as a check.
Rutgers University	Only occasionally is Board called upon to confirm actions of president.
Tennessee, University of	President makes annual statement to the Board and asks for confirmation of procedures and operations. Only occasionally does Board challenge the report.
Vermont, University of	Approval generally given in advance. Considerable freedom given to president.
Virginia Poly-Technic Inst.	Board does not interfere as long as work is satisfactory.
West Virginia University	President given all freedom that is permissible under State Law.

TABLE 12

BOARD CONTACTS WITH FACULTY, STUDENTS, AND ALUMNI

Institution	Faculty Contact	Student Contact	Alumni Contacts-How Secretary Financed.
Alabama Polytechnic Inst.	Frequent; informal.	Frequent; informal.	Strong nucleus; secretary paid by institution.
Alabama, Univ. of	On invitation.	On invitation.	Very harmonious; secretary paid by institution.
Amherst Coll.	Yes; informal.	Yes; informal	Secretary paid by alumni.
Arizona, Univ. of	Very little.	Very little.	
Arkansas, Univ. of	Has been close.	Has been close.	Secretary paid jointly by Board and alumni.
California, Univ. of	No	No	Pressure not abused. Secretary paid by alumni.
California, Univ. of, at Los Angeles	No	No	Pressure not abused.
California, Univ. of Southern	No	No	No pressure.
Citadel, The	No; may appeal.	No; may appeal.	Secretary receives no salary. College finances office.
Clemson Agric. College	Social contact encouraged.	May Appear occasionally.	
Colorado A. and M.	May upon request.	May upon request.	Harmonious; secretary paid by institution.
Colorado, Univ. of	May upon request.	May upon request.	Harmonious; secretary paid by institution.
Connecticut, Univ. of	Only through president.	Only through president.	Secretary paid by institution.
Cornell Univ.	No	No	Secretary paid by institution.
Delaware, Univ. of	No	No	Secretary paid by institution.
Florida State Univ.	Only through president.	Only through president.	No pressure; secretary paid jointly by Board and Alumni.
Florida, Univ. of	Only through president.	Only through president.	Helpful; no secretary at present.
Georgia Board	No	No	
Georgia School of Technology	No	No	Secretary paid jointly by school and alumni.
Georgia, Univ. of	May through president.	May through president	No pressure; university contributes $3000 toward salary of secretary.
Harvard Univ.	Only through visiting committee.	No	Secretary serves without salary.
Idaho, Univ. of	No	Only by request of student.	Secretary paid jointly by alumni, students and institution.
Illinois, Univ. of	Only through president.	Only through president.	Alumni Association subsidized by university to extent of $40,000. Secretary not member of administrative staff.
Indiana, Univ. of	Through president.	Through president.	Cooperative. Secretary paid by institution.
Iowa State A. and M.	Through president.	Through president.	Cost of operation by director shared jointly.

TABLE 12 (continued)

BOARD CONTACTS WITH FACULTY, STUDENTS, AND ALUMNI

Institution	Faculty Contact	Student Contact	Alumni Contacts-How secretary Financed
Iowa, State Univ. of	Through president.	Through president.	Cooperative. University appoints secretary.
Kansas State College	Through president.	Through president.	Cordial. Secretary paid by alumni.
Kansas, Univ. of	Through president.	Through president.	Cordial. Secretary paid by alumni.
Kentucky, Univ. of	Right of appeal.	Right of appeal.	Secretary paid by institution.
Louisiana State Univ.	Through president.	Through president.	Little pressure. Secretary paid by institution.
Louisiana, Southwestern Inst.	Through president.	Through president.	Little pressure; not very strong.
Maine, Univ. of	Frequently with deans.	Convocations.	Secretary paid by alumni. Institution furnishes office facilities.
Maryland, Univ. of	Yes	Can submit matters.	No pressure. Secretary paid by institution.
Massachusetts, Univ. of	Reasonably close.	Appear at times.	Secretary paid jointly by alumni-30%; institution 70%.
Miami, Univ. of	No; could appear through president.	No; could appear through president.	No pressure. Secretary paid by institution.
Michigan State Coll.	No; could appear through president.	No; could appear through president.	Alumni director selected by president; office expenses paid by college.
Michigan, Univ. of	Through president.	Through president.	Cooperative; secretary paid by alumni.
Minnesota, Univ. of	No; may appear through president.	No; may appear through president.	Cooperative; secretary paid jointly by alumni and university.
Mississippi State Coll.	Through president.	Through president.	No pressure; secretary paid by alumni.
Mississippi State Coll. for Women	Through president.	Through president.	No pressure; secr ry paid by Board.
Mississippi, Univ. of	Through president.	Through president.	No pressure; secreta. aid by institution.
Missouri, Univ. of	Accessible; social functions.	Accessible; social functions.	Secretary paid by institution.
Montana State Univ.	Informal.	Informal.	Alumni director paid by institution.
Nebraska, Univ. of	May through chancellor.	May through chancellor.	Secretary not on university payroll. Board subsidizes alumni association to $8250.
Nevada, Univ. of	Through records.	Through records.	Secretary paid by alumni. Institution furnishes office.
New Hampshire, Univ. of	Not officially.	Not officially.	Association not strong.
New Mexico, Univ. of	Through president.	Through president.	No pressure. Secretary paid by university.
N. Y. State Coll. for Teachers	No	No	Secretary paid by alumni.

TABLE 12 (continued)

BOARD CONTACTS WITH FACULTY, STUDENTS, AND ALUMNI

Institution	Faculty Contact	Student Contact	Alumni Contacts-How Secretary Financed
N.C. State Coll. of A. and E.	Yes through visiting committee.	yes through visiting committee.	Many of trustees are alumni. Secretary paid jointly by alumni and college.
N.C., Women's Coll. of the Univ. of	Yes through visiting committee.	Yes through visiting committee.	Many of trustees are alumnae. Secretary paid by college.
North Dakota, Univ. of	No; may appear through Commissioner.	No; may appear through Commissioner.	Secretary subsidized by university for specific tasks.
Ohio State Univ.	Through president.	Through president.	Alumni Association financed in part by university.
Oklahoma A. and M.	Through president.	Through president.	No pressure. Secretary paid by institution.
Oklahoma Coll. for Women	May through president.	May through president.	No pressure. No alumnae secretary.
Oklahoma, Univ. of	May through president.	May through president.	No pressure. Secretary paid by alumni.
Oregon State College	No	No	
Oregon State System	Individual members visit.	Very little.	
Oregon, Univ. of			Secretary paid by institution 82%.
Pennsylvania State Coll.	No, but may be heard.	No, but may be heard.	Secretary paid by institution.
Purdue Univ.	Yes.	Yes.	Cooperative. Secretary paid by alumni.
R. I. State College	Occasional.		Secretary paid by college.
Rutgers Univ.	No	No	Secretary paid by alumni.
San Francisco State Coll.	No	No	No contact. Secretary paid by alumni.
San Jose State College.	None whatever.	No	No contact; placement service paid by state.
South Carolina, Univ. of	Yes through president.	Yes through president.	Secretary paid by institution.
South Dakota, Univ. of	May through president.	May through president.	Active nucleus. Secretary does not receive salary from alumni as such. As staff member, he is good liason officer.
South, Univ. of	Yes frequently.	Yes	Nearly all regents are alumni. Secretary paid jointly by alumni and institution.
Stanford Univ.	Individual; informal.	Individual; informal.	Alumni employees paid by alumni.
Tennessee, Univ. of	No; representatives appear occasionally.	No; representatives appear occasionally.	Secretary paid by institution.
Texas A. and M.	Limited.	Limited.	Secretary paid by former students' association.
Texas College of Mines	Little opportunity.	Little opportunity.	No pressure; alumni young group. Secretary paid jointly by alumni and institution.

TABLE 12 (continued)

BOARD CONTACTS WITH FACULTY, STUDENTS, AND ALUMNI

Institution	Faculty Contact	Student Contact	Alumni Contacts-How Secretary Financed
Texas Technological Coll.	May through president	May through president.	Considerable pressure; secretary paid by alumni.
Texas, Univ. of	Very little.	May through president.	No pressure; secretary paid by alumni.
Tuskegee Institute	No information given.		Secretary paid jointly by institution and alumni.
Utah State Agric. Coll.	Very limited.	Very limited.	Pressure limited to athletics; secretary paid by state funds.
Utah, Univ. of	No; has liason committee.	No	Secretary paid by alumni.
Vanderbilt Univ.	Informal.	Informal.	Secretary paid by institution.
Vermont, Univ. of	Only social.	Practically none.	Through fraternities. Secretary paid by institution.
Virginia Military Institute	Yes	Yes	Yes. A considerable number of board members are alumni. Secretary paid by alumni.
Virginia Polytechnic Inst.	No; may appear before committee.	No; may appear before committee.	Secretary paid by alumni.
Virginia, Univ. of	Not close.	Has student committee.	
Washington, State Coll. of	Generally, no.	Generally, no.	Jointly by alumni and institution.
Washington, Univ. of	No; some contacts with deans.	No	Secretary paid on cooperative basis.
West Virginia Univ.	May appear upon request.	May appear upon request.	Secretary paid jointly by alumni and institution.
William and Mary, Coll. of	Faculty active in attempting influence.	Are invited to appear.	Secretary paid by institution.
Wisconsin, Univ. of	Through regent-faculty committee.	Little contact.	Very cooperative; secretary paid by alumni.
Wooster, Coll. of	Through trustee-faculty committee.	Through student-faculty committee.	Secretary paid by institution.
Wyoming, Univ. of	No	No	No pressure; secretary paid by institution.
Yale University	No	No	Secretary paid by institution.

TABLE 13

FINANCES

Institution	Appropriated by Lump Sum or Line Item	How Disbursed	Jurisdiction of Fees	Appearance of Board Before Legislature
Alabama Polytechnic Inst.	Lump sum for maintenance and support.	Directly to institution.	Institution retains.	Does not appear. Board will approve budget requests first time 1947.
Alabama, Univ. of	Lump sum under large heads.	Directly to institution.	Institution retains.	Advisory.
Amherst Coll.	Lump sum.	Directly.	Institution retains.	Private control.
Arizona, Univ. of	Lump sum.	Directly.		Finance Committee of Board presents.
Arkansas, Univ. of	Lump sum under large heads.	By university treasurer, countersigned and paid by state treasurer.	Institution retains.	Members appear before Legislative Committee.
California, Univ. of	Lump sum.	Requisition on state director of finance.	Institution retains.	Regents represented by Controller.
California, Univ. of, at Los Angeles	Lump sum.	Requisition on state director of finance.	Institution retains.	Regents represented by Controller.
California, Univ. of Southern	Lump sum.	Directly.	Institution retains.	Private control.
Citadel, The	Lump sum for wages, salaries and operations.	Monthly vouchers drawn on state treasurer.	State retains.	Appears only upon request.
Clemson Agric. College	Lump sum for maintenance.	Monthly vouchers drawn on state treasurer.		Chairman of Executive Committee appears.
Colorado A. and M.	Lump sum.	By state treasurer.	Institution retains.	None.
Colorado, Univ. of	Lump sum under large heads.	Directly.	Institution retains.	None.
Connecticut, Univ. of	Lump sum under large heads.	Directly.	University retains.	Appears only upon request.

TABLE 13 (Continued)

FINANCES

Institution	Appropriated by Lump Sum or Line Item	How Disbursed	Jurisdiction of Fees	Appearance of Board Before Legislature
Cornell Univ.	Lump sum except maintenance and operation.	By state comptroller on voucher.	University retains.	Merely authorizes administration to request.
Delaware, Univ. of	Lump sum under large heads.	Through state treasurer.	Finance Committee of Board of Trustees.	Board Chairman appears.
Florida State Univ.	Line item.	Voucher by state comptroller on state treasurer.	State retains.	Appears before Appropriation Committee.
Florida, Univ. of	Lump sum under large heads.	Voucher by state comptroller on state treasurer.	University controls.	Board presents budget.
Georgia Board	Lump sum.	Board allocates		Does not appear.
Georgia School of Technology	Lump sum.	Directly.	Treasurer of Board of Regents and accounted for to state.	Does not appear.
Georgia, Univ. of	Lump sum.	Directly.	University retains.	Private control.
Harvard Univ.		University treasurer.	Institution retains.	Private control.
Idaho, Univ. of	Lump sum.	Board controls.	Board controls.	Appear before Finance Committee.
Illinois, Univ. of	Lump sum under large heads.	Individual voucher on state treasurer.	State retains.	Assist in presenting budget.
Indiana Univ.	Lump sum under large heads.	Directly.	Retained by institution.	Usually not active.
Iowa State A. and M.	Lump sum.	Directly.	Institution retains.	One or more members attend.
Iowa, State Univ. of	Lump sum.	Directly.	Institution retains.	One or more members attend.

TABLE 13 (continued)

FINANCES

Institution	Appropriated by Lump Sum or Line Item	How Disbursed	Jurisdiction of Fees	Appearance of Board Before Legislature
Kansas State College	Lump sum under large heads.	Warrant on state treasurer.	Remitted to state & expended as other state funds.	Legislative Committee of Board assist administration funds.
Kansas, Univ. of	Lump sum under large heads.	Warrant on state treasurer.	Included in appropriations.	Member of board presents budget.
Kentucky, Univ. of	Lump sum under large heads.	Directly on requisition.	Remitted to state for university use.	Appears only on request.
Louisiana State Univ.	Lump sum under large heads.	Directly.	University retains.	By written report.
Louisiana, Southwestern Inst.	Line item.	Directly.	State retains.	Submits budget to Appropriations Committee.
Maine, Univ. of	Lump sum.	Directly.	University retains.	President of Board usually appears.
Maryland, Univ. of	Lump sum under large heads.	By state treasurer	State holds for university use.	Board appears upon request.
Massachusetts, Univ. of	Line item.	Directly, but under supervision.	State retains.	Legislative Committee of Board active.
Miami, Univ. of	Lump sum.	Directly.	Institution retains.	Private control.
Michigan State College	Lump sum under large heads.	Directly.	Institution retains.	Does not appear, except as individuals.
Michigan, Univ. of	Lump sum.	Directly.	Institution retains.	Occasional, but executive officers usually represent university.
Minnesota, Univ. of	Lump sum for maintenance.	Directly.	Institution retains.	Presents budget.
Mississippi State College	Lump sum.	Directly.	Institution retains.	Contacts for appropriations.
Mississippi State Coll. for Women	Lump sum.	Directly; income check from state.	Institution retains.	Appears before Appropriations Committee.
Mississippi, Univ. of	Lump sum.	Directly.	Institution retains.	Appears before Appropriations Committee.
Missouri, Univ. of	Lump sum.	Directly.	University retains.	Appears before legislature.

FINANCES

Institution	Appropriated by Lump Sum or Line Item	How Disbursed	Jurisdiction of Fees	Appearance of Board Before Legislature
Montana State Univ.	Lump sum under large heads.	Directly.	State retains.	Ordinarily, backing is moral support.
Nebraska, Univ. of	Lump sum.	By approved voucher on state treasurer.	Deposited with state treasurer to credit of university.	Board presents budget.
Nevada, Univ. of	Lump sum.	Partly through state office.	Institution retains.	Chairman of Board frequently appears.
New Hampshire, Univ. of	Lump sum.	Directly		Very little contact.
New Mexico, Univ. of	Lump sum.	Directly.	Institution retains.	Does not appear.
N.Y. State Coll. for Teachers	Line item.	Directly, but through state office.	State retains.	No assistance by Board.
N.C. State Coll. of A. and E.	Line item.	By state treasurer on draft.	State retains.	Appears before committees from time to time.
N.C., Women's Coll. of the Univ. of	Lump sum within classifications.	By state treasurer on draft.	Deposited with state to credit of college.	Appears before committees from time to time.
North Dakota, Univ. of	Lump sum under large heads.	Directly.	Retained by state.	Ex-officio committee presents bill to Appropriations Committee.
Ohio State Univ.	Lump sum under large heads.	Directly, but funds remain in state treasury.	State retains.	Board not active with legislature.
Oklahoma A.& M.	Lump sum.	By state regents.		Does not appear.
Oklahoma, College for Women	Lump sum under large heads.	By state regents, handled by voucher by institution on state treasurer.	Institution retains, but amount is charged as estimated income in following year's budget allocation.	Does not appear.

TABLE 13 (continued)

FINANCES

Institution	Appropriated by Lump Sum or Line Item	How Disbursed	Jurisdiction of Fees	Appearance of Board Before Legislature
Oklahoma, Univ. of	Lump sum.	By state regents.	Deposited in treasury for university.	Members appear before Appropriations Committee.
Oregon State College	Lump sum.	By State Board of Higher Education.	"unrestricted" use.	Not unless invited.
Oregon State System	Lump sum.	By State Board of Higher Education.	Board distributes on basis of need.	One or two members usually appear at legislative hearings.
Oregon, Univ. of	Under Oregon State System by State Board of Higher Education. Distributes on basis of need.			
Pennsylvania State College	Lump sum under large heads.	Directly.	Institution retains.	Members may be called if desired.
Purdue Univ.	Lump sum, generally.	Directly; received monthly from state treasurer.	Institution retains.	Does not appear unless requested.
R. I. State College	Lump sum.	Directly,	State retains for college use.	Represented at hearings.
Rutgers Univ.	More than 50% lump sum; partly specified.	Directly, through state budget director.	University retains.	Members appear before state Appropriations Committee.
San Francisco State College	Lump sum under large heads.	Through state office of Education.	State retains.	Does not appear.
San Jose State College	Lump sum under large heads.	Through state.	State retains for credit to college.	Does not appear.
South Carolina, Univ. of	Lump sum.	Directly by monthly draft on state treasurer.	State retains.	Does not appear.
South Dakota, Univ. of	Lump sum under large heads.	Directly by voucher method.	State retains.	Budget presentation in presence of regents.

TABLE 13 (continued)

FINANCES

Institution	Appropriated by Lump Sum or Line Item	How Disbursed	Jurisdiction of Fees	Appearance of Board Before Legislature
South, Univ. of	Lump sum.	Directly.	Institution retains.	Private control.
Stanford Univ.	Lump sum.	Directly.	Institution retains.	Private control.
Tennessee, Univ. of	Lump sum.	Directly.	Institution retains.	Board works with staff in securing funds. Appears occasionally.
Texas College of Mines	Line item.	Directly.	Institution retains.	Appears with president.
Texas Technological College	Line item.	Requisition on state controller for each item.	Institution retains.	Appear before Appropriations Committee.
Texas, Univ. of	Line item, theoretically; lump sum actually.	By voucher on state treasurer.	Institution retains.	Appear before Legislative Committees on invitation to assist president.
Tuskegee Inst.	Lump sum.	Directly.	Institution retains.	Some aid with selected projects.
Utah State Agric. College	Lump sum.	By requisition on state.	State retains.	Board assists on invitation of president.
Utah, Univ. of	Lump sum under large heads.	Through state Department of Finance.	State retains for university use.	Board assists president when called upon.
Vanderbilt Univ.	Lump sum.	Directly.	Institution retains.	Private control.
Vermont, Univ. of	Lump sum.	Directly.	Institution retains.	Nearly all members of Board are members of legislature.
Virginia Military Inst.	Lump sum for maintenance and operations.	Quarterly, through state treasurer.	State retains.	Members appear before legislative committee.
Virginia Polytechnic Inst.	Lump sum for operations.	Directly, through state controller.	State retains.	Sometimes appears before committees.
Virginia, Univ. of	Lump sum except salaries.	By state treasurer as bills submitted.		Appears before legislative committees when called upon.

TABLE 13 (continued)

FINANCES

Institution	Appropriated by Lump Sum or Line Item	How Disbursed	Jurisdiction of Fees	Appearance of Board Before Legislature
Washington, State Coll. of	Line item.	State funds available through state office.	Institution retains.	Appears before Appropriations Committee.
Washington, Univ. of	Lump sum under large heads.	Directly, but drawn on state treasurer.	State retains tuition fees.	Visit Appropriation Committee when asked.
West Virginia Univ.	Lump sum under large heads.	By state auditor after approval.	Institution retains.	Appears on occasion.
William and Mary, Coll. of	Combination of lump sum and line item.	Quarterly allotment through state.	State controls.	Does not appear.
Wisconsin, Univ. of	Line item.	Directly.	Institution retains.	Presentation of budget made by designated Board member.
Wyoming, Univ. of	Lump sum under large heads.	Checks signed by state auditor.	Institution retains.	Members not normally present.
Yale University	Lump sum.	Directly.	Institution retains.	Private control.

TABLE 14

ASSETS

Institution	Total Assets	How Assets are Distributed	By Whom Held
Alabama Polytechnic Institute	$ 9,510,913	$ 6,649,262 in physical plant 1,231,711 endowment and trust fund 101,266 fraternity loans receivable 1,528,672 other current assets	Board
Alabama, Univ. of	27,850,142	19,108,312 in land, buildings and equipment 7,400,681 endowment	Board
Amherst College	21,159,519	19,823,360 in fixed assets 1,336,159 in current funds	Board
Arizona, Univ. of	8,350,000	8,250,000 land, buildings & equipment 100,000 endowment	All but land held by Board
Arkansas, Univ. of	10,130,000	10,000,000 lands, buildings & grounds 130,000 endowments	Board
California, Univ. of	100,000,056	63,909,000 land, buildings & equipment 36,000,146 endowments	Board
California, Univ. of, at Los Angeles	Included in California, University of, and Comprising about 20% of total		
California, Univ. of Southern	22,000,000	16,000,000 land, buildings & equipment 1,250,000 endowment 2,400,000 Hancock Foundation 2,000,000 surplus	Board
Citadel, The	5,372,552		State
Clemson Agric. College	7,562,100	7,250,000 buildings, grounds & equipment 284,000 various funds 20,000 loan funds 8,100 gifts	Board
Colorado A. and M.	7,212,531	5,071,678 land, buildings and equipment	State Board of Agriculture.
Colorado, Univ. of	18,617,330	11,481,270 land, buildings & equipment 927,599 endowment funds	Board
Connecticut, Univ. of	11,500,000		Trustees
Cornell Univ.	70,100,000	21,000,000 endowed colleges 9,100,000 state colleges 40,000,000 endowment	Board
Delaware, Univ. of	Not given	Practically all buildings on campus are from private gifts. Maintenance and operation, state 90%; private sources 10%. Most buildings given by DuPont executives and many maintained by endowments.	Board
Florida State Univ.	6,292,000	6,000,000 land, buildings, etc. 140,000 endowment 152,000 loan funds	State
Florida, Univ. of	11,382,784	11,010,411 land, buildings, etc. 320,344 endowment 52,029 loan funds	State Board of Education
Georgia Board	See Georgia Technological College and Georgia, University of.		
Georgia School of Technology	12,676,275	12,071,735 land, buildings, & equipment 604,538 endowment 100,000 current assets	Board

TABLE 14 (continued)

ASSETS

Institution	Total Assets	How Assets are Distributed	By Whom Held
Georgia, Univ. of	$ 11,592,091	$ 8,413,883 land, buildings & equipment 948,589 endowment 1,356,826 loan fund 936,009 current assets	Board
Harvard Univ.	Not given		Board
Idaho, Univ. of	Not given		Board
Illinois, Univ. of	60,721,151	5,686,240 current funds 406,990 loan funds 2,102,783 endowment 52,493,562 plant funds 31,574 agency funds	Board
Indiana Univ.	27,998,325	1,347,181 current funds 198,847 loan funds 22,690,500 plant 565,391 enterprise 92,685 agency 31,838 scholarships 3,071,881 endowments	Major holdings in name of Board. Rest by state.
Iowa State A. and M.	22,744,170	3,061,686 current funds 122,570 loan funds 1,288,994 endowment 18,145,960 plant funds 124,960 agency funds	State Board of Education.
Iowa, State Univ. of	31,556,274	152,128 student loan funds 3,611,706 current funds 220,955 agency funds 1,283,964 endowment 2,592,000 capital funds 23,695,521 property and equipment	State Board of Education.
Kansas State College	7,985,986	64,604 student loan funds 551,841 endowment funds 4,822,883 land, buildings equipment 223,536 supplies 1,233,307 unexpended plant funds 1,099,821 other unexpended funds	State
Kansas, Univ. of	21,896,264	12,392,186 land, buildings, equipment 166,642 loan funds 1,230,022 endowment 6,912,869 cash 1,194,543 unexpended building funds	Majority by state
Kentucky, Univ. of	13,201,624	11,291,186 land, buildings & equipment 2,009,537 - by - 901 - by -	State Board of Trustees Haggin Estate
Louisiana State Univ.	30,177,540	23,432,696 land, buildings, equipment 6,744,844 cash and securities	Board
Louisiana, Southwestern Inst.	4,860,000	3,660,000 land, buildings, equipment 1,200,000 state appropriations	State
Maine, Univ. of	7,500,000	Land, buildings and endowment (1,200,000 endowment)- by - 100,000 Foundation)- by -	90% state; 10% trustees trustees University of Maine Foundation.

TABLE 14 (continued)

ASSETS

Institution	Total Assets	How Assets are Distributed	By Whom Held
Maryland, Univ. of	Not given		State, except endowments.
Massachusetts, Univ. of	$ 5,000,000	($162,000 Trustee Endowment Fund) Buildings financed by alumni are self-liquidating and ceded to state.	State, except Trustee Endowment fund.
Miami, Univ. of	2,662,043	$2,362,886 land, buildings, etc. 116,957 expansion fund 175,061 plant fund 7,139 scholarship fund	Board
Michigan State Coll.	36,803,688	19,201,739 land, buildings, equipment 4,497,212 current funds 3,000,286 trust and agency	State Board of Agriculture.
Michigan, Univ. of	101,715,083	7,096,628 current funds 804,084 student loan funds 17,258,715 endowment funds 73,780,597 plant funds 2,775,058 agency funds	Regents
Minnesota, Univ. of	79,588,796	6,120,626 current funds 486,719 loan funds 27,155,176 endowment funds 95,768 agency funds 1,288,580 unexpended plant funds 44,441,924 invested plant funds	Board
Mississippi State Coll.	7,685,484	6,109,000 land, buildings, equipment 1,576,484 securities and cash	State
Mississippi State Coll. for Women	2,675,767	2,407,941 land, buildings, equipment 267,826 securities and cash	State
Mississippi, Univ. of	5,676,584	4,588,525 land, buildings, equipment 755,710 endowment 332,349 cash and securities	State
Missouri, Univ. of	24,585,705	19,572,478 land, buildings, equipment 31,592 unexpended plant funds 2,356,476 endowment funds 347,901 student loan funds 261,968 agency funds 2,051,285 current funds	Curators
Montana State Univ.	4,469,266	188,228 current funds 14,322 student loan funds 156,557 endowment funds 109,497 agency funds 4,000,661 plant funds	State
Nebraska, Univ. of	19,554,221	15,340,816 land, buildings, equipment 1,151,719 endowment 537,440 student loan funds 2,524,244 cash	Regents
Nevada, Univ. of	4,342,096	3,442,498 land, buildings, equipment 70,500 unexpended plant funds 752,710 endowments 76,387 loan funds	Land grants by state, other endowments by regents.

TABLE 14 (continued)

ASSETS

Institution	Total Assets	How Assets are Distributed	By Whom Held
New Hampshire, Univ. of	$ 8,953,820	$ 644,835 current assets 450,095 loan funds 1,424,771 endowment 410,151 plant funds for construction 6,023,968 physical plant	Jointly, by state and regents.
New Mexico, Univ. of	4,000,000	2,685,000 land, buildings, equipment 1,000,000 endowment 300,000 cash and current assets	Board
N. Y. State Coll. for Teachers	Not given	50,000 loan fund	State
N.C. State Coll. of A. and E.	13,200,000		State holds 12 million, rest by foundations.
N.C., Women's Coll. of the Univ. of	7,830,636	7,651,636 land, buildings, equipment 179,000 permanent improvement fund	State
North Dakota Univ. of	7,551,006	3,447,437 land, buildings, equipment 1,700,000 grant lands 2,403,569 current funds	State Board of Higher Education.
Ohio State Univ.	48,589,647	2,647,419 current funds 300,000 student fees 513,000 bonds and deposits 509,657 inventories 12,360,341 state appropriations 2,178,037 investments 30,080,940 lands, buildings, equipment	State
Oklahoma A. and M.	11,748,789	7,939,413 buildings 2,167,062 equipment 760,000 books 410,991 improvements 293,324 land 177,997 loan funds	
Oklahoma Coll. for Women	1,677,523	1,364,655 land, buildings, improvements 312,867 equipment	State
Oklahoma, Univ. of	9,001,998	4,473,646 buildings 4,293,349 land, equipment, improvements 230,642 loan funds	Board
Oregon State College	See Oregon State System. State College comprises half the total state.		
Oregon State System	20,000,000	Also small endowments held by separate foundations.	State
Oregon, Univ. of	See Oregon State System. University comprises half the total state.		
Pennsylvania State Coll.	36,957,220	26,423,780 physical plant 10,533,449 current funds	State
Purdue Univ.	27,254,754	1,422,215 current funds 22,364,065 physical plant 231,270 auxiliary enterprise 27,355 scholarships 3,107,770 endowments 102,079 student loan fund	Trustees hold cash securities and most of land; rest by state.

TABLE 14 (continued)

ASSETS

Institution	Total Assets	How Assets are Distributed	By Whom Held
R. I. State College	$ 5,516,800	$ 5,381,112 land, buildings, equipment 135,688 various funds	Board
Rutgers Univ.	28,000,000	3,500,000 public funds	Jointly; most by trustees.
San Francisco State Coll.	2,423,827		State
San Jose State College	9,750,000	4,000,000 land 5,000,000 buildings 750,000 equipment	State
South Carolina, Univ. of	7,836,000	No endowment 70,000 scholarships	State State
South Dakota, Univ. of	3,500,000	2,500,000 land, buildings, equipment 95,000 current funds 400,000 appropriations 50,000 medical school 402,375 fees and earnings	State, except scholarship and loan funds.
South, Univ. of	5,000,000		Board
Stanford Univ.	58,000,000	17,000,000 land, buildings, equipment 38,000,000 endowment 3,000,000 cash	Board
Tennessee, Univ. of	12,653,000	9,903,000 land, buildings, equipment 2,300,000 furniture, lab equipment 400,000 endowment 50,000 gifts	Trustees
Texas, A. & M.	Not given		
Texas Coll. of Mines	2,024,000	1,235,000 lands, buildings, equipment 613,000 endowment 175,000 cash	State
Texas Technological College	5,999,905	4,137,889 lands, buildings, equipment - by - 268,300 fees - by - Balance appropriations & inventory	State Board
Texas, Univ. of	102,663,336	31,594,536 land, buildings, grounds 65,256,007 endowment 5,368,988 other income 443,803 loans and scholarship funds	State holds permanent and available funds; investments controlled by accountable officers
Tuskegee Inst.	Not given		
Utah State Agri. Coll.	4,000,000	3,500,000 buildings, grounds, equipment 500,000 endowments and funds	Board
Utah, Univ. of	Not given		
Vanderbilt Univ.	40,638,000	30,468,000 endowment 8,386,000 plant Balance scholarships and trusts	Board
Vermont, Univ. of	8,600,000	60,000 from state Balance from private sources	Board (One building by State)

TABLE 14 (continued)

ASSETS

Institution	Total Assets	How Assets are Distributed	By Whom Held
Virginia Military Institute	$ 3,766,961	$ 445,953 endowment	State, except endowments and foundations.
Virginia Polytechnic Inst.	10,800,000	9,000,000 buildings, land equipment 300,000 endowment 1,500,000 appropriations 10,000 alumni donations	State, except endowments and gifts
Virginia, Univ. of	23,000,000	10,000,000 buildings and grounds - by - 13,000,000 endowment - by -	State Visitors
Washington, State Coll. of	24,312,145	8,742,655 land, buildings, equipment 10,813,208 endowment 4,209,910 current funds 107,636 agency funds 438,733 other assets	State; the rest by the regents.
Washington, Univ. of	56,943,975	20,243,975 land, buildings, equipment 18,200,000 biennial operations 17,000,000 biennial building 1,500,000 scholarships and research	State
West Virginia Univ.	13,505,000	13,000,000 buildings, capital outlay 400,000 operating fund 105,000 land grant endowment	State
William and Mary Coll. of	7,700,000	6,000,000 - by - 1,700,000 endowment - by -	State Board of Visitors and Endowment Assn.
Wisconsin, Univ. of	47,691,155	35,572,545 land, buildings, equipment 4,991,031 endowment 209,894 loan funds 6,836,684 current funds & inventory	Regents
Wooster, Coll. of	6,611,535	3,673,280 endowment 2,688,898 buildings and grounds	College
Wyoming, Univ. of	11,459,257	5,318,972 lands, buildings, equipment 4,263,560 endowment 9,825 prepaid insurance 62,953 inventories 209,458 notes and accounts receivable 1,594,507 cash	Board
Yale Univ.	127,426,009	123,112,370 endowment 4,313,639 current funds	Board

TABLE 15

FUNCTIONS OF BOARDS AS TO

Institution	Educational Policy	Academic Standards	Faculty & Administrative Appointments	Political Interference
Alabama, Polytechnic Inst.	Yes	Yes	Yes	
Alabama, Univ. of	Responsible for "management and control" but delegates to president matters of internal administration. President refers matters not specifically delegated to the Executive Committee or to Board.			No
Amherst College	Yes	Yes	Yes	No
Arizona, Univ. of	Yes	Yes	President recommends	No
Arkansas, Univ. of	Yes	Yes	Yes	No
California, Univ. of	No	No	Yes, above rank of instructor.	No
California, Univ. of, at Los Angeles	No	No	Yes, above rank of instructor.	No
California, Univ. of Southern	No	No	Administration only	No
Citadel, The	Yes	Yes	Yes	No
Clemson Agric. College	Yes	Yes	Yes	No
Colorado A. and M.	No	No	Yes	No
	"General supervision and control"			
Colorado, Univ. of	Yes	Yes	Yes	No
Connecticut, Univ. of	Entirely legislative; not administrative.			No
Cornell Univ.	Yes	No	Yes, above rank of instructor.	No
Delaware, Univ. of	Yes	No	Yes	No
Florida State Univ.	Yes	No	Yes	No
Florida, Univ. of	Yes		Yes	No
Georgia Board	Yes	Yes	Yes	No
Georgia School of Technology	Yes	Yes	Yes	No
Georgia, Univ. of	Yes	Yes	Yes	No
Harvard Univ.	No	No	Yes	No
Idaho, Univ. of	Yes	Yes	Yes	No
Illinois, Univ. of	Yes	Yes	Yes	No
Indiana Univ.	Yes	Yes	Yes	No
Iowa State A. and M.	Yes	Yes	Yes	No
Iowa State Univ.	Yes	Yes	Yes	No
Kansas State College	Prescribes general policies.			Financial control

TABLE 15 (continued)

FUNCTIONS OF BOARDS AS TO

Institution	Educational Policy	Academic Standards	Faculty & Administrative Appointments	Political Interference
Kansas, Univ. of	Yes		No, except president	No
Kentucky, Univ.	No	No	Yes	No
Louisiana State Univ.	Yes	Yes	Yes	No
Louisiana, Southwestern Inst.	Yes	Yes	Yes	State Department of Education politically inclined.
Maine, Univ. of	Yes	Yes	Yes	No
Maryland, Univ. of	Yes	No	Deans only	No. Abolishing controls.
Massachusetts, Univ. of	Yes	Yes	Yes, above assistant professor.	No
Miami, Univ. of	No	No	Yes	No
Michigan State Coll.	Yes	Yes	Yes	No
Michigan, Univ. of	Yes	Yes	Yes	No
Minnesota, Univ. of	Yes	No	Yes	No
Mississippi State Coll.	Yes	Yes	Yes	No
Mississippi State Coll. for Women	Yes	Yes	Yes	No
Mississippi, Univ. of	Yes	Yes	Yes	No
Missouri, Univ. of	Yes	No	Yes	No
Montana State Univ.	General control	Only to avoid duplication	Yes	No
Nebraska, Univ. of	Yes	Yes	Yes	No
Nevada, Univ. of	Yes	Yes	Yes	No
New Hampshire, Univ. of	Yes	Yes	Yes	No
New Mexico, Univ. of	Yes	No	Yes	No
N.Y. State Coll. for Teachers	No	No	President only	No
N.C. State Coll. of A. and E.	Yes	No	Yes	No
N.C., Women's Coll. of the Univ. of	Yes	No	Yes	No
North Dakota, Univ. of	Yes	Yes	Yes	No
Ohio State Univ.	Yes	Yes	Yes	No
Oklahoma A. and M.	General control		Yes	No
Oklahoma Coll. for Women	General control		Yes	No

TABLE 15 (continued)

FUNCTIONS OF BOARDS AS TO

Institution	Educational Policy	Academic Standards	Faculty & Administrative Appointments	Political Interference
Oklahoma, Univ. of	General control		Yes	No
Oregon State College	Yes	Entrance requirements	Yes	No
Oregon State System	Yes	No	Yes	No
Oregon, Univ. of	Yes	No	Yes	No
Pennsylvania, State Coll.	Yes	Yes	Yes	No
Purdue Univ.	Approval	Yes	Yes	No
R. I. State College	Yes	No	Yes	No
Rutgers Univ.	Yes	Yes	Yes	No
San Francisco State Coll.	Yes	Yes	Yes	No
San Jose State College	Yes	Yes	Yes	No
South Carolina, Univ. of	Yes	Yes	Yes	No
South Dakota, Univ. of	Yes	Yes	Yes	No
South, Univ. of	No	No	Yes	No
Stanford Univ.	No	Yes	Yes	No
Tennessee, Univ. of	Yes	Yes	Yes	No
Texas A. and M.	Delegates	Delegates	Yes	
Texas Coll. of Mines	Yes	Yes	Yes	No
Texas Technological Coll.	Yes	Yes	Yes	No
Texas, Univ. of	Yes	Yes	Yes	No
Tuskegee Inst.	Has veto powers; president has authority.			No
Utah State Agric. Coll.	Yes	Yes	Yes	No
Utah, Univ. of	No; can veto.	No; can veto.	Yes	No
Vanderbilt Univ.	Approves	Yes	Yes	No
Vermont, Univ. of	Yes	Yes	Yes	No
Virginia Military Inst.	Yes	Yes	Yes	No
Virginia Polytechnic Inst.	Yes	Yes	Yes	No
Virginia, Univ. of	Yes	Yes	Yes	No
Washington, State Coll. of	Yes	Indirectly	Confirms	No
Washington, Univ. of	No	No	Approves	No
West Virginia Univ.	Yes	Yes	Yes	No
William and Mary, Coll. of	Yes	No; has power	Yes	

TABLE 15 (continued)

FUNCTIONS OF BOARDS AS TO

Institution	Educational Policy	Academic Standards	Faculty & Administrative Appointments	Political Interference
Wisconsin, Univ. of	Yes	Yes	Yes	No
Wooster, Coll. of	Yes	Yes	Yes	No
Wyoming, Univ. of	Yes	Yes	Yes	No
Yale Univ.	Yes	Yes	Yes	No

TABLE 16

TUITION AND FEES

Institution	Rates and Changes in Tuition and Fees
Alabama Polytechnic Institute	Increase in tuition the past five years from $80 to $90 for two semesters and $110 to $120 for a full year, plus curriculum fee ranging from $1.50 to $9.50 in Veterinary Medicine, which is the laboratory fee, plus student activities fee of $16.40 for normal year.
Alabama, University of	Increase in tuition for the past five years. No state tuition as such except in law and medicine. Fee system changed 3 years ago, formerly overall fees, $61.50 plus lab and special course fees. Now $114 for general course and $126 for science courses including lab fees.
Amherst College	Tuition has not been increased to any class of students in the last five years, but are considering increasing it in 1947.
Arizona, University of	No increase in tuition for in-state (now $30 a year). Non-residents pay $30 plus a non-resident fee of $300. Increase of $100 in 1939-40.
Arkansas, University of	Increase in tuition past five years: In-state, increased $9 a year; out-of-state from $30-$100 (graduated) to $150 a year now. Student health costs taken out of registration fee; student activity fee, $9; lab fees in some courses. Total matriculation fee, $94 a year.
California, University of	No tuition for in-state students. Tuition for out-of-state students has doubled in past five years (now $300 a year). All students pay health and athletic fee ($27.50 a term).
California, University of, at Los Angeles	No tuition for in-state students. Tuition for out-of-state students has doubled in past five years (now $300 a year). All students pay health and athletic fee of $29 a term, $58 a year.
California, University of Southern	Tuition increase of 13% for all students in 1947. Present tuition $434 for full program, 2 semesters, law and engineering, $450; medicine, $600.
Citadel, The	Tuition increased in 1945 from $60 a year to $80 a year for state students. Increase from $200 to $250 a year for out-of-state students, by action of General Assembly.
Clemson Agric. College	Tuition raised by legislature in 1945 from $60 to $80 a year, in-state, and from $200 to $250 for out-of-state. State puts 43% into a student's education.
Colorado A. and M.	Increase in tuition, over-all, for residents $53, from $115.50 to $168.50 per year of 3 quarters. Increase for non-residents, $153, from $165.50 to $318.50.
Colorado, University of	No increase in tuition for past five years for residents of state; ranging according to departments from $40 to $47. Non-resident, Boulder campus, increase from $25 to $42 per quarter over resident fees. Medical School in Denver, increase for residents from $91 to $125 per quarter and for non-residents reduction of $82 to $75 plus resident fees. These fees include Health, General Student Fee, Laboratory, Library. Additional increase in tuition of $5 for resident students and $10 to non-resident students now under consideration.
Connecticut, University of	The University is not permitted by statute to charge tuition. The University, however, does charge an all-University fee of $125 per resident student. This fee has not been raised during the past 8 years.
Cornell University	In 1945 the tuition rate in the endowed colleges was raised from $400 to $500 and in the state colleges from $200 to $300 for the academic year. In the state colleges tuition is free to bonafide residents of New York State. All students, residents and non-residents of the state pay the same tuition in endowed colleges and the $300 tuition rate in the state college applies only to non-residents.

TABLE 16 (continued)

TUITION AND FEES

Institution	Rates and Changes in Tuition and Fees
Delaware, University of	Out-of-state students, $200 (1941-42); $250 (1946-47). In-state students: tuition is free to all state students, but all state students are subject to a maintenance fee of $95 (1941-42), $175 (1946-47).
Florida State University	No tuition for in-state students. No increase in matriculation fee in past five years. Present fee, $21 for 9 months. No lab fees. Student activity fee and Health Fee, $33 for 9 months. Out-of-state tuition raised from $100 to $200 in 1945.
Florida, University of	No tuition for in-state students; fees for residents (1939-40), $61; (1946-47), $161. Fees for non-residents, (1939-40), $161; (1946-47), $300.
Georgia School of Technology	No increase in tuition past five years. In-state, $139.50. Out-of-state, $300. Student activities, $22.50 per year.
Georgia, University of	Increase in tuition in past five years; resident of state, $122.50 to $142.50 for 9 months' term, including fees, tuition, student health and activity fees, and everything except lab fees which at present average $5 per year per student, but will be abolished in 1948 in an over-all fee. Non-resident fee increased from $274.50 to $442.50.
Harvard University	No increase in tuition during the past five years. Except in the Graduate School of Business Administration, fees are based on a charge of $200 for a 16-week term, or $400 for the normal academic year. In the Business School they run to $300 per term.
Idaho, University of	By constitutional provision there is no tuition for residents of Idaho. Non-resident tuition is now set at $75 per semester.
Illinois, University of	No increase in tuition for in-state students for the past five years. Present rate, $40 per semester for all students; $80 a semester for out-of-state students. These are not all-inclusive. Additional for all students - Union Fee, $5, Health Fee, $5, Lab, Library and Service Fee, $8. Students buy own athletic tickets.
Indiana University	No increase in fees for past five years for in-state students. Present rate, $48.75 per semester in general courses to $117.50 per semester in Dentistry. Increase in fees for out-of-state students from $64.25 to $153.75 per semester in general courses and from $153 to $213.75 per semester in Dentistry. These are all-inclusive, such as health, registration, library, laboratory, but does not include athletic tickets.
Iowa State A. and M.	In past five years registration fee has increased from $123 to $138 for the academic year. Out-of-state tuition (additional) has increased from $40 a year to $150 a year. These are all-inclusive fees, including lab fees, hospital, library, Student Union, athletics, concerts, lectures, debates, student publications.
Iowa, State University of	Student fees for state residents ranged from $65 to $112 in 1942-43; $65 to $115 for 1947-48. For non-residents, additional tuition, from 0 to $132 in 1942-43; $50 to $130 for 1947-48. These fees are all-inclusive.
Kansas State College	Resident tuition formerly $25 a semester less lab fees, changed to $40 per semester, including lab fees; veterinary medicine fee $10 higher per semester. Non-resident tuition $75 a semester, plus lab fees, increased to $90 a semester including lab fees. Veterinary Medicine $10 additional. Semester charges for activity fee $7.50, student union, $5, student health, $7.50. Matriculation fee for residents, $10, for non-residents, $20. No increase in fees.

TABLE 16 (continued)

TUITION AND FEES

Institution	Rates and Changes in Tuition Fees
Kansas, University of	Increase in semester tuition for state residents, from $25-$30 to $40-$100. Coincidental with these increases, specific lab and course fees were abolished. The change was not intended to increase the total income of the University. Other required fees include: Matriculation, $10 resident, $20 non-resident; Health Service, $7.50 a semester; Activity, $7.00 a semester, plus taxes, Student Union, $5 a semester.
Kentucky, University of	Tuition increased from $100 to $112.50, June, 1942, annually, for in-state students; $126 to $172.50 for out-of-state students.
Louisiana State University	No tuition increase since 1939-40. No state tuition. Out-of-state on reciprocal basis. Lump student fee for all students for health, athletics, etc. of $30 per semester or $60 per year. Will add $10 in 1947 to this and abolish all lab fees.
Louisiana, Southwestern Inst.	No tuition charges, $13 per semester registration fee, which covers athletics, lyceum, etc. No student health fee. No increase in registration fee. Living expense increase from $124 to $142 a semester; out-of-state, $50 a semester.
Maine, University of	$175 per year for residents of Maine, an increase of $25 which became effective July 1, 1946; $300 for out-of-state students, a $50 increase.
Maryland, University of	In-state students pay $188 tuition a year. $313 for out-of-state. Lab fees, special course fees, etc., are additional charges.
Massachusetts, University of	No increase in tuition in either in-state or out-of-state categories during the past five years.
Miami, University of	Tuition in 1941, $250; tuition in 1947, $360--an increase of approximately 40%.
Michigan State College	Increase in tuition 17.5% for in-state students in past five years. Present rate, $47 per quarter in general courses, $92 in veterinary medicine. Increase of 61.6% in course fees for out-of-state students. Present rate, $97 in general course, $142 in veterinary medicine. These are all-inclusive -- registration, health, library, athletic tickets, lectures and concerts, Union, class, student newspaper, etc.
Michigan, University of	Increase in tuition 16-2/3% for in-state students in past five years. Present rate, $70 per semester in general courses to $140 per semester in medicine. Increase in fees for out-of-state students from $100 to $150 per semester in general courses and from $200 to $225 in medicine. These are all-inclusive, such as health, registration, library, laboratory, athletic, Michigan League and Union, but does not include special laboratory courses.
Minnesota, University of	In past five years, average increase, undergraduate colleges, resident students, 50%. Corresponding non-resident increase 87%. Tuition ranges (1939-40) from $20 to $75 for residents, from $40 to $125 for non-residents. Present range from $30 to $75 for residents, and from $75 to $120 for non-residents. Rates given per quarter.
Mississippi State College	No state tuition; out-of-state tuition levied on out-of-state students, $100 a semester; matriculation $25 a semester, other college fees $26.25 a semester; student activities fee per semester $9; room, heat, lights, $25 a semester.
Mississippi State Coll. for Women	No state tuition. Matriculation fee, $50 a year - has not been, but will be increased to $65 per year. All fees will be increased from $90 to $115 in 1948.
Mississippi, University of	No state tuition. Matriculation fee, $25 a semester. No increase. Health and athletics and publications voted by students, $13.50 a semester. Also library, etc., $25 more a semester. Total, $63.50 a semester.

TABLE 16 (continued)

TUITION AND FEES

Institution	Rates and Changes in Tuition and Fees
Missouri, University of	Non-resident tuition fees from $45 to $150 for 18 weeks. Other fees, on 18 weeks' basis, Library, Hospital and incidental fee, $36; Student Activities Building Fee, $1.25; Supplementary Medical School fee, $20 (12 weeks); Course fees from $1 to $16; Military deposit, $5; Music fee, $30.
Montana State University	Resident students charged no tuition. Non-resident fee increased from $25 per quarter to $100 per quarter, effective September, 1947.
Nebraska, University of	Increase in tuition fees in the past five years for in-state students from $2.50 to $3 per credit hour per semester, 20% increase effective September 1, 1946. For out-of-state students, increase from $25 to $75 per registration minimum per semester. University has been on a reciprocal non-resident basis so that actual increase is $25. Registration, matriculation, graduation fees the same. Student Health Fee increased 100% from $2.50 to $5.00 a semester. Laboratory fees extra, but no increase.
Nevada, University of	Law provides no tuition can be charged at University. Board in University dining room has gone from $32.50 to $40 per month. Room rent remains the same.
New Hampshire, University of	Tuition rates have been increased as follows: In 1941, $10 for both in-state and out-of-state; fall of 1946, $100 increase for out-of-state students.
New Mexico, University of	Increase of tuition from $30 to $40 a term for in-state, and out-of-state increase of $25 per term or from $105 to $140. Building fee for all students raised from $2 to $10 per term.
N. Y. State Coll. for Teachers	No increase in tuition for in-state students for past five years. Tuition of out-of-state students increased $100, that is from $200 to $300.
N. C. State Coll. of A. and E.	Tuition increased in 1942 by $10 for in-state students, and from $225 to $288 for out-of-state students.
N.C., Women's Coll. of the University of	Tuition unchanged for years. $50 annually for in-state, plus a $20 fee. Out-of-state fee is $288 annually (increased from $175 June, 1946.)
North Dakota, University of	No changes have been made in either in-state or out-of-state fees at the University during the last five years.
Ohio State University	Increase of 50% in fees for in-state students during past five years. From $20 to $30 per quarter. In Medicine from $110 to $150, including laboratory fees. Increase in fees for out-of-state students, additional, $50 per quarter now increased to $75 per quarter. Same increase for professional courses. These fees are not all-inclusive, but there are additional charges for athletics, student activities, laboratories, except Medicine.
Oklahoma A. and M.	No tuition for resident students; $25 per semester for non-residents. No increase in past five years. Out-of-state medical students $350 per year; student fee including health, library, Union, etc. $14.75 per semester; athletic fee optional about $11 a year; laboratory fees according to course.
Oklahoma Coll. for Women	No in-state tuition or matriculation fee. No increase in health fee, $3 per semester; student activities fee, $6 per semester; art fee (lab) $1-$4 per semester; physical education, $1 per semester; all lab fees run from $1-$4 per semester; total $13-$21 per semester. Out-of-state fee, $50 a year.

TABLE 16 (continued)

TUITION AND FEES

Institution	Rates and Changes in Tuition and Fees
Oklahoma, University of	No tuition for resident students; $50 per semester non-resident fee; no increase in tuition in past five years; out-of-state medical students, $350 per semester; physical education, $1 per semester; all lab fees run from $1-4 per semester; total $13-21 per semester. Out-of-state fee, $50 a year.
Oregon State College	See Oregon State System.
Oregon State System	No income from tuitions.
Oregon, University of	No increase in tuition fees for last five years.
Pennsylvania State College	No increase in tuitions for either in-state or out-of-state students during the past five years.
Purdue University	No increase in fees for in-state students for past five years, $54 per semester (includes registration, laboratory and library, medical and infirmary, student activity, recreation fees (athletic tickets) plus laboratory deposits for special courses). Out-of-state tuition increased from $50 per semester general and $75 per semester engineering to $100 per semester for all.
R. I. State College	No increase in out-of-state tuition during past five years. No tuition for residents of the state. Residents pay a general fee of $70 a semester. This became effective in 1943, replacing miscellaneous fees of varying amounts, depending upon courses taken. In general it represented some increase, perhaps $10 to $15 a semester, over the average fee paid previously.
Rutgers University	No increase in tuition fees during the past five years.
San Francisco State College	No increase in tuition for regular courses. Slight increase in tuition for summer session ($5 per course).
San Jose State College	No increase in tuition for regular courses. Slight increase in summer session (20%).
South Carolina, University of	Tuition increased in 1946 from $30 to $40 per term (2 semesters plus summer short term, for in-state). Out-of-state from $100 to $125 per term.
South Dakota, University of	No increase in tuition for in-state students in past five years except in Medicine. Present rate $35 per semester in general courses, $50 in Law, $100 in Medicine. Present rate for out-of-state students $52.50 per semester in general courses, $75 in Law, $225 in Medicine. These do not include registration, health, library, Athletic tickets, student union, student publications, etc. Fees approximately $35 per semester.
South, University of	No distinction between in-state and out-of-state students. Special rates for residents of Franklin County, sons of clergy and theological students. Tuition increased slightly in 1946.
Stanford University	Tuition increase, 1946, from $444 annual fee to $500, including health, athletic and student activity fee.
Tennessee, University of	Tuition increased from $45 to $50 a quarter in 1946 for in-state. $30 to $75 for out-of-state.
Texas A. and M.	No information.
Texas College of Mines	No increase in tuition ($50 a year in-state), out-of-state, same. Bill pending in 1947 to increase out-of-state. Laboratory fees very low.
Texas Technological College	No tuition increase in recent years. State law fixes fees to be charged and amounts. In-state tuition, $25 a semester, $50 a year; out-of-state charge same as out-of-state charge for state from which student comes.

TABLE 16 (continued)

TUITION AND FEES

Institution	Rates and Changes in Tuition and Fees
Texas, University of	Student Activity fee (optional) $12.13 for two semesters; Hospital fee (optional) $3 for 9 months; Union fee (required) $1 a semester.
Tuskegee Inst.	Tuition and fees range from $32.50 to $65 per quarter.
Utah State Agric. Coll.	No increase in tuition for in-state students in past five years (now $17 per quarter). No increase in non-resident entrance fees in past five years ($45 additional). Increase in athletic fees from nothing to $6. General Student Body fee, no increase, now $12; plus registration $10, class fee, $1, Building fee, $20.
Utah, University of	There has been no substantial increase in tuition fees except for the Medical School, which has expanded from a two-year to a four-year program and has increased its fees from $65 to $137. Student Activity fee has increased from $10 to $15.
Vanderbilt University	Tuition increased 1946-47 about one-third in the various schools and departments. No difference between in-state and out-of-state students. General tuition about $400 per year. Specialized schools higher.
Vermont, University of	No increase in tuition during the past five years.
Virginia Military Institute	Tuition increased from $200 to $230 annually in 1940, and will be raised to $300 in 1947.
Virginia Polytechnic Inst.	Tuition raised in 1946 from $40 to $50 per quarter for Virginians, and $80 to $100 for out-of-state. Veterans charged out-of-state. Extension in Daville, Norfolk and Richmond, $200 a year. Virginia Polytechnic Institute especially caters to children of industrial and agricultural classes.
Virginia, University of	Tuition has been increased approximately $25 for 9 months' session for Virginians, and $50 per 9 months' session for non-Virginians.
Washington, State College of	No increase in tuition for in-state or out-of-state students during the past five years.
Washington, University of	Increases, in-state, from $30 to $40 a quarter; non-resident from $65 to $90 a quarter. These fees are all-inclusive.
West Virginia University	No increase in tuition in last five years. Tuition, including athletic and health fees, $40 a semester for in-state; $115 for out-of-state per semester. Additional fees for certain professional schools.
William and Mary, College of	No increase in tuition for years. Slightly lower than in 1942 due to reduction in athletic fee.
Wisconsin, University of	No increase in tuition for either in-state or out-of-state students for past five years, but increase is contemplated of possibly 25% in incidental fee paid by both resident and non-resident. Present rate $48 a semester. Plan to increase to $60. This is all-inclusive. Athletic tickets and student publications optional. Fees range from $48 a semester in general colleges, to $55 in Law, $112.50 in Medicine. Non-residents' fee $100 additional.
Wooster, College of	Tuition and fees inclusive, $400 per year. Increase of $75 in last five years.
Wyoming, University of	Increase in tuition for in-state students from $25.50 per quarter (1939-40) to $39.50 per quarter, including Student Activities fee. Increase for out-of-state students from $48 per quarter (1939-40) to $109.50 per quarter, including Student Activities fee. Student Activities fee includes Associated Students of University of Wyoming fee, health fee, union dues, and entertainment items, increased from $7.50 to $9.50.
Yale University	Tuition has been increased 50% in the past five years. It is the same for in-state or out-of-state students.

TABLE 17

SALARY SCALES *

Instructor	Asst. Prof.	Assoc. Prof.	Professor	Dept. Head	Dean	Top Admin. Personnel	President	Increase Since Pearl Harbor
1. 2500-3200	3250-3900	4000-4900	5000-8000	No additional	3500-8000	10,000	15,000+	10%
2. 2820-3720	3240-4320	3780-4980	4260-6180	4260-6180	+40 to 80		8,820	$45 per mo
3. 3000-aver.	3000-3800	3700-4290	3700-4700	3700-4700		4,500-4700	7,500+	15%
4. 2400-3000	2700-3600	3000-4000	3600-5000	4000-5000	6000	6,500	7,500	35%
5. 1800-2700	2800-3500	3600-4100	4200-4500	4500-5000	5000-7500	7,500	12,000+	30%
6. 2220-2700	2820-3900	3960-4200	4080-4800	4380-5100	4380-6300	3,900-6000	10,000+	
7. 2400-3000	3000-3500	3500-4000	4000-5000	4200-5000	6000	4,250-5000	8,400+	26.5%
8. 1800-2400	2500-3000	3100-3600	3700-4125	-4500	-6000	6,000	8,500+	35%
9. 1800-2100	2200-2500	2600-3000	3100-3900	4000-4200		4,500	7,000+	25%
10. 1600-2400	2400-3000	3000-3600	3600-4200	3600-4200	4800-5500	6,000-6600	8,000	6%
11. 2400-3000	3000-4000		4000-5000	4000-5000	5000-6000	4,100-7000	7,750	35%
12. 1700-2250	2250-3000	3000-3600	3750-4500	4000-5000	5000-6000	6,500	7,500+	15%
13. 1800-2600	2300-2900	2500-2980	2500-3100	2900-3800	3600-4500	4,500	7,000+	17%
14. 2000-3200	2700-4000	3200-4000	3800-5000	4000-4800	5500-6500	8,000	11,000	20%
15. 2200-3000	2800-3800	3200-3800	3060-4200	4200	5500	4,300-6000	8,000+	
16. 2000-2900	3000-3200	3300-3600	3700-4400	4000-4400	4900		10,000	35%
17. 2250-3200	3000-4000	3500-4500	4200-6750	4200-6750	5750-9000	7,000	10,000	29%
18. 1958-2429	3034-3638	3840-4243	4445-5184	5184	6462	5,508	10,000	20%
19. 1800-2450	2500-2950	3000-3650	3700-4850	3700-4850	4000-6500	4,000-6500	10,000	20%
20. 2500-3000	3000-4000		4000-5500		4000-6000	6,000	10,000+	20%
21. 2000-3300	2500-4000	3200-4500	3600-6750	6500	7020-7600	5,000-8000	10,500+	40%

* These scales apply to institutions having enrollments of under 3000.

TABLE 17 (continued)

SALARY SCALES **

Instructor	Asst. Prof.	Assoc. Prof.	Professor	Dept. Head	Dean	Top Admin. Personnel	President	Increase Since Pearl Harbor
1. 1780-3150	2525-3780	2855-4725	3630-7500	No additional	4500-8110	5750	11,050+	30%
2. 2000-3000	2500-3500	3000-4000	3500-up	3500-up	5000-5600	5750	12,500	35%
3. 2820-3720	3240-4320	3780-4980	4260-6180	No additional	+40 to 80		8,820	$45 mo.
4. 1800-3200	2400-4500	2900-4600	3800-6000	4500-5500	4500-6500	4200-5700	8,500+	43%
5. 2400-3600	3000-4800	3800-6000	4500-7000		7500	7500	8,500+	43%
6. 1950-2500	2500-3500	3100-3900	4000-4500	+150 to 300			4500-10,000	25%
7. 1800-3000	2500-3500	3000-4000	3500-4800	3500-4800	6000	6800	11,000+	10%
8. 2500-3800	3200-4125	3700-4500	4200-5100	4500-5500	5500-6400	5000-6250	8,500+	36%
9. 1680-2912	2100-3850	2800-4180	3360-4620		3978-6344	3978-6344	10,200	15%
10. 1800-2900	2400-3600	2800-4000	3400-5000	No additional	5000-6200	4000-7500	10,000	25%
11. 1800-2200	2400-3000	3000-3600	3750-4800	4000-5000	5000-6500	9000	7,500+	15%
12. 2000-up	2400-up	2620-up	3255-up					17%
13. 2000-up	salary range has been abandoned.					7000	7,500	30%
14. 1500-2200	2100-2800	2700-3400	3300-4000	3500-4200	5400	3300-4780	8,920	27%
15. 2000-2200	2200-2700	2700-3100	3200-3800	+200	5700	6700	10,200+	10%
16. 2200-3300	2700-4200	3500-4700	3900-5400		5600-6500	6000-6500	9,500+	49%
17. 2000-3025	2500-3800	3100-4200	3800-9000	5000-9000	7500-12000	10000-12000	15,000+	15%
18. 2160-2697	2832-3638	3840-4646	4848-6144	4848-6144	6462-7416	7734-8688	10,000+	18%
19. 2000-2600	2800-3400	3750-4250	4500-6000		+500-1000		15,000	20%

** These scales apply to institutions having enrollments of from 3000 to 6000.

TABLE 17 (continued)

SALARY SCALES ***

Instructor	Asst. Prof.	Assoc. Prof.	Professor	Dept. Head	Dean	Top Admin. Personnel	President	Increase Since Pearl Harbor
1. 2160-3000	2760-3600	3120-4380	3840-5520	2840-5520	4500-6600	4500-6600	10,500+	25%
2. 2000-2900	3000-3600	3700-4600	4200-6000	4200-6000	4600-7800	5800-7800	12,000+	30%
3. 2500-up	3000	In process of adjustment.		No minimum.				30%
4. 2300-3800	3600-4500	4600-5500	5600-7000	+200	5500-9500	5100-7800	10,000+	30%
5. 2040-3840	2520-4400	3180-5700	4080-7440	4080-7440	4080-7440		11,800+	$400 yr.
6. 1900-3000	3000-4000	3400-4500	4000-9000	6000-10000	7000-10000	11000-15000	20,000+	35%
7. 2400-4100	2860-4800	3200-5000	4200-6400	No additional	5600-7400	4000-6500	8,500+	25%
8. 1800-3200	2800-4000	3000-4800	3600-6000		6800-7800	5500-7000	12,000+	40%
9. 1950-2500	2500-3500	3100-3900	4000-5000	+150-300	5500-7000		10,000	45%
10. 1900-4000	2400-4400	2200-5500	3000-7000	3000-7000	4200-7500	4700-6600	12,000+	45%
11. 1800-3900	2000-4560	3000-4800	3600-5500	3800-5150	6000-8400		9,500	23%
12. 2400-up	3000-up	3600-up	No minimum.		7500-10000	5000-7000	17,500	
13. 2500-3000	3125-3500	3750-4000	4500-5000	No additional	5600-7000	5600-8500	9,500+	35%
14. 2000-3800	2900-4300	3400-5000	3550-6000	No additional	3500-10000	6300-12000	12,000+	25%
15. 2400-3300	3300	3800	4500	5600	6000-7500	7500	10,000+	
16. 1800-3800	2400-4600	2700-5000	3200-6280	4180-6750	7300-10000	11000	20,000	35%
17. 2400-3000	2800-3600	3400-4500	4500-5000	4500-6000	5500-7000	8000	9,100+	30%
18. 2000-3025	3000-3800	3400-4438	3950-5200	3850-5500	6200-6500	4200-6200	12,100+	25%
19. 1800-3450	2300-3800	2800-4800	3600-4800	4000-6000	5200-6500	6500	17,500+	12-1/2%
20. 3000-3700	3700-4400	4400-5000	5000-6500	5000-6500	6500-8000	6000-8000	18,000	45%
21. 2400-3500	3800-5000	5000-7000	7000-12000		6500-8000			

*** These scales apply to institutions having enrollments of from 6000 to 10,000.

TABLE 17 (continued)

SALARY SCALES ****

Instructor	Asst. Prof.	Assoc. Prof.	Professor	Dept. Head	Dean	Top Admin. Personnel	President	Increase Since Pearl Harbor
1. 3600–	3900-4500	4800-5700	6000-7200	No additional	+ 1000-1500		17,500+	35%
2. 3600	3900-4500	4800-5700	6000-7200+	No additional	+ 1000-1500		13,000+	35%
3. 2600-2800	3200-3800	4000-5000	4800-6000+	No additional	6000-10000	18,000+	32,000+	45%
4. 3000	4000-4250	4800-8400	9600-12000		+ 1000-3000		25,000	
5. 3000-up	4000-up	5000-up	6000-up		8750-13000	10,000-18,000	20,000+	35%
6. 2650-3950	3540-5400	4050-7000	4200-8650	No additional	8000-10800	10,000	15,000	39%
7. 1800-4200	3000-7000	3500-9000	4200-10040	No additional	7181-11000	4,300-14,000	14,000+	35%
8. 2250-3300	3000-4800	3300-5400	4000-7000	6000-9000	9000-10500	6,500-9,000	14,000+	35%
9. 2200-2800	2800-3400	3400-4000	4000-4600	4400-5900	7000-11000	10,000	15,000	20%
10. 3000-3500	3500-4200	4250-5300	5400-6600	5400-6600	6600-9600	10,000	12,000+	35%
11. 2750-3850	3300-5100	4350-5900	5000-8500	6050-8600	10000-11500			33%
12. 2700-up	3500-up	3500-7500	4000-8000		5900-11400	6,000-15,000	15,000	15%
13. 2100-3600	2700-4000	3300-5500	4000-7000		7000-10000	8,500-11,000	15,000	
14. 2400-3300	3000-3900	3900-4800	4500-10000	4500-10000	+ 7500-15000	9,200	15,900+	25%
15. 2000-2300	2208-2930	2650-3956	2981-4451	3312-4945	4800-7000	3,900-7,200	12,000+	
16. 1800-up	2200-up	2600-up	3000-up		4500-up	5,000	12,000+	15%
17. 2000-4800	2500-5340	3000-6000	3600-8000	4500-8500	6000-12000	6,000-14,000	15,000+	30%
18. 2400-3600	3200-4400	4000-5200	4800-6000		6000-13000	6,000-20,000	20,000	
19. 2400-3000	3100-3600	3700-4400	4500-8700		5700-10700	10,610	18,610	20%
20. 2000-4750	2800-4750	3500-6500	4250-9500	4350-9400	9000-11000	8,000-11,000	15,000+	25%

**** These scales apply to institutions having enrollments of over 10,000.

TABLE 18

TEACHING LOAD

Institution	Increase in Teaching Load	Normal Load, Hours	Largest Class
Alabama Polytechnic Inst.	Some increases, but extra pay.		150
Alabama, Univ. of	Some increases, but extra pay.	15	450
Amherst Coll.	No increase on the average.		
Arizona, Univ. of	No appreciable increase, but larger classes.		800
Arkansas, Univ. of	No increase.		200
California, Univ. of	Normal still holds but some have voluntarily taken heavier load.	9	950
California, Univ. of, at Los Angeles	Normal still holds but some have voluntarily taken heavier load.	9	
California, Univ. of Southern	No increase.	12-15	1250
Citadel, The	No increase.		
Clemson Agric. Coll.	Little appreciable increase.		
Colorado A. and M.	No increase.	14	262
Colorado, Univ. of	No increase.	7-15	250
Connecticut, Univ. of	No increase.	12-15	
Cornell Univ.	No increase.		
Delaware, Univ. of	Increase negligible.		
Florida State Univ.	No appreciable increase. Veterans' normal 15 hour load extended to 18.	15	
Florida, Univ. of	No increase.		
Georgia School of Technology	No increase.	15	
Georgia, Univ. of	No appreciable increase.	15	400
Harvard Univ.	No information.		
Idaho, Univ. of	High during 1946-47. Expected normal 1947-48.		
Illinois, Univ. of	No information.		
Indiana Univ.	No increase.	7-10	450
Iowa State A. and M.	No increase.	12-15	250
Iowa, State	No increase.	10-15	
Kansas State College	No increase.	15	570
Kansas, Univ. of	No increase.	8-15	
Kentucky, Univ. of	No general increase, but larger classes.		
Louisiana State Univ.	No appreciable increase.	12-15	300

TABLE 18 (continued)

TEACHING LOAD

Institution	Increase in Teaching Load	Normal Load, Hours	Largest Class
Louisiana, Southwestern Inst.	No appreciable increase.		132
Maine, Univ. of	No information.		
Maryland, Univ. of	No information.		
Massachusets, Univ. of	Teaching loads not seriously increased.		
Miami, Univ. of	No increase except with overtime pay load decreased.		250
Michigan State College	No increase.	12-14	300
Michigan, Univ. of	No increase.	8-16	1200
Minnesota, Univ. of	No increase.	8-15	1100
Mississippi State Coll. for Women	No increase. Classes decreased due to lost enrollment during war.	15	30
Mississippi State Coll.	No appreciable increase.		83
Mississippi, Univ. of	No appreciable increase.	12	300
Missouri, Univ. of	No information.		
Montana State Univ.	No increase.		
Nebraska, Univ. of	No increase.	11	290
Nevada, Univ. of	Increase 2 or 3 hours, in each case exceeds 18 hours.		
New Hampshire, Univ. of	No appreciable increase.		
New Mexico, Univ. of	No increase.	12	225
N.Y. State Coll. for Teachers.	No information.		
N. C. State Coll of A. and E.	No increase.		
N.C., Women's Coll. of the Univ. of	No appreciable increase.		
North Dakota, Univ. of	Negligible.	13.25	204
Ohio State Univ.	Little change.	7-12	500
Oklahoma A. and M.	No appreciable increase.		200
Oklahoma Coll. for Women	No appreciable increase.	16	84
Oklahoma, Univ. of	No appreciable increase.		150
Oregon State College	No information.		

TABLE 18 (continued)

TEACHING LOAD

Institution	Increase in Teaching	Normal Load, Hours	Largest Class
Oregon State System	No increase.		
Oregon, Univ of	No information.		
Pennsylvania State Coll.	Teaching load has always been high and remains so.		
Purdue Univ.	No increase.	12-16	400
R. I. State Coll.	Increases negligible.		
Rutgers Univ.	No appreciable increase.		
San Francisco State Coll.	No increase. Load reduced.		
San Jose State College	Teaching load reduced.	12	
South Carolina, Univ. of	No increase.		
South Dakota, Univ. of	No increase.	12	190
South, Univ. of	No increase.	15 Top	
Stanford Univ.	No increase.		
Tennessee, Univ. of	No appreciable increase.		
Texas A. & M.	No information.		
Texas College of Mines	No appreciable increase.	12-15	204
Texas Technological Coll.	No appreciable increase.		200
Texas, Univ. of	No appreciable increase.	12	200
Tuskegee Inst.	No information.		
Utah State Agric. Coll.	No increase.	14	200
Utah, Univ. of	Increase 30%.		
Vanderbilt Univ.	No increase.		
Vermont, Univ. of	No increase, except in size of classes.		
Virginia Military Inst.	No increase.		
Virginia Polytechnic Inst.	No increase.		
Virginia, Univ. of	No increase. Increase on number of staff.		
Washington, State Coll. of	Appreciable increase.	12-16	400
Washington, Univ. of	No information.		
West Virginia Univ.	No appreciable increase.	15	
William and Mary, Coll. of	No increase in teaching load. Number of faculty increased.		
Wisconsin, Univ. of	No increase.	10	700
Wooster, Coll. of	No increase.	16	80
Wyoming, Univ. of	No increase.	12-16	150
Yale Univ.	No appreciable increase.	12	

TABLE 19

ENROLLMENT

| Institution | Prewar | | | Present | | |
	Men	Women	Total	Men	Women	Total
Alabama Poly-technic Inst.			4100	5301	1010	6300
Alabama, Univ. of		5000-5500		5200	1910	10000
Amherst Coll.			850			1150
Arizona, Univ. of			2922	3100	1487	4487
Arkansas, Univ. of			2500	3853	1048	4901
California, Univ. of			23898			40800
California, Univ. of, at Los Angeles			10000	8000	5000	13799
California, Univ. of Southern			16218	19000	5000	23688
Citadel, The			1980			1793
Clemson Agric. Coll.			2381			2965
Colorado A. and.M.	1375	583	1958	2575	491	3066
Colorado, Univ. of	2747	1598	4345	5030	2216	7246
Connecticut, Univ. of			4200	7400	1800	9200
Cornell Univ.			6900			9400
Delaware, Univ. of			900			1700
Florida State Univ.			1857	664	2673	3337
Florida, Univ. of			3000	7213	160	7373
Georgia School of Technology			2910			4487
Georgia, Univ. of			3408	4439	1802	6241
Harvard Univ.			8583			12183
Idaho, Univ. of			3047			3707
Illinois, Univ. of	10636	3498	14134	19950	5488	25438
Indiana Univ.	4273	2213	6486	9287	3823	13110
Iowa State A. and M.	5700	2404	8104	8000	3500	11500
Iowa, State Univ. of	5772	3312	9084	8209	3779	11988
Kansas State College	2879	1229	4108	4922	1345	6267
Kansas, Univ. of	2949	1405	4354	6306	2218	8524
Kentucky, Univ. of			3800	4940	1684	6624
Louisiana State Univ.			8550	9200	2800	12000

TABLE 19 (continued)

ENROLLMENT

Institution	Men	Prewar Women	Total	Men	Present Women	Total
Louisiana, Southwestern Inst.			1867	2300	850	3151
Maine, Univ. of			2000	3300	700	4000
Maryland, Univ. of			6500			8500
Massachusetts, Univ. of			1550			2100
Miami, Univ. of			1375	4886	1335	6221
Michigan State College	4660	2350	7010	9670	3223	12893
Michigan, Univ. of	8412	3639	12051	13678	4915	18593
Minnesota, Univ. of	10179	5381	15560	19677	7426	27103
Mississippi State Coll.			2400	2809	113	2922
Mississippi State Coll. for Women			1200			1120
Mississippi, Univ. of			1500	2562	610	2832
Missouri, Univ. of	6743	2809	9552	12800	2326	15126
Montana State Univ.			2036			3657
Nebraska, Univ. of			7176	7182	2322	9504
Nevada, Univ. of			1267			1725
New Hampshire, Univ. of			2200	2310	890	3400
New Mexico, Univ. of			1713	2637	1010	3662
N. Y. State Coll. for Teachers			932			1360
N.C. State Coll. of A. and E.			2521	4800	100	4902
N.C., Women's Coll. of the Univ. of			2254			2123
North Dakota Univ. of	1395	565	1960	2106	786	2892
Ohio State Univ.	9000	4000	13000	47000	18000	65000
Oklahoma A. and M.			7921	8729	3118	11847
Oklahoma Coll. for Women			1048			806
Oklahoma, Univ. of			9141	9277	3446	12723
Oregon State College			4659			6951
Oregon State System			11500			17600

TABLE 19 (continued)

ENROLLMENT

Institution	Men	Prewar Women	Total	Men	Present Women	Total
Oregon, Univ. of			3700	3700	2000	5700
Pennsylvania State Coll.			7200			10000
Purdue Univ.	5788	1333	7121	9905	1893	11798
R. I. State College			1200			2200
Rutgers Univ.			7600			14000
San Francisco State Coll.	563	1155	1718	1257	1186	2443
San Jose State College			4067	3394	2347	5741
South Carolina, Univ. of			2000	3000	1000	4000
South Dakota, Univ. of			920			1661
South, Univ. of			325			450
Stanford Univ.			4300	5260	1944	7200
Tennessee, Univ. of			3834	5800	1500	7344
Texas A. & M.			6981			8650
Texas Coll. of Mines			1082	1182	582	1764
Texas Technological Coll.			3890	3841	1525	5366
Texas, Univ. of			11100	12747	4361	17250
Tuskegee Inst.			1407			2591
Utah State Agric. Coll.			3126	3336	1133	4469
Utah, Univ. of			4632	5949	2663	8612
Vanderbilt Univ.			1700	2235	715	3050
Vermont, Univ. of			1450	1300	700	2000
Virginia Military Inst.			730			780
Virginia Polytechnic Inst.			3052	3972	152	4124
Virginia, Univ. of			3000			4300
Washington, State College of			4100			7200
Washington, Univ. of			10905			15594
West Virginia Univ.			3474			6010
William and Mary, Coll. of	At Williamsburg only		1315	At Williamsburg (All, 6000)		1800
Wisconsin, Univ. of	8500	4000	12500	13500	5200	18700
Wooster, College of	447	481	928	680	632	1312
Wyoming, Univ. of			2100	2250	750	3000
Yale Univ.			5300			8651

TABLE 20

GRADUATES

Institution	Percentage of Freshmen Enrollees Graduated	Percentage Including Transfers
Alabama Poly-technic Institute		35
Alabama, Univ. of		50-55
Amherst College		80
Arizona, Univ. of		33
Arkansas, Univ. of		50
California, Univ. of		50
California, Univ. of, at Los Angeles		
California, Univ. of Southern		
Citadel, The	33	
Clemson Agric. Coll.		40
Colorado A. and M.	40	
Colorado, Univ. of		20
Connecticut, Univ. of		
Cornell Univ.		57 (prewar)
Delaware, Univ. of		60
Florida State Univ.	35	
Florida, Univ. of		40
Georgia School of Technology		45
Georgia, Univ. of		50-60
Harvard Univ.		66
Idaho, Univ. of	No percentage available.	
Illinois, Univ. of		30
Indiana Univ.	38	51
Iowa State A. and M.	40	55
Iowa, State Univ. of	25	
Kansas State College		63
Kansas, Univ. of	28	Nearly 100
Kentucky, Univ. of		40
Louisiana State Univ.		60
Louisiana, Southwest-ern Institute		25
Maine, Univ. of	52	
Maryland, Univ. of	61	
Massachusetts, Univ. of	75	slightly higher
Miami, Univ. of	33	41
Michigan State Coll.	25-30 (prewar)	
Michigan, Univ. of		18.8
Minnesota, Univ. of		40-50
Mississippi State Coll.	25	45-50
Mississippi State Coll. for Women	43	49
Mississippi, Univ. of		50
Missouri, Univ. of		15-18
Montana State Univ.		39
Nebraska, Univ. of		47
Nevada, Univ. of	35-40	
New Hampshire, Univ. of	60	
New Mexico, Univ. of		8

TABLE 20 (continued)

GRADUATES

Institution	Percentage of Freshmen Enrollees Graduated	Percentage Including Transfers
N.Y. State Coll. for Teachers		75
N.C. State Coll. of A. and E.		30-40
N.C., Women's Coll. of the Univ. of		50
North Dakota, Univ. of		30
Ohio State Univ.	35	
Oklahoma A. and M.		30-35
Oklahoma Coll. for Women	27	31
Oklahoma, Univ. of		40
Oregon State Coll.		
Oregon, Univ. of	30	40
Pennsylvania State College	56	
Purdue Univ.		50
R. I. State College	60 (prewar)	
Rutgers Univ.	60	
San Francisco State College	45	45
San Jose State Coll.	No percentage available.	
South Carolina, Univ. of		40 (prewar)
South Dakota, Univ. of	30	50
South, Univ. of		16-2/3
Stanford Univ.	52 (prewar)	
Tennessee, Univ. of	28	38
Texas A. and M.		40
Texas College of Mines	26	
Texas Techno-logical College		50
Texas, Univ. of	30	
Tuskegee Institute	47	
Utah State Agric. College	30	55
Utah, Univ. of		65
Vanderbilt Univ.		33-1/3
Vermont, Univ. of	45	55
Virginia Military Institute		37
Virginia Poly-technic Institute	42	
Virginia, Univ. of		
Washington, State College of	40	
Washington, Univ. of	No percentage available.	
West Virginia Univ.		20-25
William and Mary, College of	No percentage available.	
Wisconsin, Univ. of	50	
Wooster, College of		53
Wyoming, Univ. of		30-35
Yale Univ. of	85	

Attention is called to the wide variation in the above figures, which are those furnished by the institutions themselves.

TABLE 21

FACULTY MEMBERS ACTIVE IN PROFESSIONAL ASSOCIATIONS

Institution	Faculty members Active in Professional Associations & Expenses Paid by Whom
Alabama Polytechnic Institute	College pays expenses of speakers, officers, delegates, and in some cases one-half expenses of others who attend.
Alabama, University of	University pays expenses for speakers and officers, and one-half for those who merely attend.
Amherst College	Not active.
Arizona, University of	Active in state and regional associations. University policy is to help with expenses within reason.
Arkansas, University of	Association of State Colleges hold regular meetings. Some faculty members active in state, regional and national associations. University pays expenses of speakers and half expenses for limited number of others.
California, University of	Faculty members active in state, regional and national educational associations. University has a travel budget and if university benefit is involved, funds are available for travel.
California, University of, at Los Angeles	Active. University has travel budget and funds are available for travel when university is benefited.
California, University of Southern	Faculty members active in state, regional, and national associations. University pays full expenses of such memberships for deans and heads of departments, and half for faculty when representing university.
Citadel, The	Active. College pays expenses of officers or participants of such meetings.
Clemson Agric. College	Active. College pays travel expense.
Colorado A. and M.	Active. On college business, as speakers or officers, college pays full expenses. On others, round trip coach fare only.
Colorado, University of	Active. University pays expenses for participants, speakers and officers, but not for mere attendance. This fund administered by faculty itself.
Connecticut, University of	Active. University finances participants and delegates attending meetings.
Cornell University	Active. University financing of attendance very limited. More generous plan under consideration.
Delaware, University of	University fiances officers or participants in national association meetings.
Florida State University	Active. College pays institutional dues and traveling expenses for officers and speakers on programs.
Florida, University of	Active. College pays institutional dues and traveling expenses for officers and speakers on programs.
Georgia School of Technology	Active. Allows travel cost to delegates and speakers and pays half of expense for other members who attend.
Georgia, University of	Active. University pays institutional dues and expenses for regularly appointed delegates.
Harvard University	Faculty members at liberty to join any professional association. These connections mostly financed by individuals themselves.
Idaho, Univ. of	Active. University assists in financing attendance.
Illinois, University of	Active. Reasonably generous travel allowance for attendance. University pays expenses for representatives.
Indiana University	Active. University finances expenses to those appointed officially to represent institution in associations of which university is a member. University does not finance expenses of individual faculty members simply on basis of their individual membership associations. $35,000 expended in 1947.

TABLE 21 (continued)

FACULTY MEMBERS ACTIVE IN PROFESSIONAL ASSOCIATIONS

Institution	Faculty Members Active in Professional Associations & Expenses Paid by Whom
Iowa State A. and M.	Travel allowance granted to staff members who are actively identified with learned societies, either as officers or as participants in programs. Others pay own expenses.
Iowa, State University of	Active. University rarely pays expenses of a staff member to the meetings of his own professional society.
Kansas State College	Active. Joint board fixes sum for out-of-state travel expenses; for professional meetings, railroad fare or its equivalent allowed; when on college business, all travel and subsistence expenses allowed. Fund administered by deans.
Kansas, University of	Active. University pays expenses for participants, speakers and officers in such meetings, but not for mere attendance. Expense fund administered by faculty members.
Kentucky, University of	Generally, university helps finance faculty members' attendance at professional meetings.
Louisiana State University	Very active. University generous in providing expenses for faculty.
Louisiana, Southwestern Inst.	Active. Expenses are paid within limitations of travel budget for members on programs or who go for specific purpose. Travel budget too limited.
Maine, University of	Active. University has travel allowance for attendance at regional and some national meetings.
Maryland, University of	Active. University finances attendance on limited scale.
Massachusetts, University of	Very active. University finances attendance of faculty members to at least one meeting a year.
Miami, University of	Active. University pays travel where member participates in program or is officer, but does not pay dues. Contributes to transportation extensively where meetings are merely attended.
Michigan State College	Active. Liberal travel allowances to representatives of college at meetings of learned societies; at least one representative sent with full expenses paid to all meetings of major societies, more if meeting is comparatively near.
Michigan, University of	Active. Full expenses of institutional representatives are usually paid and at least transportation of faculty members who give papers before learned societies or take part in their meetings as officers, committee chairmen, etc.
Minnesota, University of	Active. University pays expenses for those who are designated as representatives at meetings of professional associations. Owing to size of university, it is impossible to finance expenses for all invited to read papers, or attending. General policy liberal.
Mississippi State College	Active. Expenses paid by the institution within limits provided by budget, and such activity is encouraged.
Mississippi State Coll. for Women	Active. College pays expenses for members only when sent by college.
Mississippi, University of	Active, University pays travel and necessary expense for participation.
Missouri, University of	Active. University pays travel expenses to professional meetings.
Montana State University	Active. University has $6000 annual budget to subsidize travel expenses of faculty members.
Nebraska, University of	Active. University finances expenses to meetings of associations of which the university is a member, often when faculty members give serious papers or are sent to secure information for the institution. Individual members pay their own expenses for mere attendance.

TABLE 21 (continued)

FACULTY MEMBERS ACTIVE IN PROFESSIONAL ASSOCIATIONS

Institution	Faculty Members Active in Professional Associations & Expenses Paid by Whom
Nevada, University of	Not active. University does not pay expenses normally.
New Hampshire, University of	University encourages attendance by helping with expenses.
New Mexico, University of	Active. University helps with expenses of members delivering papers.
N. Y. State Coll. for Teachers	Active. In some instances, travel expenses to attend meetings are met by college.
N.C. State Coll. of A. and E.	Active. College helps to finance.
N.C., Women's Coll. of the University of	Active. College helps to finance.
North Dakota, University of	Active. Expenses paid by institution subject to approval of Commissioner and Governor for out-of-state travel.
Ohio State University	Active. Full expenses of representatives of institution are usually paid. At least transportation expenses are paid for faculty members who give papers for learned societies or take part in their meetings as officers of and as chairmen. Individual members are not paid for mere attendance.
Oklahoma A. and M.	Active.. College pays expenses of speakers and regularly appointed delegates; liberal distribution of expense funds within limits of budget.
Oklahoma Coll. for Women	Active. Institution pays expenses of speakers and representatives.
Oklahoma, Univ. of	Active. Institution pays expenses of speakers and representatives.
Oregon State College	Active. Expenses paid to national and regional meetings.
Oregon, Univ. of	Active. Expenses paid to national and regional meetings.
Pennsylvania State College	Active. Travel expenses of delegates paid by college.
Purdue University	Active. Expenses partially paid by university. University's representatives' expenses paid; others at own expense.
R. I. State College	Active. College assists in financing attendance.
Rutgers University	Active. University assists in financing attendance.
San Francisco State College	Faculty interested in state, regional and national associations. 90% in California State Teachers Association; 60% in NEA. College does not help finance memberships.
San Jose State College	Faculty interested in associations. State pays for memberships but does not finance expenses outside state.
South Carolina, University of	Active. Expenses paid partly by institution, partly by faculty members.
South Dakota, University of	Active. University pays all expenses for faculty members who present papers or are officers.
South, University of	Active. Reasonable allowance in university budget for this purpose.
Stanford University	Very active. University contributes substantially to expenses of faculty members.
Tennessee, University of	Active. University pays expenses for memberships.
Texas, A. and M.	Active. College pays expenses of officers or participants of national scientific societies.

TABLE 21 (continued)

FACULTY MEMBERS ACTIVE IN PROFESSIONAL ASSOCIATIONS

Institution	Faculty Members Active in Professional Associations & Expenses Paid by Whom
Texas College of Mines	Very active. College assists in expenses of delegates who bring benefit to institution.
Texas Technological College	Active. Institution pays travel when members are on program, subject to restrictions by state law to original researches or state business.
Texas, University of	University pays transportation for members who present reports on original research.
Tuskegee Inst.	Active. Institution pays expenses on recommendation of department heads and approval of president.
Utah State Agric. College	Active. College pays transportation for authorized representatives. Provision reasonably generous.
Utah, University of	Active. University has membership and travel allowance for participants.
Vanderbilt Univ.	Active. Memberships and trips financed by university.
Vermont, University of	Active. University assists by financing travel to attend professional meetings.
Virginia Military Institute	Board assigns funds to enable faculty men to join academic societies.
Virginia Polytechnic Inst.	Active. Institution pays expenses of out-of-state trips for officers or participants.
Virginia, Univ. of	Some activity.
Washington, State College of	Active. College pays transportation.
Washington, University of	Active. University finances to a considerable extent.
West Virginia University	Active. University pays traveling expenses.
William and Mary, College of	College helps finance attendance.
Wisconsin, University of	Active. University pays expenses of faculty members officially designated to represent institution, but not otherwise. Must have president's approval to travel outside the state at university expense.
Wooster, Coll. of	Active. College helps finance attendance.
Wyoming, University of	Active. University expends $5000 a year to enable faculty members to attend meetings as representatives of the university.
Yale University	Active, but members pay own way.